The Challenge and Spirituality
of Catholic Social Teaching

The Challenge and Spirituality
of Catholic Social Teaching

Marvin L. Krier Mich

Louisville, Kentucky

Cover image by Fielding Jezreel
Book design by Kirby Gann

ISBN 0-9765203-1-1

First Edition
Published by Sowers Books and Videos, a division of JustFaith, Inc.
Louisville, Kentucky

PREFACE

I have been blessed with many opportunities to experience the power of God's Spirit alive in the Catholic community. My ministry within the Catholic community as an educator and activist for over thirty years has focused on the social justice dimensions of the gospel. The vision of Pope John XXIII has been a guiding framework for this ministry. His vision for the church called for (1) an updating of its structures and theology, (2) a focus on issues of justice and peace, and (3) reaching out to other Christians, the interfaith community, and all people of goodwill. The Second Vatican Council set the Catholic Church on the path of realizing the three dimensions of Pope John's vision for the church. Pope John called the church to tackle issues of justice and peace by his challenging social encyclicals.

In *Mater et Magistra,* released in 1961, Pope John taught that Catholics should not only be educated in Catholic social teaching, but more importantly should live it out in each person's particular vocation and society setting. This is a central challenge for the church, namely, to teach our social tradition and to be transformed by it. In *Pacem in Terris* the pope described how respect for human rights is the basis for lasting peace.

In 1971, the Synod of Bishops reinforced Pope John's commitment to social justice by stating that "action on behalf of justice and participation in the transformation of the world fully appear to us as a constitutive dimension of the preaching of the Gospel." Action on behalf of justice is not only an essential part of living and preaching the gospel, it is also the way we will be transformed by God's Spirit into authentic disciples of Jesus.

Action on behalf of justice will transform us. Actually, it is God's Spirit that will transform us when we take the risk of working on behalf of justice. As we work to create a community of justice and peace, we will experience God's power and God's Spirit in our lives. This Spirit will transform us. We will move beyond education to transformation. We will no longer look at the world with the same eyes. We will see new realities and injustices that our eyes may have missed before. We will hear new voices, the voices of those muffled by the lack of power, wealth, and access to resources. We will be filled with a new hope, a new courage that knows that we are doing God's work in the world.

This book is primarily a story of transformation. More accurately, it presents stories of transformation in the Spirit. While it unpacks the core themes of Catholic social teaching, it also tells the stories of our saints, contemporary and ancient, who under the power of the Spirit live out the meaning of the "glad tidings to the poor," the Gospel of Jesus Christ. Each chapter brings forth insights from the biblical tradition, which is the narrative of God's Spirit at work in the world. I hope this work can be part of your education and transformation as a follower of Jesus.

I would like to thank Jack Jezreel, the director of JustFaith, for the invitation to work on this text. Jack wanted a text that would be invigorating. As Christians we are invigorated by God's Spirit. I can only hope that something of that invigorating Spirit is evident in these pages.

I am grateful to my wife Kristine and children Rachel and Nathaniel for their patience as I used many weekends to work on this project. Thanks also to Bob Land, who reviewed the text; to Peggy Rosenthal, who took the first draft and shaped it into a readable text; to Brigit Hurley, for her careful reading of the text; and to Linda Stearns and Scott Gates, who helped in the revision process.

It is an honor and a joy to share the stories of our Catholic social tradition, the principles, the biblical insights, and the stories of holy men and women who make that tradition a lived reality by the witness of their lives.

CONTENTS

The Challenge and Spirituality
of Catholic Social Teaching

INTRODUCTION

A New Breed of Men and Women

Jesus invites us into a new way of living, a new way of being in the world. In baptism we were plunged into the waters of death; we died to the old way of living. To symbolize our new identity we were given a new set of clothes, the white garment; we were given the light of Christ, to enlighten our path in a world of darkness. We were anointed with the oil of catechumens to strengthen us for the battle with evil, self-doubt, and lethargy. As my pastor, Father Bill Donnelly, puts it, we have been rubbed with the oil of baptism so we could slip out of the grasp of the devil. We were welcomed into a new family, a new community, committed to living the values of Jesus. The second anointing was with Chrism to remind us of our high calling to be "priest, prophet, and king."

What a marvelous gift: to be welcomed into the community of the beloved disciples, to be claimed for Christ, to be reborn into a life of grace, rejecting the clamor of evil. What a high calling! What an honor! What has happened since our welcome into the church? What has happened to the church itself since its baptism by the Spirit on that first Pentecost? How has the church been an agent of the Spirit renewing the face of the earth?

Each of us as Christians could tell our own story of discipleship, a story of faithfulness and grace and infidelity and sin. The Catholic Church could also tell the saga of fidelity and infidelity, the story of wrestling with the meaning of God's word in new circumstances and, at times, missing the mark. The church, like individual Christians, has had its moments of grace and sin, yet throughout the journey we are confident that the love of God calls us back and continues to sustain us. When the church or individual Christians have missed the mark or been unfaithful, we know that God is waiting for our return.

1

The story of Christian discipleship is complex and multileveled, not only through history, but in our own day as well. History reveals many paths to being a faithful servant of God's work in the world. This is true for individuals and for denominations. In Christianity, as in life, one size does not fit all. Each Christian follows God's calling, revealed in the circumstances of her life, discovered in her unique gifts and talents and in the longing of her hearts. There are many paths winding through the forest, many tributaries flowing into the river of discipleship. This diversity of Christianity should not be surprising to us, because from the very beginning of Christianity there were diverse interpretations of how to live out the good news. We have twenty-seven books in the Christian Scriptures (New Testament); we do not have just one way of telling the story or one way of living it out. No one approach exhausts the meaning of Christian faith. Even within specific denominations there are diverse and, at times, competing interpretations of discipleship.

One ancient way of describing the diversity of discipleship and ministry is found in the baptismal rite itself: "as Jesus was anointed Priest, Prophet, and King, so may you live as child of God." The Christian is anointed with the oil of Chrism to be priestly, prophetic, and kingly. These three images highlight three distinct aspects of ministry and discipleship.

The priestly ministry focuses on calling the community together for worship and connecting the sacrifices of our lives with the sacrifice of Christ. The priestly ministry tends to focus on the needs of the community and its members and to celebrate the sacred rituals of the liturgy and sacraments that give meaning to our lives.

The prophetic ministry is not so interested in comforting the community as it is in challenging the community to be faithful to God's word and work. The prophet sees the world in black and white, no shades of gray. The prophetic community is willing to take hard stands, such as the Catholic Worker community and its pacifist position and Pope John Paul II's Gospel of Life. The prophetic voice names injustice and stands with the poor and others who are victims of oppression. While the prophet criticizes injustice, he or she also energizes the community with the clarity of God's word.

The kingly ministry is a service that is concerned with worldly realities, the governance of the secular community, the common good, and public order. In the kingly focus, the impulses and concerns of the prophetic and the priestly are redirected into the practical secular arena and the political arena. The church's kingly ministry seeks to shape social policy and advise presidents, mayors, and legislators. While being rooted in the faith language of the Christian community, the kingly approach seeks to articulate its moral and social positions in reasonable ways so as to be accessible to the wider community. The tradition of the just war ethic fits into this kingly style of teaching. The arguments are presented in ethical language, not in theological terms.

While the prophetic calls the church to reach for the ideal, the kingly cautions that idealism with the realism of what is possible, what is responsible. "Yet it is precisely the effort to be *both* prophetic and responsible that distinguishes Catholic social teaching." David O'Brien and Thomas Shannon believe that "the church as a whole is trying to be both idealistic and realistic because that is what it is called to be."[1]

As individual Christians, we are called to be prophetic, responsible, and sacramental. These three ministries give full expression to Christian discipleship, yet no one person perfectly balances all three ministries. Each Christian generally emphasizes one ministry with less attention given to the others. The same is true for the various Christian denominations that tend to highlight one of these types of ministry and even shift its focus through history. In general, Christianity was more prophetic in the first three centuries and then shifted to more kingly and priestly emphases in succeeding centuries. Religious movements within Catholicism often attempted to reclaim and give prominence to the prophetic dimension. St. Francis of Assisi, for example, is one among many leaders who called the church to the prophetic message of radical love and evangelical poverty.

The Catholic Church includes all three types of ministry. Our leaders too may be prophetic on one occasion and priestly or kingly on the next occasion. For instance, Pope John Paul II was prophetic when he visited Poland and supported Solidarity, the workers' movement; he was kingly when he met with world leaders, and priestly when he led in worship, baptized, and ordained ministers for the church.

The social documents of the Catholic Church also reflect the different hues of these three metaphors. The social documents tend to have a kingly role in urging leaders and laity to work for a just social order. Often there are prophetic edges in the documents. Some documents as a whole are prophetic. The 1971 Synod document *Justice in the World*, with its strong language about injustice in the Third World, stands out in this regard; the 1993 encyclical of John Paul II, *Gospel of Life*, in naming a "culture of death," has a prophetic tone. At times the priestly ministry is evident in the social documents when the bishops and pope urge the community to be rooted in prayer and fasting as essential components of building a more just world. The 1986 pastoral letter, *The Challenge of Peace*, is a clear example of prayer and fasting as a way to open hearts to the way of peace.

This book highlights the prophetic strain of Catholic social teaching and witness. The prophetic voice attempts to wake us up, to see the gospel in a fresh way. The prophetic voice challenges the accommodation of the Christian faith to American culture. The prophetic voice asks the church to take sides in the struggle for justice, as the bishops suggested in the 1971 Synod document, *Justice in the World*: "If instead the Church appears to be among the rich and the powerful of this world its credibility is diminished."[2]

THE CHURCH'S SOCIAL MISSION

The Christian community has from its very beginning been concerned about social issues. The pages of the New Testament are filled with stories of Jesus and his followers caring for the sick, the poor, and the needy. The early church also took on a prophetic role as it criticized the abuses of the Roman Empire and has continued to the present time its critique of social injustice. In the last one hundred years the Catholic Church has been more intentional about its social mission. Our discussion of the church's social mission is located within the Roman Catholic tradition. In this text, when speaking of "church" we are generally referring to the Roman Catholic Church. The more intense emphasis on the social mission of the church is due to four factors:

1. The first factor was new emphasis on the *pastoral and theological dimensions of the church*. Since Vatican II the Catholic Church has emphasized its sacramental and pastoral dimensions, in contrast to previous centuries when the church emphasized its institutional structures and offices. The emphasis on the institutional dimensions of the church in previous centuries was in response to the Protestant Reformation, which had denied the authority of papal offices and church institutions such as monasticism, celibacy, and major portions of the sacramental system. In reaction to the claims of the Protestant reformers the Catholic Church defended its institutional structures and offices from the sixteenth through the mid-twentieth century.

According to theologian Francis Schussler Fiorenza, "a sea change took place in the 20th century."[3] This sea change was that the Catholic Church finally moved beyond a defensive attitude toward Protestantism. The church also moved away from a negative response toward the values of the modern, secular world, including the values of equality, human rights, individual freedom, and secular autonomy. The Second Vatican Council placed the theological and pastoral treatment of the church at the forefront. Vatican II emphasized the images of the church as the people of God, the body of Christ, and the sacrament of salvation. Less attention was given to the church's institutional identity as a hierarchical organization. With this new emphasis, the social mission of the church acquired a new meaning. The social mission was no longer one of the specific tasks that the institutional church performs. Instead, the social mission of the church became a symbol and sacrament of the very essence of the church. The social mission of the church "is the church in action, expressing and symbolizing itself in practice."[4]

In this new vision, the social mission of the church expresses the very essence of what it means to be church. This is what the 1971 Synod of Bishops said in *Justice in the World*:

Action on behalf of justice and participation in the transformation of the world fully appear to us as a constitutive dimension of the preaching of the Gospel, or in other words, of the Church's mission for the redemption of the human race and its liberation from every oppressive situation.[5]

2. A second factor in the new emphasis on the social mission of the church is a *new understanding of society* itself. After the French Revolution and the American Revolution, the understanding of secular society changed. No longer did Europeans and Americans view society, social status, and occupational roles as divinely ordered. Instead, societies and social structures are seen as historically conditioned, subject to change, and open to transformation. If social structures and social class are not divinely ordered, then they are humanly ordered and humanity is responsible for the way we organize society, including its economic and political dimensions. Gradually the Catholic Church realized that monarchy is not the only form of government that is acceptable to God. We realized that forms of government and the institutions of the economy are the result of human creativity and ingenuity. Thus, we are responsible for shaping more just forms of government and economic life.

Because of this new insight, the church realized that it must preach conversion not only to individuals, but also to our unjust social arrangements. The church's social mission was expanded to include not only the behavior of individuals, but the structural arrangements of power and wealth within and among nations.

3. A third factor was the *growing awareness of social injustice*. This awareness followed from the insight that humans are responsible for the institutions in society, as discussed above. While there has always been hunger and poverty, today we name these problems as social injustice and not simply a situation of nature that must be accepted. We have become aware of the political, economic, and social causes of poverty and hunger. Hunger and disease could be lessened if structural changes were made, such as sharing of wealth, less military expenditures, restructuring of international debt, and more equitable forms of taxation. This awareness "makes clear," Fiorenza concludes, "that the church's social mission is much more than engaging in works of mercy but involves a mission to social, political, and economic life."[6]

4. A fourth factor that contributed to a new understanding of the social mission of the church was the new understanding of the *relationship of theory and practice*. Earlier understandings of the relationship emphasized theory as knowledge and practice as the application of this knowledge. In this perspective social ministry was considered merely a matter of skill and application. The new understanding of the theory-practice relationship gives a new status and higher priority to practice. "Practice is no longer merely the aftermath of theory so that practice reflexively flows from theory." As Fiorenza explains, "Instead practice is a source of experience that affects theory and influences how we interpret the world

and our tradition."[7] Practice is not simply an acquired skill in applying knowledge to concrete practice. Practice is a way of life, a source of knowledge by which we come to new insights. To convey this richer understanding of practice, the Greek word "praxis" is often used. In this view of practice, the practice or praxis of the church and its social mission are new sources of knowledge and insight.

In this new understanding, the insights of lived Christian experience are another source of knowledge and authority, along with scripture, tradition, and human reason. This richer understanding of praxis has led to a new appreciation of the importance of reflecting on the Christian's lived experience. New methods of reflection developed which stressed the importance of praxis. The methodology of the "pastoral circle," for example, outlines a four-step process that begins and ends with praxis: (1) insertion or lived experience, (2) social analysis, (3) theological reflection, and finally, (4) pastoral planning and action.[8] Theologians and social ministers who subscribe to this new understanding of practice describe theology as the second act, "what you do when the sun goes down." The commitment to service and social mission is the first act. Practice informs and shapes the theology.[9]

These four factors have placed a new emphasis on the importance and centrality of the church's social mission.

CATHOLIC SOCIAL TEACHING

Catholic social teaching is a body of principles and values that draws upon the gospel and the biblical tradition. In its modern expression, Catholic social teaching begins with Pope Leo XIII's encyclical, *Rerum Novarum*, from 1891. In this encyclical Pope Leo addressed the abuses of workers in industrialized Europe. Since that time, popes and bishops, along with lay movements, have continued to address an ever-broadening array of issues. The theology, method of moral reflection, and the guidelines for action have varied greatly over the last century.[10]

The teachings of recent popes and the Second Vatican Council have much in common with those of the earlier popes, "but they are informed by more flexible approaches to scripture and tradition and by a more positive assessment of the modern world." While Pope Leo XIII and his successors were filled with charity and a passion for justice, "these qualities were smothered by triumphalist ecclesiology, antidemocratic political values, and a conservative, even negative understanding of natural law." By contrast, the modern documents "communicate a vision of the church as servant to humanity, a renewed concern for the human person and human rights, an increasing emphasis on popular participation, and a more open and humble acknowledgment of the historically conditioned character of human life and consciousness."[11] While Catholic social teaching has always been Eurocentric, in recent decades it has incorporated perspectives and concerns from the developing nations, and through the teaching of local bishops it has become more culturally diverse.

Seven Themes—"A Starting Point"

The breadth of Catholic social teaching is immense and complex. In an effort to make this tradition more user-friendly, three committees of the National Conference of Catholic Bishops came together in 1995 to produce a summary of Catholic social teaching. This summary, entitled *Sharing Catholic Social Teaching: Challenges and Directions*, was to be used in parishes and Catholic schools.[12] The joint committee noted that it is not easy to summarize the sophisticated body of teaching that has developed over the last one hundred years. The committee distilled the main points of Catholic social teaching into seven themes, identifying them as "key themes that are at the heart of our Catholic social tradition . . . as a starting point for those interested in exploring the Catholic social tradition more fully."[13]

The seven themes identified by the U.S. bishops in *Sharing Catholic Social Teaching* are:

1. Life and dignity of the human person (*need to more fully incorporate gays & women*).
2. Call to family, community, and participation
3. Rights and responsibilities
4. Option for the poor and vulnerable
5. The dignity of work and the rights of workers
6. Solidarity
7. Care for God's creation

We use these themes as the framework for the last seven chapters of this book. (The first chapter addresses an overarching theme of "following Christ in a consumer society.") I do not follow the order listed above. Rather I rearrange the order so that we begin with creation, as the starting point of all life.

In keeping with an emphasis on the importance of praxis, we present the lived reality of these themes as they have been lived out in the saints of the church and in the lives of contemporary Christians. Their lives and their activism are sources of wisdom and insight that have helped to shape the Catholic social tradition.

In a number of chapters we link the central theme with specific issues. For example, in chapter 2 creation is linked with environmental issues; in chapter 3 human dignity is paired with abortion and the death penalty; in chapter 6 rights and responsibilities are linked with poverty and racism, and in chapter 8 solidarity is linked with the ethics of war.

The core teaching of Catholic social teaching is the dignity of human life. As the bishops point out: "This central Catholic principle requires that we measure every policy, every institution, and every action by whether it protects human life and enhances human dignity, especially for the poor and vulnerable." That one sentence is a summary of all the encyclicals and pastoral letters of the past one hundred years. This principle of the dignity of each person, especially the poor and vulnerable, also "offers consistent moral guidance for the future."[14]

The social mission of the church has emerged as a constitutive dimension of preaching the gospel. As the Second Vatican Council reminds us, the mission of preaching the gospel and transforming society has been given to the whole church. Each of us is to live out our baptismal commitment.[15] The entire Christian community participates in shaping and being shaped by this tradition. As active Catholics, we not only receive the teaching of the tradition, but we have a role to play in shaping that tradition, by the expertise of our lived experience. Because of our new understanding of the importance of praxis as a source of theological wisdom and insight, we realize that the wisdom of the entire people of God is needed for the authentic development of Catholic social teaching. There are distinctive roles for bishops, theologians, religious educators, and the laity, but each plays an important role.

Three Types of Teaching Authority

Bishop Richard Sklba, Old Testament scholar and auxiliary bishop of Milwaukee, articulated the way the various kinds of authority in the church complement each other. He identified three types of authority: the authority that comes from the *lived experience* of Christians who struggle between grace and sin; the authority that comes from competence, skill, or learning—that is, the authority of *expertise*; and the authority that comes from *delegation*. For example, an expert might know all the reasons that a person should stop smoking. Someone else with experiential authority which goes beyond the intellectual insights of the expert may have struggles with trying to stop smoking. Yet another person may have the authority to make sure that no smoking takes place in a particular building. Bishop Sklba believes that "the same kinds of diversification of authority exist in the Church." He continues by explaining the necessity of all three authorities:

> One of the roles of the bishop is not merely to represent the delegated responsibility for tradition but rather to make sure that the Church community experiences a healthy balance between those three kinds of teaching authorities. The bishop ensures that knowledge, experience, and delegation are speaking to one another.[16]

Keeping Catholics with three kinds of authority in communication with each other is not an easy task. Many of the controversial moral and social issues within the church reveal the tensions between these diverse authorities. We often think of the troubling issues related to sexuality, such as birth control, the role of women, and the rights of gays and lesbians. But I would point out that the social and economic positions of the church are equally controversial, including the limited right to private property, the role of the state in economic affairs, and the question of a just war and the morality of the death penalty. These complex questions need the insights and wisdom from all the authoritative sources within the people of God. Bishop Sklba's point is that the bishops' role is to keep these authoritative voices speaking to one another. The role of the bishop or the pope is not to prematurely stop the conversation.

The Second Vatican Council articulated this broad responsibility when it taught in *The Pastoral Constitution on the Church in the Modern World*: "With the help of the Holy Spirit, it is the task of the entire People of God, especially pastors and theologians, to hear, distinguish, and interpret the many voices of our age, and to judge them in the light of the divine Word" (no. 44).[17] In naming theologians, pastors, and the people of God, this passage is consistent with Bishop Sklba's three types of authority that must work together to discern the meaning of the gospel in today's world. The bishops of the Council also suggested that the laity take initiative in living out the gospel in their arenas of influence: "Let the layman not imagine that his pastors are always such experts, that to every problem which arises, however complicated, they can readily give him a concrete solution or even that such is their mission. Rather, enlightened by Christian wisdom and giving close attention to the teaching authority of the Church, let the layman take on his distinctive role" (no. 43).

Pope Paul VI reinforced the message in 1971 that the task of the whole Christian community is to wrestle with the meaning of the gospel in our diverse and complex world:

> In the face of such widely varying situations it is difficult for us to utter a unified message and to put forward a solution which has universal validity. Such is not our ambition, nor is it our mission. It is up to the Christian communities to analyze with objectivity the situation which is proper to their own country, to shed on it the light of the Gospel's unalterable words and to draw principles of reflection, norms of judgment and directives for action from the social teaching of the Church.[18]

This book gives voice to the three authoritative voices in the church: the official teaching of popes and bishops, the insights of theologians and spiritual leaders, and the experience of the people of God struggling to be faithful Christians.

Catholic social teaching, then, is the dynamic, living tradition of the whole

Catholic community. As the joint committee of the U.S. bishops noted, this tradition is founded on

- The life and words of Jesus who came "to bring glad tidings to the poor . . . liberty to captives . . . and recovery of sight to the blind" (Luke 4:18–19);
- The passion for justice of the Hebrew prophets calling for "justice to surge like water" (Am 5:24);
- The early martyrs, fathers, and mothers of the church;
- The bishops, popes, and councils who articulated the church's concern for justice, peace, and the poor and vulnerable; and,
- The lived experience of the People of God.[19]

The entire church receives the teaching of the tradition, and the entire church is part of shaping and passing that teaching on to the next generation. You and I are part of that living tradition. By our authentic Christian living may we become authoritative witnesses. May we also be heirs to its "prophetic vision and courageous action," as John Coleman has pointed out:

Ultimately, the future of this tradition will depend less on our ability to parrot its significant terms such as subsidiarity, a just wage, etc., and more on our ability to read the signs of the times in fidelity to the Gospel of human dignity as Leo, Pius XI and XII, John—with all their historical limitations, biases, and failures—tried to do in their times. History will surely unveil all too well our shortcomings. May it also—as it does for this legacy of the popes—show our prophetic vision and courageous action.[20]

CHAPTER 1

The Challenge of Being Prophetic:
Gospel and Culture

This first chapter reflects on the meaning of living our "prophetic ministry" given to us in baptism. How are we to be prophetic in a culture that places such a high value on material riches and pursuing a higher standard of living? We turn to the Bible, the teachings of the church fathers, and the insights of Pope John Paul II to get our bearings on this troubling question.

Many of us as American Catholics have not thought about the values of the gospel and our consumption of material possessions. It is not an easy issue to deal with. On the one hand we believe that God wants us to enjoy the good things of the earth—a good meal, a decent home, and so forth—but on the other hand we are warned not to make possessions a god.

The messages of our materialistic culture consciously and unconsciously shape our attitudes. We accept the cultural mantra to constantly improve our situation. We move from the starter home to a bigger home. We enjoy the convenience of our technological society, so we add labor-saving devices to our households and state-of-the-art computers and broadband uplinks.

As I write these words, our family is having a yard sale to unload some of our unwanted things. It's amazing how much stuff we have accumulated! Recently our nineteen-year-old daughter, Rachel, returned from seven weeks in Europe where she took a four-week course in drawing in Florence and had three weeks of backpacking in Europe. Her first comment on opening her bedroom door after living out of a backpack was, "Boy, I have a lot of stuff." She didn't realize how many possessions she had until she left the country and lived without most of it for a few weeks.

That is probably true for most of us. We go along with the expectations of our society. We want to fit in. Our children want what their friends have; we adults want what our friends have. We try to create a higher standard of living for our children. They learn from us and from our culture that life is about moving ahead, making progress, keeping the economy moving. How do we bring the values of the gospel to our consumer society? This is not an easy task. One size does not fit all. Some are called by gospel values to a more radical lifestyle of voluntary poverty. Others, the majority of us, are called by gospel values to a stewardship of our resources—striving to live simply and care for the needs of others. This first chapter, then, wrestles with that central project of our culture: being a consumer, and how to be a consumer who is attentive to the values of the gospel and the Catholic tradition.

CHRIST AND CULTURE

As Christianity spread across the Roman Empire, Greek and Roman apologists, men and women who explained and defended the Christian religion, explained its beliefs in terms of their cultural attitudes and assumptions. For example, these apologists used the natural-law thinking of the Greco-Roman culture with its roots in Stoic philosophy. The church as an institution also picked up the cultural trappings of the Roman approach to law and order. Roman terms and concepts like diocese, curia, and a hierarchy of ordination (deacon, priest, and bishop) found their way into the Roman Catholic Church. In the Edict of Milan in 312 the Emperor Constantine made peace with church, and Christianity became the religion of the empire. Previously, Christianity had been countercultural, but as the empire became Christian, Christianity lost some of its countercultural edge. As the secular political structures waned in effectiveness, the church took up some responsibility for maintaining public order and addressing the needs of the poor. There emerged a blending and an accommodating of Christianity and culture.

Since the Edict of Milan Christianity has been wrestling with its relationship with the societies and cultures in which it finds itself. This challenge continues in our day as well. Thoughtful Christians wonder if Christianity has lost its soul by accommodating to the culture. Do individual Catholics commit themselves more to cultural norms and values than the values of the gospel? The blending of culture and religion means that we may confuse our loyalty to the gospel with our loyalty to our country. Father Richard Rohr believes that "too many . . . Catholics do not understand that to be Catholic means to be Christian first and American second. They do not put the invitation of the gospel ahead of the demands of nationalism." When this happens, Rohr claims we "fall into the idolatry condemned by the prophets and rejected by Jesus."[1]

John Kavanaugh, a Jesuit priest, has focused on the challenge of "following Christ in a consumer society," which is the title of his 1981 book. Ten years after the first edition, Father Kavanaugh reflected on the response he received from Catholics to his message:

> I have found the greatest resistance and challenge to my ideas from people who might be located at either far end of the spectrum. Some of them seem to have so strongly identified faith with Americanism that they reject any critique of the United States as being communistic or even anti-Catholic. Others, it seems to me, have become so identified with American secular liberalism that they see any appeal to a radical Catholic of Christian faith as mere pietism.[2]

It is hard to follow Christ in a consumer society because the messages urging consumption surround us and shape our identity from the earliest years of our lives. The cultural mantra drones consistently: work and spend, work and spend.

Harvard economist Juliet Schor, in *The Overworked American: The Unexpected Decline in Leisure*, documents how American households find themselves locked into an insidious cycle of work and spend. Households go into debt to buy products they do not need and then work longer than they want in order to keep up on the payments. She makes the astute observation that "shopping is the chief cultural activity in the United States."[3] As American Catholics we are surrounded by the messages of our consumer society. Yet as people of faith, we want to discern what the meaning of our Christian vocation is in the midst of our American culture. We turn to authoritative voices from our Catholic tradition to help us reflect on our following of Christ in a consumer society. These voices include a German-born British economist, Pope John Paul II, the Christian Scriptures, early church teachers, and St. Francis of Assisi.

E. F. Schumacher

E. F. Schumacher was "a prophet in the guise of an economist." His message was to alert the world to the catastrophic consequences of the Western experiment in materialism. He warned, "In the excitement over the unfolding of his scientific and technical powers, modern man *sic* has built a system of production that ravishes nature and a type of society that mutilates man."[4] Here is a voice, rooted in an alternative economic theory and Catholic social teaching, that speaks of a society that emphasizes human well-being and a gracious care of the earth.

Born in Germany in 1911, Schumacher went to England as a Rhodes scholar in the 1930s. As World War II broke out he was detained as an enemy alien and sent to northern England to work on a farm. This experience of common productive labor was an important part of his formation. During this time he also became a

Roman Catholic. After the war he worked as an economic advisor to the British Commission in Germany. Then for twenty years he was the top economist and head of planning at the British Coal Board.

Schumacher grew skeptical of his discipline of economics, which, he realized, was based on a materialistic view of reality in which growth, efficiency, and production were the ultimate measures of value. Economists, he believed, ignored the spiritual dimensions of human beings while promoting a civilization headed for catastrophe. Through the 1960s and 1970s he published his unique opinions in obscure publications. In 1973 he hit the mainstream with the publication of *Small Is Beautiful*. The subtitle of the book said it all: *Economics As If People Mattered*.

As an advisor to the government of Burma, he developed an appreciation of Eastern religions, especially Buddhism. One of the chapters of his book was "Buddhist Economics," in which he explained what an economy would look like if it reflected Buddha's idea of "right livelihood." Buddhist economics would focus on permanence, equality, the reduction of desires, the alleviation of suffering, respect for beauty, and the dignity of work. He contrasted the Buddhist ethic with the Western economic system, which was sustained by waste, short-term savings, and the stimulation of avarice and envy. He quipped later that he could have called the essay "Christian Economics," but then "no one would have read it."[5]

As a convert to Catholicism, Schumacher utilized the Catholic moral framework of the four cardinal virtues of prudence, justice, fortitude, and temperance. He believed that "There is perhaps no body of teaching which is more relevant and appropriate to the modern predicament than the marvelously subtle and realistic doctrines of the 'Four Cardinal Virtues' and in particular, temperance that means knowing when 'enough is enough.'"[6]

Schumacher's works were widely read in the mid-1970s. He showed the importance of bringing moral values to economics for the sake of creation and for the sake of human survival. He contrasted the consumerist way of life, which multiplies human wants, with the simple life whose aim is to achieve maximum well-being with the minimal use of the earth's resources. His writing showed that while "economics as if people mattered" was truly rooted in Catholic social teaching, it was also a universal ethic.

Pope John Paul II

Like Schumacher, Pope John Paul II consistently warned the West about the danger of materialism and consumerism. Even though he suffered under a Communist state, Pope John Paul II believed that consumerism is a more insidious enemy of Christianity than the communism of the Soviet system.

Communism is explicitly antireligious; materialism and consumerism are more subtle enemies of gospel values.

Pope John Paul II offered a clear moral directive. "It is not wrong to want to live better; what is wrong is a style of life which is presumed to be better when it is directed towards 'having' rather than 'being,' and which wants to have more, not in order to be more but in order to spend life in enjoyment as an end in itself." Having is the goal of the consumer culture, and it presumes that we will be more if we have more.

The cultural attitude of consumerism is, in the pope's thinking, definitely connected to the ecological crisis: "Equally worrying is the ecological question which accompanies the problem of consumerism and which is closely connected to it. In his desire to have and to enjoy rather than to be and to grow, man consumes the resources of the earth and his own life in an excessive and disordered way."[7]

Pope John Paul II consistently spoke out on the need for simplicity in the Christian's life, especially for those of us living in the richer nations. In 1979 when he came to the United States, Pope John Paul II addressed an enthusiastic audience in Yankee Stadium:

> Christians will want to be in the vanguard in favoring ways of life that decisively break with the frenzy of consumerism, exhausting and joyless. It is not a question of slowing down progress, for there is not human progress when everything conspires to give full reign to the instincts of self-interest, sex, and power.
>
> We must find a simple way of living. For it is not right that the standard of living of the rich countries would seek to maintain itself by draining off a great part of the reserves of energy and raw materials that are meant to serve the whole of humanity. . . . It is in the joyful simplicity of a life inspired by the Gospel and the Gospel's spirit of fraternal sharing that you will find the best remedy for sour criticism, paralyzing doubt, and the temptation to make money the principal means and indeed the very measure of human advancement.[8]

Twenty-two years later, the U.S. bishops picked up Pope John II's lead, noting that "Our religious tradition has always urged restraint and moderation in the use of material goods." They went on to talk about an unpopular concept, "sacrifice":

> Changes in lifestyle based on traditional moral virtues can ease the way to a sustainable and equitable world economy in which sacrifice will no longer be an unpopular concept. For many of us, a life less focused on material gain may remind us that we are more than what we have. Rejecting the false promises of excessive or conspicuous consumption can even allow more time for family, friends, and civic responsibilities. A renewed sense of sacrifice and restraint could make an essential contribution to addressing global climate change.[9]

Getting our bearings about consumerism and possessions is not easy in American culture. The messages of the media are almost overwhelming on this point. It is essential that not only the pope speak about these dangers, but our local faith communities as well. In our parish in Rochester, New York, we renew our baptismal promises each Sunday during the Easter season, using the contemporary form which asks whether we "reject the spirit of consumerism and materialism which is so prevalent in our age." Our parish tries to invite us each Advent to prepare for Christmas in a way that does more good for creation and those who have less, rather than buying gifts for those who have more than they can use already. Our parish has even tried to tackle the Cinderella syndrome around Christian marriages. Is there a simpler way to celebrate the vows of two Christians? Pope John Paul II, E. F. Schumacher, and the staff of St. Mary's Church are trying to remind us of the timeless teaching of Jesus about the lure of possessions.

Christian Scriptures

While the dominant cultural message is "shop till you drop," our biblical faith offers a radically different way to think about the accumulation of possessions.

Jesus warned his followers of the dangers of attachment to wealth and the heedless acquisition of material possessions: "And he said to them, 'Take care! Be on your guard against all kinds of greed; for one's life does not consist in the abundance of possessions'" (Luke 12:15). Jesus taught that at the end of time we will be judged on how we have used the resources entrusted to us (Matt. 25:14ff). "In these ways Jesus opened up to us a new living based not upon consumption, but upon prudent use of the goods of this world with a special concern for the poor."[10]

The church of the apostles continued the vision of Jesus that rich and poor alike would share in the bounty of creation. The Acts of the Apostles gives two ideal pictures of the early followers of Jesus who "shared all things in common" (2:42–47 and 4:32–35).

The biblical vision teaches us that God created a good earth; that the earth is not ours, but God's; and that we, with creation, are to praise God. How we use the resources of the earth is not just an economic question, but a moral and theological issue as well. Use of the resources of creation, as we turn them into possessions, becomes a thorny question for Christians. Our view of possessions reveals a great deal about our attitude toward creation, our neighbor, and God.

The Bible is not a rulebook even though we find rules, such as the Ten Commandments, within its pages. The Bible is better seen as "a body of witnesses to what it means to live a human life before a creating, sustaining, and saving God."[11] In his study on the "sharing of possessions," Professor Luke Timothy Johnson of Yale Divinity School explains that when we look at the Bible in this way, we find "a great deal being said about the way people use possessions."

Johnson explains that the focus is not so much on the things themselves as "what they mean for those who claimed them." He believes that our attitude toward possessions is either one of idolatry or true faith—a stark choice indeed! Our response to possessions tells us what we perceive as of ultimate value in our lives. Possessions become an idol if they enslave worshipers of "the true God who calls humans out of such fearful, compulsive self-grasping into a new life of freedom that enables them to use things without being owned by them." He goes on to say, "The first and most fundamental meaning of possessions, then, is their expression of the human response of idolatry or faith before the mystery of existence."[12]

Before we assume that we have chosen faith rather than "idolatry" because we do not worship idols, Johnson unpacks the meaning of idolatry in contemporary terms. "Idolatry, in simple terms, is the choice of treating as ultimate and absolute that which is neither absolute nor ultimate. We treat something as ultimate by the worship we pay it." Worship in this context is not the worship of our lips or standing at the altar with incense, but the worship of service. Worship is service. Hence, my god is that which I serve. "Whatever I may claim as ultimate, the truth is that my god is that which rivets my attention, centers my activity, preoccupies my mind, and motivates my action." That for which I give up anything else is my god.[13]

The Bible focuses on riches as the classic object of idolatry, but other realities can become idols for us—beauty, power, pleasure, succeeding, stamp collecting, or a million other things.

The Gospel of Luke gives a couple of examples of idolatry. One is the parable of the Rich Man with the barns.

> [Jesus] said to them, "Take heed, and beware of all covetousness; for a man's life does not consist in the abundance of his possessions." And he told them a parable, saying, "The land of a rich man brought forth plentifully; and he thought to himself, 'What shall I do, for I have nowhere to store my crops?' And he said, 'I will do this: I will pull down my barns, and build larger ones; and there I will store all my grain and my goods. And I will say to my soul [life], "Soul, you have ample goods laid up for many years; take your ease, eat, drink, and be merry," But God said to him, "Fool! This night your soul [life] is required of you; and the things you have prepared, whose will they be?"' So is he who lays up treasure for himself, and is not rich toward God." (Luke 12:15–21)

Johnson comments that Jesus explicitly and emphatically rejects the identification of "life" with "abundance of possessions." The man in the parable is not a fool because he is rich. "He is a fool because he identifies his very existence with the security he thinks comes from having grained stored in barns." He has made the mistake of equating his life, his being, with what he has. Rather than realizing his life is in God's hands he trusts in his possessions. This man identified his life with his possessions. He identified his being with his having, which is a fatal mistake. (Pope John Paul II makes this same distinction.) The Bible teaches us to only trust in God, but we are tempted to trust in our possessions or some other god.

A few chapters later Luke makes the reference to Lot and his wife when Sodom and Gomorrah burned. When Lot's wife turned back to look at Sodom she became a pillar of salt. Luke believed that she turned back in longing for the possessions she had left behind. So he says, "Remember Lot's wife. Whoever seeks to gain his life will lose it, but whoever loses his life will preserve it" (Luke 17:33). Luke believed that Lot's wife was "tragically confused." She identified her *being* with her *having*, her life with her possessions. She could not respond to God's call, and so she lost the life that she had tried to build up by what she possessed. Johnson maintains that "there is no doubt about the sharpness of Jesus' teaching here." The sentence, "Whoever seeks to gain his life will lose it" could also be translated as "Whoever seeks to possess his life will lose it" because the Greek word that Luke used really means "to possess." Luke's point is simply that one who would try to hold onto life as a possession will lose it.[14]

"The mandate of faith in God is clear: we must, in some fashion, share that which has been given to us by God as a gift. To refuse to share what we have is to act idolatrously." Johnson gives us an image that expresses our attitude toward God and our possessions, a clenched hand:

> The significance of the sharing of possessions, whether by once-for-all donation or by steady almsgiving or by a community of goods . . . expresses our self-disposition toward God and the world. The clenched hand, the stance of holding and hoarding our possessions . . . manifests and makes real our closure against God and the world. The open hand, the sharing of possessions . . . reveals and makes actual our availability to God and the world.[15]

Johnson suggests that there is no one way to share our possessions. Some examples from the Christian Scriptures include:

- The disciples dropped their fishing nets and ran after a preacher they had just met.
- Martha and Mary made space for Jesus in their home and likewise made room for his teaching in their hearts.
- The first believers in Jerusalem who were "one of heart and mind" and shared all without discrimination.[16]

Two passages from Acts of the Apostles are very clear about the early Christian community's attitude toward possessions:

> They devoted themselves to the apostles' instruction and the communal life, to the breaking of bread and the prayers. A reverent fear overtook them all, for many wonders and signs were performed by the

apostles. Those who believed shared all things in common; they would sell their property and goods, dividing everything on the basis of each one's need. They went to the temple area together every day, while in their homes they broke bread. With exultant and sincere hearts they took their meals in common, praising God and winning the approval of all the people. (Acts 2:42–47)

. . . .

Now the whole group of those who believed were of one heart and one soul, and no one claimed private ownership of any possession, but everything they owned was held in common. With great power the apostles gave their testimony to the resurrection of the Lord Jesus, and great grace was upon them all. There was not a needy person among them, for as many as owned lands or houses sold them and brought the proceeds of what was sold. They laid it at the apostles' feet, and it was distributed to each as any had need. (Acts 4:32–35)

This picture of a community that shares all, so that the needs of all would be met, is an ideal picture, an image of sharing by which later communities could judge themselves.[17] The phrase, "there was none needy among them," is a reference to Deuteronomy 15:4, which promised that when the laws of almsgiving were perfectly kept there would be no more needy persons. Luke is suggesting that the first Christian community fulfilled the Jewish desire for a community without poverty. As the history of Christianity unfolded, the monastic tradition emerged as an attempt to keep alive in the church this tradition of sharing possessions.

The Letter of James clearly teaches that a living faith is to be expressed by responding to the needs of others in love. Avoiding injustice is not enough; "faith in God demands fidelity to the needy."[18] "If a brother or sister is ill clad and in lack of daily food, and one of you says to them, 'Go in peace, be warmed and filled,' without giving them the things needed for the body, what does it profit? So, faith by itself, if it has no works is dead" (2:15–17).

James restates the traditional Jewish belief for the followers of Jesus: "Religion that is pure and undefiled before God and the Father is this: to visit orphans and widows in their affliction, and to keep oneself unstained from the world" (1:27). According to James, care for the needy is not some optional program of social reform; care for the needy is an expression of faith in God.

Early Church Tradition

The teaching of Jesus on the dangers of possessions and the importance of sharing God's gifts with the needy permeated the early church. The writings of the early church after the biblical era are compelling and eloquent on this point, as a few selections can demonstrate.

At the end of the first century the author of the *Didache*, which is Greek for "teachings," instructs the early Christians and us: "Give to anyone that asks, without looking for any repayment, for it is the Father's pleasure that we should share his gracious bounty with all people. . . . Never turn away from the needy; share all your possessions with your brother, and do not claim that anything is your own. If you and he are joint participators in things immortal, how much more so in things that are mortal?"[19]

In the second century, *The Shepherd of Hermas*, concerned about the welfare of the rich as well as the poor, teaches that the rich must become detached from their wealth before they can be genuine Christians. One proves that he or she is detached by a willingness to help all who are in trouble financially, emotionally, and spiritually. "Instead of fields, then, buy souls that are in trouble. . . . Look after widows and orphans and do not neglect them. Spend your riches and all your establishment you have received from God on this kind of field and houses."[20]

The early church wrestled with the question of whether a rich person could be saved. After considerable conversation and prayer, the church concluded that "they were allowed a chance of salvation if they lived modestly and distributed their possessions generously to the poor."[21]

Clement of Alexandria, writing in the early third century, reaffirmed the scriptural position that the source of all humanity's troubles is the desire for wealth. Clement did not see a value in poverty. He was trying to appeal to the cultured and the rich of Alexandria. He offered a moderate principle that we use the resources of the earth to meet our needs. What is beyond our basic needs must be shared with the needy.

Clement mocked rich people's need for extravagant bathroom facilities: "It is farcical and downright ridiculous, for men to bring out urinals of silver and chamberpots of transparent alabaster, as if grandly ushering in their advisers, and for rich women in their silliness to have privies made of gold. It is as if the wealthy were not able to relieve nature except in a grandiose style!"[22]

John Chrysostom, the greatest preacher of the early church (354–407), picked up the danger of serving greed rather than the goal of serving God. He saw that greed had become an idol. The avaricious man is a slave of money, a double agent who masks his real allegiance, a Christian who worships Mammon, not Christ. In response to the charge of idolatry, Chrysostom has the rich reply: "But I've never made an idol . . . nor set up an altar nor sacrificed sheep nor poured libations of wine; no, I come to church, I lift up my hands in prayer to the only-begotten Son of God; I partake of the mysteries, I communicate in prayer and in all other duties of a Christian. How then . . . can I be a worshiper of idols?" Chrysostom goes on to say, "You pretend to be serving God, but in reality you have submitted yourself to the hard and galling yoke of ruthless greed."

Chrysostom preached that the rich injure themselves as well as the poor by their neglect of the poor. "Don't you realize that, as the poor man withdraws silently, sighing and in tears, you actually thrust a sword into yourself, that it is you who received the more serious wound?" With blunt language, Chrysostom turns the tables on the rich: "The rich are in possession of the goods of the poor, even if they have acquired them honestly or inherited them legally." If they do not share, "the wealthy are a species of bandit." He goes on to explain the patristic principle of the universal purpose of creation: "Do not say 'I am using what belongs to me.' You are using what belongs to others. All the wealth of the world belongs to you and to others in common, as the sun, air, earth, and all the rest."[23]

The right of all people to benefit from the resources of the earth is a persistent teaching of the early church. St. Ambrose, the archbishop of Milan, explained this principle to his fourth-century audience. "God has ordered all things to be produced so that there should be food in common for all, and that the earth should be the common possession of all. Nature, therefore, has produced a common right for all, but greed has made it a right for a few."

The early church leaders were not attacking the rich. Rather, they attacked greed and avariciousness. Ambrose "deplores the ruthless greed of the avaricious, their heartless exploitation of the poor, and the ostentation of their luxury." The archbishop of Milan believed that giving to the poor was actually restitution for stolen goods. "You are not making a gift of your possessions to the poor person. You are handing over to him what is his."[24]

The early church leaders taught a care for the earth and the universal purpose of the goods of the earth in continuity with the biblical tradition. This teaching echoed through the centuries and rang with exceptional clarity in the life of Francesco Bernardone, Francis of Assisi.

Francis of Assisi

Francis was born on the right side of the tracks in 1182. His father, Pietro Bernardone, was a wealthy cloth merchant in Assisi, a modest-sized town nestled in the Umbrian hills between Rome and Florence. Francis was one of the "privileged young men of Assisi, attracted to adventure and frivolity as well as tales of romance." But sickness and a battle wound gave him time to think about the direction of his privileged life. As he recovered from his illness he was much more aware of his own vulnerability and dependence on God. The turning point of his conversion was an encounter with a leper. God's grace allowed him to overcome his revulsion for all that the leper stood for. He embraced the leper and claimed the embrace changed "bitterness to sweetness." "From that moment on, Francis would make his home with the lepers and marginalized of the world, and there find Christ, the suffering, crucified Savior."[25]

Francis dramatically left his life of privilege when he stripped naked before the bishop in the public marketplace. Handing back his rich clothing to his shocked father, he said, "Hitherto I have called you father on earth; but now I say, Our Father, who art in heaven." The bishop quickly had him covered with a peasant's frock, which Francis marked with a cross. Francis took the gospel as his rule of life.

When he was twenty-three years old he would find direction for his life in the voice of the crucified who spoke to him from a cross in the ruined church of San Damiano. He heard the Lord tell him to "rebuild my church." He interpreted the message as instructing him to physically rebuild the dilapidated church in which he was praying. Francis began reconstructing the crumbling walls and continued to serve the needs of the lepers. "The spectacle which Francis presented—the rich boy who now camped out in the open air, serving the sick, working with his hands, and bearing witness to the gospel—attracted ridicule from the respectable citizen of Assisi." But his radical conversion had "a subversive appeal." Before long, other young men and women followed his example.

Seeking further direction from the gospel, Francis and his companions came across those passages wherein Jesus instructed his disciples to take nothing for the journey, as he sent them out to preach conversion and the kingdom of God. This instruction would be their mandate. He now realized that the command of Jesus to rebuild the church did not mean its bricks and mortar but a call to the church to "the radical simplicity of the gospel, to the spirit of poverty, and to the image of Christ in his poor."[26]

In his conversion he turned toward the poor and away from the "sacred violence" of his day, the Crusades, as he opted for radical nonviolence.

Francis turned to nature with a radically new appreciation. All things great and small, living and inanimate reflected the Creator's love and were, therefore, deserving of reverence and respect. According to the Franciscan Leonardo Boff, a Brazilian theologian, what allowed Francis to enter into the fraternity of all creation was the asceticism of poverty. For Francis, poverty "is a way of being by which the individual lets things be what they are; one refuses to dominate them, subjugate them, and make them objects of the will to power."[27]

According to Boff, poverty requires the "renunciation of the instinct to power, the dominion over things," because the desire for possessions is what stands between true communication between persons with each other and with all creation. As Francis became poorer, he became more fraternal; he saw poverty as the way into the experience of universal fraternity with creation. Francis realized that he was a creature, a fellow companion with all the rest of creation. He was "not over things, but together with them, like brothers and sisters of the same family."[28]

Francis came to embrace creation by first embracing his fellow human beings, especially the poor. The poor reminded him of his true nature: a dependent creature unable to be self-made, self-sufficient, or self-fulfilled. Francis entered into a radical companionship with the poor, and through them, with all of creation. His life and his new relationship with all of creation—which included the elements, the stars, animals, the poor and the sick, sultans and crusaders, princes and prelates—represented "the breakthrough of a new model of human and cosmic community."[29]

A NEW BREED OF MEN AND WOMEN

Our Christian vocation is to be a disciple of Jesus as Americans. We can celebrate all that is life-giving and good about our cultural values, but we must have a discerning eye and ear regarding the messages of American culture. Father Richard Rohr reflects his Franciscan spirituality as he points out the paradox of Christian discipleship and spiritual growth: "Paradoxically, our soul does not grow by being fed. It does not develop by taking more and more into itself, by adding experience, by increasing information or activity. Spiritual development is not a matter of addition but subtraction. It is not an aggressive activity but a passive activity, not by taking in but in letting go."[30] Our spirits are filled not by acquiring more, but by enjoying the gifts in our lives already: our family, our community, our faith, our modest home, our work, and creation. We are enriched not by adding more stuff, but in seeing the goodness and beauty in our present situation.

While our culture imbues us with the message that possessions bring happiness, our faith tradition teaches us that possessions do not bring us happiness. Rather, pursuing the lasting values of fidelity, love, community, justice, and peace opens the door to everlasting joy. The voices of our Catholic tradition invite us to discern our attitude toward our possessions. Some of us will be called to the radical witness of *voluntary poverty*—a holy poverty that is full of joy and a deeper richness. I saw the joy of radical poverty in the Missionaries of Charity when I was a graduate student in Rome. One evening the sisters asked if I could drive them to the train station in the middle of the night in Rome. Mother Teresa had just reassigned four of them to open a house in Sicily, so they were catching the night train. They packed a few belongings in a cardboard box, and within a few hours they had said their good-byes and were off to a new place. I remember how they giggled and laughed as we lifted their "fancy luggage" onto the train. They were such a contrast to the dower faces of the other passengers on the platform. How could women who have so little be so joyful? How could these women who have let go of so much be so full of life? Their commitment to radical poverty and gospel living had filled them with a different kind of richness.

Others in the Christian community are called to a *stewardship* of what we have and a tempering of our desire for more. Most of us are not called to voluntary poverty, but the gospel does invite us to be joyful stewards of what we have. I personally feel very blessed to have a modest home in the city of Rochester, New York.

We have a small city lot, but the yard is filled with flowers, bushes, a birdfeeder, squirrels, birds, and an occasional woodchuck, skunk, or opossum. I enjoy the richness of this setting as I sit outside with my laptop computer working on this book. Giving thanks for what we have, even if it is less than others have, is an important part of being a faithful steward.

When I look around my church, when I look around my workplace, I find many holy people who are living the gospel values in our consumer society. They use their resources instead to strengthen the community and care for the needy. I see Brigit, my coworker, and her husband Jeff who are raising their three children on a modest income. Jeff is a social worker and Brigit works part-time so she can home-school their children. While they do not have a lot of creature comforts, they decided to adopt a baby girl from China. They are putting their resources, their money, and their energy into creating a home for one of God's unfortunate children. Brigit and Jeff have taken our gospel values and made them real for this little girl from China. That is what Christian stewardship looks like. This is what Christian passion and holiness look like. As John Kavanaugh notes, "Holiness will never occur where there is no passion or zeal for justice." For Kavanaugh holiness "will never be found where there is no sense of one's own personal poverty nor a correlative love of the poor." He explains what he means by sanctity:

> Sanctity is the acceptance of one's humanity, the acknowledgment that one is a loved sinner, and the overflowing of that experience of being unconditionally loved into compassion and honest labor. . . . The saint does the only utterly new and sacred thing on the face of the earth. The saint has learned to give all—even his or her very self—freely away in a true revolution of life and love.[31]

Brigit and Jeff, the Missionaries of Charity—these people are among the saints of our time. They remind us of the sanctity and compassion of Jesus. They make that sanctity and compassion real in our time and in our place. They keep alive the passion and vision of the followers of Jesus as found in the early church. This vision of sanctity is expressed in the words of the *Epistle to Diognetus* written at the end of the second century to the tutor of the emperor Marcus Aurelius. The author explains that in gratitude for God's gifts, as Christians we should imitate God by loving our neighbors: "Happiness is not found in dominating one's fellows, or in wanting to have more than his weaker brethren, or in possessing riches and riding roughshod over his inferiors." The author explains, "No one can become an imitator of God like that, for such things are whole alien to his greatness." To imitate God the following is required: "But if a man will shoulder his neighbor's burden; if he be ready to supply another's need from his own abundance; if, by sharing the blessings he has received from God with those who are in want, he himself becomes a god to those who receive his bounty—such a man is indeed an imitator of God."[32]

The early Christians lived a "reversal of values" in the pagan culture. Athenagoras of Athens, a Greek Christian, noted in the year 180 that Christians did not place great importance on their property, their reputations, and their freedom. These were not the focus of their highest values. Athenagoras pointed out that Christians' belief in an all-bountiful God resulted in an astonishing reversal of current pagan values and has brought into existence "a new breed of men and women who refuse to abandon the poor and the helpless to fate, but who rush to their assistance in times of crisis."[33] Jeff, Brigit, and the Missionaries of Charity are this new breed of men and women in our day.

☙

A Prayer for Social Justice

Almighty and eternal God, may your grace enkindle in all persons a love
of the many unfortunate people whom poverty and misery reduce to a
condition of life unworthy of human beings.

Arouse in the hearts of those who call you Father a hunger and thirst
for social justice and for fraternal charity in deeds and in truth.

Grant, O Lord, peace in our days, peace to souls,
peace to our community and peace among nations. Amen.[34]

—Pope Pius XII

CHAPTER 2

God's Gift of Creation

H oward Hunter is an apple farmer in Delta Township, Michigan. At age ninety-eight he has had time to reflect on his many years of working the land and tending his orchard. "The orchard taught us how to raise apples and to cooperate with nature, not control it." His philosophy is rooted in a belief that things will turn out fine even if the outcome is not what you expected. Hunter remembers an unseasonably cold, clear evening years ago. His son, Stan, came to his father and said, "It's a beautiful night, but I think the apples are frozen." Hunter looked at the apples himself and saw that they were frozen but said to his son, "It's still a beautiful night."

Tending his apple trees has taught Hunter and his family about the vicissitudes of farming as a challenge toward strength, knowledge, and humility. These lessons have been absorbed by Hunter's granddaughter Cindy, who visits with her three-year-old son. "Every time I step into this house or walk through the orchard, I feel a sense of well-being.... It is not unlike what one might feel walking into a church.... A great many people have felt this same sacredness when they've come for apples at Hunter's Orchard."[1] Respect for life begins with appreciating the sacredness of creation. The Hunter family in Michigan has come to appreciate that truth.

As we reflect on the first of the seven starting points of Catholic social teaching, we discuss those working to defend their environment in Central America and Brazil; we examine in some detail the biblical themes toward creation, and the impact of St. Boniface and St. Francis, key points of the Catholic environmental ethic and sacramental view of creation.

Just as the Hunter family in Michigan appreciates the sacredness of their land, so are the peasant farmers of central Honduras trying to protect their tropical forests. These farmers are upset that their tropical forests and water resources are being ruined by the greed of the wealthy landowners of the region. Landowners are cutting down the forests with little regard for the impact on the environment and people who live in the mountainous region. The peasant farmers and religious leaders claim that indiscriminate logging has dried up water sources and increased their poverty.

Thousands of farmers joined Father José Andres Tamayo on a seven-day, 120-mile "March for Life" on June 19, 2003, to protest the destruction of their region. The purpose of the march was to demand a moratorium on logging in central Honduras until a forest audit could be conducted and plans developed for sustainable use of the forest. After years of working to protect the forests of the isolated region, Father Tamayo, other priests, religious, and the people were taking their protest to the nation's capital, Tegucigalpa.

"I'm walking to seek justice," said Father Raymundo Osorto, a parish priest from La Union. "There are villages that have been plunged into poverty and desperation after a few rich businesspeople extracted millions and millions of dollars of timber."[2] Bertha Oliva, one of the marchers, explained, "The march isn't an end in itself, but a means to take back Honduras from those who commit ecological genocide in order to profit from nature. [They are] violating the basic right of people to life."

Father Tamayo led ten thousand marchers into the capital to the Presidential Palace. The marchers received the support of the cardinal of Tegucigalpa, Oscar Rodriguez Maradiaga, who joined them as they entered the city. The bishop of the province of Olancho, Tomas Mauro Muldoon, an advocate for the environment, also joined the march. As they approached the Presidential Palace the president refused to talk with the marchers; he told them to meet with a group of his assistants.

Father Tamayo has been working on this problem for some time. Previous efforts included blocking highways to prevent logging trucks from driving through the region and a public fast for a month to protest the deforestation. His activism on behalf of the peasant farmers and the forests has not gone unnoticed by the owners of the logging companies. Timber company owners pooled forty thousand dollars to pay for the priest's assassination if Father Tamayo did not leave the country by the end of May 2003. Father Tamayo rejected their threat: "Those who want me dead won't go to heaven by fabricating a hell here on earth. I'm afraid of dying, but I won't leave Honduras."

The government did not want a martyr on its hands, so they provided security for the march. A military bodyguard was never far from Tamayo's side. When the marchers entered the capital, police guarded Father Tamayo closely. While Father Tamayo escaped harm, a month later another leader of the group, Carlos Reyes, was assassinated. Carlos was a staff member of the environmental ministry of the diocese of Juticalpa. His death sparked the government to take notice of the marchers' concerns. A formal dialogue was set up, but as the sessions dragged on, popular anger over environmental abuse dissipated. Church leaders admitted that they had not worked hard enough at building coalitions with other groups. No one was charged with Reyes's killing.[3]

Father Tamayo and his community were not defeated. A year after the first march to the capital Father Tamayo organized another seven-day "march for life" to protest the systematic destruction of the country's tropical forests by illegal loggers and corrupt officials in the state forestry corporation. The latest report is that "as thousands descended on the capital, Teguciglapa, President Ricardo Maduro agreed to set up two joint committees to consider short-term measures for protecting watersheds and farmland threatened by erosion."[4]

A number of lessons emerge from this story in the central highlands of Honduras. First, the work of defending the environment is controversial and dangerous because there are powerful forces that benefit from the status quo; second, the work will experience setbacks; finally, the church cannot do it alone. The church needs to be in coalitions with other groups and organizations to build an effective alliance.

Despite these setbacks, Father Tamayo and his community seem determined to witness their belief that the resources of the earth are meant for the benefit of all, not only the wealthy who control the land. They are fighting to reverse the attitude that creation can be dominated and exploited for the benefit of the few. These farmers and religious leaders witness to the ancient biblical truth that has been distorted and forgotten because of human arrogance and greed: the earth and its resources are not a possession of the few but meant to serve the needs of the entire community.

Father Tamayo and his community are activists who are putting their lives on the line in their defense of the environment and the poor who suffer because of ecological abuses. They are taking courageous stands. These men and women are confronting the exploitation of nature by their fellow Christians. Their struggle and the respect for creation shown by the Hunter family make them authoritative voices who help shape our Catholic social tradition. We review other authoritative voices in our tradition, including the story of creation in the book of Genesis, the Sabbath and Jubilee traditions, the Christian Scriptures, saints, the teachings of our bishops, and insights of theologians. As we examine the Catholic attitude toward creation, we discover that past misunderstandings of the biblical teaching may have actually been part of the problem.

"LET THEM HAVE DOMINION": THE HEBREW SCRIPTURES

The Bible teaches that God created the heavens and the earth. Genesis also teaches that humanity had a special role in creation:

> Then God said, "Let us make man in our image, after our likeness. Let them have dominion over the fish of the sea, the birds of the air, and the cattle, and over all the wild animals and all the creatures that crawl on the ground...." God blessed them, saying: "Be fertile and multiply; fill the earth and subdue it. Have dominion over the fish of the sea, the birds of the air, and all the living things that move on the earth." (Gen. 1:26, 28)

The lesson of Genesis is that humanity has responsibility over nature and some level of power over it, as a steward has some level of authority over the resources of the owner.

Some commentators believe that the misinterpretation of this text has actually led to the exploitation and domination of nature. Historian Lynn White, in particular, suggested that by vigorously embracing the Genesis mandate to hold "dominion" over the earth and to "fill and subdue it," the Judeo-Christian tradition broke the hold of animistic belief in the intrinsic sacredness of nature. White's thesis is that the Judeo-Christian tradition taught that exploiting people is wrong, but that exploiting nature is right and proper. With these attitudes Christianity set the stage for the emergence of modern science and technology in the West and thus bears a heavy burden of responsibility for ecological degradation.

While the Judeo-Christian tradition may have been part of the problem, White also believes that it can be part of the solution:

> Both our present science and our present technology are so tinctured with orthodox arrogance toward nature that no solutions for our ecological crisis can be expected from them alone. Since the roots of our trouble are so largely religious, the remedy must also be essentially religious, whether we call it that or not. We must rethink and refeel our nature and our destiny.[5]

A biblical scholar, Sister Dianne Bergant, gives evidence that White's criticism has some truth to it. Sister Bergant reminds us of this misunderstanding of the Genesis text. "After all, are we not superior to all of creation? Have we not been told to subdue the earth and have dominion over the fish and the birds and every living thing (cf. Gn 1:26, 28)?" She points to Catholic catechetical materials. Some catechisms showed a pyramid with mineral creation on the first level, vegetative life on the second level, animate life on the next level, and finally humanity at the top of the pyramid. "In this way, we learned that God created the lower levels of the natural world to serve the ends of the higher level. How well this was illustrated; how well we learned it, and how wrong we have been!"

According to Sister Bergant, such a human-centered (anthropocentric) worldview is "certainly not biblical." The Bible has a God-centered (theocentric) worldview. "It is false to think that humankind is itself the measure of everything. God is! The value of creation does not lie in its usefulness for us. It lies in the fact of its existence from God. The Bible is very clear on this point. The world is not ours; it is God's. . . . We are stewards. We are accountable to God."[6]

Rabbi David Saperstein concurs with Sister Bergant's interpretation of the Genesis text from the Hebrew Scriptures (the Old Testament). The rabbinic tradition taught that "the right to subdue was subservient to the obligation to subdue for a purpose. That purpose was to protect the earth, to be a guardian of the earth. . . . It is important for us to exercise dominion in the context of replenishing the earth." According to Saperstein, the codirector of the Religious Action Center of Reform Judaism, Jews "acknowledge that we have no rights of ownership or authority over the world. We enjoy only a borrowed authority; God remains the master of God's creation."[7]

In Genesis 2 we find the second account of creation, in which God asked Adam to name his fellow creatures:

> The Lord God said: "It is not good for the man to be alone. I will make a suitable partner for him." So the Lord God formed out of the ground various wild animals and various birds of the air, and he brought them to the man to see what he would call them; whatever the man called each of them would be its name. The man gave names to all the cattle, all the birds of the air, and all the wild animals; but none proved to be the suitable partner for the man. (Gen. 2:18–20)

The text continues with the story of God taking a rib from the man and creating woman, who is a suitable partner and companion.

In naming the animals, the man establishes a relationship with each creature. God sees that it is not good for the man to be alone, that being in relationship with other creatures is good. The best relationship is with other humans, but humanity is also in relationship and companionship with all creatures. Fathers Michael Himes and Ken Himes, who are brothers, believe it is time to recover this theme of companionship. "Companionship implies mutuality. It excludes the reduction of either side of the relationship to a tool of the other's purposes."[8] The natural world is not intended for domination and subjugation by humans, but for companionship.

The Himes brothers argue that "companionship" is a better image for our relationship with creation than the image of "stewardship." The stewardship theme can be interpreted as God having begun creation and then handing creation over to humanity. When the image of stewardship dominates our imagination, God can be removed from the scene as human beings are given oversight of the earth. In a subtle way, human beings move to center stage in the drama of caring for creation. Stewards are not anxious for the master to return; humans enjoy being in charge and may forget that we do not own creation, that we are only caretakers.

In many ways, it is better to speak of our companionship with all of creation, rather than our stewardship over creation.[9]

The second account of creation teaches that humanity is in a relationship of caring for creation. This text also teaches that God is understood as in a relationship with the Hebrew people through the covenant; humanity, which is made in God's image, must be relational. "Humanity is sexed in order that human beings may be driven into relationship with one with another."[10] The only God that the Hebrew tradition knows is One who is relational, so the creature created in the image of that God must be relational. We explore this dimension more fully in the chapter on community, family, and participation.

In Genesis we also learn that God, through Noah, makes a covenant with all of creation that includes all humanity and all creatures of the earth (Gen. 8:21–22). When the flood recedes, God pledges that never again shall the earth be destroyed.

The Hebrew Scriptures are also aware, as we are today, that the sins of human beings destroy the earth as well. The prophet Hosea cries out:

> There is no fidelity, no mercy, no knowledge of God in the land. False swearing, lying murder, stealing and adultery. In their lawlessness, bloodshed follows bloodshed. Therefore, the land mourns, and everything that dwells in it languishes: the beasts of the field, the birds of the air, and even the fish of the sea perish. (Hos. 4:1b–3)

In the biblical vision, injustice results in suffering for all creation.

The Sabbath and the Jubilee year were biblical traditions that were meant to restore the proper balance to creation and human relationships when they were distorted by sin or exploitation. In their 1991 statement *Renewing the Earth*, the U.S. bishops point out that "the Sabbath rest gave relief from unremitting toil to workers and beasts alike. It invited the whole community to taste the goodness of God in creation."[11] The Jewish tradition also developed the Sabbath year. Every seventh year, the land and the people were to rest. Nature would be restored by human restraint. Finally, after seven sets of seven years, a special "year of favor from the Lord" would take place. In that year, the Jubilee year, not only would the land lie fallow to be restored, but debts would be forgiven so that human relationships would be restored and the poor would have a new beginning.

The prophets called the people back to their covenant with God. They condemned those who had broken faith with God by their injustice toward the poor and needy, the migrant worker and day laborer, the orphan and the widow. Conversion back to God meant not only shattering the idols but also "doing justice" to those who were needy, especially orphans and widows. The Word of the Lord to those who had turned away from God was simply to "keep justice, and do righteousness" (Isa. 56:1).

The conversion that the prophets called for was a conversion to just relationships, not only with God but with those treated unjustly, especially with the poor. The prophets' vision of justice linked God, neighbor, and possessions:

> In the preaching of the prophets . . . we see that the human use of possessions directly symbolizes and makes real the fundamental human response to God, and it does this precisely in the way possessions are taken from or given to other human beings. We respond to our neighbor as we respond to God. How we use possessions reveals both.[12]

When Shadrach, Meshach, and Abednego were thrown in the fiery furnace they broke into prayer in which they invited all of creation to praise God with them:

> Let the earth bless the Lord;
>   praise and exalt him above forever.
> Mountains and hills, bless the Lord;
>   Praise and exalt him above all forever.
> Everything growing from the earth, bless the Lord;
>   Praise and exalt him above forever.
> You springs, bless the Lord;
>   praise and exalt him above forever.
> Seas and rivers, bless the Lord;
>   praise and exalt him above forever.
> You dolphins and all water creatures, bless the Lord;
>   praise and exalt him above forever.
> All you birds of the air, bless the Lord;
>   praise and exalt him above forever.
> All you beasts, wild and tame, bless the Lord;
>   praise and exalt him above forever.
>
>   (Dan. 3:74–81)

The book of Psalms, used in the Liturgy of the Word and the Liturgy of the Hours, echoes the praise that creation gives to God along with humanity. "The heavens declare the glory of God, and the firmament proclaims his handiwork" (Ps. 19:2).

CHRISTIAN SCRIPTURES

Jesus continues the Jewish tradition of proclaiming the Jubilee year in which humanity and creation are liberated: "The spirit of the Lord is upon me," he announced in the synagogue in Nazareth, "to announce a year of favor from the Lord" (Luke 4:18–19). Paul teaches that creation, too, is waiting for liberation: "Yes, we know that all creation groans and is in agony even until now . . . while we await the redemption of our bodies" (Rom. 8:22–23).

Jesus constantly used the beauty of creation to illustrate his message of salvation. The birds of the air and the lilies of the field were a reminder of God's care. Wisdom about the spiritual life was to be gained by observing the fig tree: "Notice the fig tree, or any other tree. You observe them when they are budding, and know for yourselves that summer is near. Likewise when you see all the things happening of which I speak, know that the reign of God is near" (Luke 21:29). Jesus saw in the seed cast on the ground a lesson of the Word of God trying to take root in our lives (Luke 8:11).

Jesus used the earthy realities of bread, wine, oil, and water to symbolize the new covenant he established with humanity and all creation. This new covenant overcomes all hostility and restores the order of love that God intended from the creation of the earth. Christ is the firstborn of a new creation that participates in God's grace and God's salvation.

FROM BONIFACE TO FRANCIS OF ASSISI

As the Christian faith spread throughout Europe it carried with it both an appreciation of creation but also a fear of pagan religions that worshiped nature. Christianity's praise of creation was tempered by its fear of idolatry. St. Boniface stands out in the eighth century as a symbol of this confrontation with nature worship. An Anglo-Saxon by birth, Boniface left England when he was forty to preach the gospel to the people of Saxony, Germany. Boniface was willing to adapt Christianity as far as possible to the local culture. But he was unwilling to accept the worship of trees, a common feature of German folk religion. So in 723 Boniface took an ax to a tree dedicated to the god Thor. A crowd of onlookers expected that lightning bolts would rain down upon Boniface for his sacrilege. When he remained unscathed, his challenge to the idol Thor demonstrated to the people the truth of Christianity. Boniface's act of defiance inspired a wave of conversions.[13] An unintended consequence of his action was a diminished awe for the sacredness of nature.

For a thousand years Christianity in Europe confronted the worship of nature in pagan religions. This confrontation with pagan nature worship meant that Christian theology and practice overreacted to the fear of idolatry and downplayed the importance of respect for nature. Five hundred years after Boniface, Francis of Assisi opened a new chapter of Christian theology and spirituality regarding creation. With the threat of the worship of nature resolved, Francis turned to nature with a radically new appreciation. All things great and small, living and inanimate, reflected the Creator's love and were, therefore, deserving of reverence and respect.

As we discussed in the first chapter Francis entered into the fraternity of all creation. The humility and poverty of Francis were the keys to this new appreciation of nature. For Francis, poverty "is a way of being by which the individual lets things be what they are; one refuses to dominate them, subjugate them, and make them objects of the will to power."[14] Consequently, as Francis became poorer, he became more fraternal; he saw poverty as the way into the experience of universal fraternity with creation. Francis realized that he was a creature, a fellow companion with all the rest of creation. He was "not over things, but together with them, like brothers and sisters of the same family."[15]

Francis entered into a radical companionship with the poor and, through them, with all of creation. His new relationship with all of creation represented "the breakthrough of a new model of human and cosmic community."[16]

CHICO MENDES

Contemporary saints, such as Chico Mendes, have come to the same understanding as Francis of Assisi regarding the care of the earth and its link to our care of the poor. The son a rubber tree tapper in the Amazon, Mendes began organizing rubber workers in 1977. At first, his intention was to protect the rights and livelihood of the workers from the encroaching big landowners and ranchers who preferred to burn and clear the forests to make room for cattle. This activity threatened the livelihood of the workers who made a living by tapping the renewable resource of the rainforest in northwest Brazil. Gradually, Mendes realized that burning the forest was not only a disaster for the rubber workers, but also for the environment of the region, a disaster that had global consequences. Burning the forest contributed to the greenhouse effect in a number of ways. The smoke from the fires added to the atmospheric pollution, and the loss of the forest meant a loss of oxygen-producing trees. Cutting the forests ruins the land and ultimately threatens the health of the whole planet. Chico Mendes made the connection between the cry of the poor and the cry of the Earth.

The landowners and ranchers used threats and violence to attack the rubber workers and their union, for which Mendes and his supporters responded with nonviolent tactics. Mendes was repeatedly threatened with death. His wife, Ilza, described his resolve: "Sometimes I'd say to Chico, 'Chico, they're going to kill you! Why don't you take care of yourself and go away?' But Chico wasn't afraid of death. He told me that he would never stop defending the Amazon forest—never!"

The workers' struggle attracted international support. In 1987 Mendes was awarded the United Nations' Global 500 Award for Environmental Protection. He was call "the Gandhi of the Amazon." Soon after this the government of Brazil granted reserve status to four areas of rainforest, but this recognition did not protect him from violence. On December 22, 1988, Chico was shot and killed by a rancher and his son.

Ilza, now a widow, captured the faith and hope of many of those who are working for just causes. "Chico had a lot of faith. When he died, I was filled with despair. But God comforted me and inspired me to work alongside others to carry on Chico's work. They killed him, but they didn't kill his ideals or crush the struggle."[17]

The Catholic tradition embraces Chico, Francis, Chrysostom, and Hosea as it articulates a contemporary appreciation of and respect for the cosmos.

CONTEMPORARY CATHOLIC SOCIAL TEACHING

Contemporary Catholic social teaching continues the themes of Scripture, the early church, and the witness of the saints. This section surveys key themes and orientations in current Catholic social teaching in regard to creation.

The Catholic understanding begins with the recognition that human well-being must be attained in harmony with our whole, single earth community. Since we are an integral part of this created order, Pope John Paul II reminds us that "we must take into account the nature of each being and of its mutual connection in an ordered system which is precisely the 'cosmos.'"[18]

A fundamental theological principle to guide us in our reflection is that "all of God's creatures have intrinsic value, in and of themselves. Nature is not just useful to us humans, but is valued and love in itself, for itself, by God."[19]

Sacramental View of the Universe

Because creation is sacred, the elements of creation are holy. The Catholic liturgical tradition recognizes the goodness of creation and uses "earthy" components of creation—water, ashes, oil, fire, wine, and bread—in sacred worship. Bishop Anthony Pilla of Cleveland states, "Catholic sacramental practice embraces the gifts of creation and uses them for praise and thanksgiving. Fundamental to that practice is the conviction that creation is itself holy and appropriately used for worship."[20]

Sacraments reveal God's love for us; they reveal grace. "By being thoroughly itself, a sacrament bodies forth the absolute self-donative love of God that undergirds both it and the entirety of creation." We think of the seven sacraments of the church as revealing God's grace. "But *every creature, human and nonhuman, animate and inanimate, can be a sacrament.*"[21] This discovery that every part of creation, including ourselves, is a sacrament of God's love is the beginning of a great reverence for creation. The sacraments of creation are to be appreciated and respected for what they are, and not seen as a tool to achieve human goals.

Trappist monk Thomas Merton captures this sacramentality a little more poetically. He calls creation "saints":

> The forms and individual character of living and growing things, of inanimate beings, of animal and flowers and all nature, constitute their holiness in the sight of God. . . .
> The special clumsy beauty of this particular colt on this April day in this field under these clouds is a holiness consecrated to God by His own creative wisdom and it declares the glory of God.
> The pale flowers of the dogwood outside this window are saints.
> The little yellow flowers that nobody notices on the edge of that road are saints looking up into the face of God. . . .
> The lakes hidden among the hills are saints, and the sea too is a saint who praises God without interruption in her majestic dance.
> The great, gashed, half-naked mountain is another of God's saints.
> There is no other like him. He is alone in his own character; nothing else in the world ever did or ever will imitate God in quite the same way. That is his sanctity.[22]

Merton reminds us to notice the flowers by the side of the road, to appreciate the mountains and all creatures as God's saints; all are expressions of God's love.

Central Themes of Catholic Social Teaching on Creation

The U.S. bishops, in their 1993 statement called *Renewing the Earth*, offer a summary of the themes of Catholic social teaching regarding the environment. They state:

> We believe that the following themes drawn from this tradition are integral dimensions of ecological responsibility:
>
> - A God-centered and *sacramental view of the universe*, which grounds human accountability for the fate of the earth;
> - A *consistent respect for human life*, which extends to respect for all creation;
> - A world view affirming the ethical significance of *global interdependence* and the *common good*;
> - An ethics of *solidarity* promoting cooperation and a just structure of sharing in the world community;
> - An understanding of the *universal purpose of created things*, which requires equitable use of the earth's resources;
> - An *option for the poor*, which gives passion to the quest for an equitable and sustainable world;
> - A conception of *authentic development*, which offers a direction for progress that respects human dignity and the limits of material growth.[23]

In this summary we see how the themes of Catholic social teaching on creation are interconnected with other basic principles. Talk about creation is impossible without linking it to the common good, the option for the poor, respect for life, and solidarity. All of this is set in a sacramental worldview that sees all people and all of creation as a holy reflection of God. While each of these themes deserves a fuller discussion, we are limiting our commentary to two themes: common good and option for the poor.

When discussing the common good and the environment, we must speak in terms of an international or planetary common good because of the way our environment is limited by national borders. When speaking about issues of climate and air quality the bishops state that

> Global climate is by its very nature a part of the planetary commons. The earth's atmosphere encompasses all people, creatures, and habitats.... As Pope John Paul II has said, "We cannot interfere in one area of the ecosystem without paying due attention both to the consequences of such interference in other areas and to the well being of future generations."[24]

The bishops of the Northwest remind us that "the community and individual *needs* take priority over private *wants*. The right to own and use private property is not seen as an absolute individual right; this right must be exercised responsibly for the benefit of the owner and the community as a whole." The common good expands to include the good of the whole ecosystem: "We urge people to be conscious of, and respectful toward, the watershed as our common home and as the provider of necessities for the good of the whole ecosystem."[25]

In the 1990 World Day of Peace Message, entitled "Peace with All Creation," Pope John Paul II focused on the "ecological crisis" specifically. He noted, "In our day there is a growing awareness that world peace is threatened not only by the arms race, regional conflicts and continued injustice among peoples and nations, but also by a lack of due respect for nature, by the plundering of natural resources and by a progressive decline in the quality of life."[26] The planetary common good and world peace are threatened when creation is abused.

The pope also linked concern for the poor with respect for the environment, as the Bible and St. Francis had done before him:

> It must also be said that the proper ecological balance will not be found without directly addressing the *structural forms of poverty* that exist throughout the world. Rural poverty and unjust land distribution in many countries, for example, have led to subsistence farming and to the exhaustion of soil. Once their land yields no more, many farmers move on to clear new land, thus accelerating uncontrolled deforestation.[27]

Catholic theologian Elizabeth Johnson also developed the linkage between the poor and the abuse of the earth. She took it one step further and suggested that "nature" could be viewed as the "new poor." "Solidarity with victims, option for the poor, and action on behalf of justice widens out from human beings to embrace life systems and other species to ensure vibrant communion in life for all."[28] Johnson extended the option for the poor and concern about justice for the oppressed to include the rest of the family of creation. The poor suffer doubly, from poverty and from the devastation of the environment.

- The peasant farmers in Honduras suffer along with the earth as the forests are cut without regard for the future.

- In the factories along the Mexican-U.S. border, thousands of young people, mostly women, make consumer goods for export in factories known as *maquiladoras*, while they live and work in unhealthy squalor. Their environment is spoiled by toxic waste. In visits to this region, I saw deformed children and workers with cancer resulting from exposure to the chemicals. Even the dirt roads in the barrios were patched with a toxic chemical by-product from producing freon—a chemical outlawed in the United States, but tolerated in Mexico. The children walked barefoot on these chemically laden roads, which became even more dangerous when it rained.

- Agribusiness farming in developing countries focuses on cash crops, such as strawberries or bananas for the North, which creates wealth for a few from the backbreaking labor of the many. In the Dominican Republic I saw orange groves whose juice is exported, while in the same country Coca-Cola markets its orange flavored soda, *Fanta*, which has no nutritional value.

- In the United States, the poor suffer doubly as well. While the well-off can choose to live amid acres of green, the poor are housed on cheap land near factories, refineries, or in homes and apartments with chipping lead paint. The results are not surprising: birth defects, general ill health and disease, and mental and emotional disabilities resulting from environmental abuses.

Fellow theologian Rosemary Radford Ruether joins her colleague Elizabeth Johnson in issuing a challenge:

> The environmental movement needs to be about more than saving seals and defending public parks from lumber companies, although these are worthy causes. It needs to speak of environmental racism and classism, about the poisoning of the environments where poor black, Latino, and indigenous people live in inner cities and rural areas. An environmental movement that does not make these connections across class and racial lines is an escapism for hikers, and not a serious call for change in the industrial system's disregard of its ecological base.[29]

If there was any doubt about the importance of ecological issues from a Christian perspective, Pope John Paul II made it clear that the Christian "duty toward nature and Creator are an essential part of their faith." Pope John Paul II also invited the pro-life community to include creation in its purview: "Respect for life and for the dignity of the human person extends to the rest of creation, which is called to join man in praising God."[30]

In addition to the papal statements on the environment, local bishops' conferences, regions, and specific dioceses have produced helpful statements and offered leadership on this issue. In fact, local religious leaders have produced more than fifty statements from around the world on environmental problems.[31] One excellent example of Catholics providing leadership on ecological issues comes from the northwestern region of the United States and one diocese in Canada, where we find the Columbia River and its watershed.

THE COLUMBIA RIVER WATERSHED

The bishops, along with the religious and secular leadership of British Columbia (Canada), Montana, Idaho, Washington, and Oregon worked together for four years on a pastoral letter on the environment. What brought them together was the Columbia River and tributaries in Montana, Idaho, Washington, and Oregon, which begins in British Columbia and after 1,200 miles flows into the Pacific Ocean. The Columbia watershed covers 259,000 square miles.

This international pastoral letter on the environment brings four distinctive features to our discussion:

1. Its attitude toward the wisdom of Native Americans who inhabited this area long before the Europeans arrived.
2. The letter's view of humanity as part of creation and not at the top of the food chain or the pyramid of creation.
3. The process for writing the letter, which was inclusive and open to the public (which is not the way Roman Catholic magisterial statements are normally written).
4. The recognition of conflict among diverse parties who utilize the river.

The letter notes that the first human communities entering the watershed generally adapted themselves to the *Che Wana*, the Great River, fishing for salmon, hunting wild game, and gathering roots and berries. Then we find the following respectful paragraph:

> Native religions taught respect for the ways of nature, personified as a nurturing mother for all creatures. They saw the salmon as food from this mother, and the river as the source of their lives and the life of the fish. They adapted themselves to the river and to the cycles of the seasons.

Among the *Wanapum*, the River People, some elders were set apart as dreamers and healers, respected for their visions and healing powers.

A few pages later the bishops expressed their gratitude and apologies:

> The indigenous peoples have a wealth of spirituality, culture and traditions that call forth a need for appropriate respect and preservation. We are brothers and sisters in God's creation and we are grateful to the First Nations and the Native Americans for the lessons they teach about respect for nature. We apologize for cultural insensitivities and lack of justice, both past and present.

This is a truly catholic stance—to be open and grateful for the wisdom and insight of all people, even those who are not Christian. History reveals that church leaders have not always been appreciative of the culture and religion of indigenous peoples. The bishops then extend a hand of cooperation and collaboration:

> Today, we extend an offer of peace and friendship to native peoples of our region. We pledge to work with them to seek equitable resolutions of conflicts over treaty rights, to work with them to enhance their engagement with other cultures, to foster their economic development and to participate with them to promote care for creation. We call upon the members of our parish communities, government officials, those with economic interests and the general public to join in these efforts.[32]

The second contribution of this letter is a more humble attitude for humanity in the order of creation. Earlier Roman Catholic attitudes, which are still present in the church, saw human beings as the apex of creation, empowered by God to use nature to our benefit, and too often in the process exploiting nature.

The bishops of the Northwest are very sensitive to the biblical theocentric view and place humanity within the ecological community, not above it:

> People live in the world of nature, not apart from it. They need to alter that world at times in order to provide for their needs. . . . We can live in greater harmony with our surroundings if we strive to become more aware of our connection to, and responsibility for, the creation that surrounds us.
>
> Such a challenge can be met only if we implore the assistance of the God who creates the universe and who continually sends forth the Spirit for the ongoing renewal of the human race and for the renewal of the face of the earth.[33]

The Catholic Church has many ways of producing official documents. Sometimes the process is closed and secretive; other times it is open and transparent. Since the Second Vatican Council the U.S. bishops have used an open and transparent approach in writing on nuclear weapons and on the economy.

Archbishop Rembert Weakland, who chaired the committee drafting the pastoral letter on the economy, commented on the importance of the process as creating a community of moral discourse and "forming church."[34]

The bishops of the Northwest continued the tradition of an open process. Sometimes the process is more transformative than the final product. To help pay for the staff and many meetings of the open process, the bishops garnered grants from the Environmental Justice Program of the United States Catholic Conference and the National Religious Partnership for the Environment.[35] An international steering committee was formed in 1997, including representatives of the Canadian and U.S. dioceses, and Catholic colleges and universities. After this steering committee was formed, the process included the following steps:

- Eight sessions were held to "read the signs of the times." These analysis sessions included representatives from industry, agriculture, fishing, education, and indigenous groups.
- After these sessions a draft of perspectives was prepared, enhanced by the advice of theologians, natural and social scientists, and church representatives.
- A Web site was established, inviting comments from the public.
- The first draft of the letter was released on May 12, 1999.
- Seven listening sessions took place from June through December 1999.
- The final draft was released on January 8, 2001.

The bishops did not see the publication of the letter as the end of the process, but rather as part of "an ongoing conversation process, to resolve regional conflicts with respect, . . . and to promote sustainable ecological relationships."[36]

The bishops and the steering committee of the Northwest are to be commended for a text written in a nonsexist manner that draws upon the wisdom of many disciplines and traditions. They have made a real contribution to the living Catholic social tradition and to the process of forming church. They drew upon diverse, authoritative voices in articulating Catholic social teaching on the environment.

The steering committee, which was composed of diverse parties who have an interest in the river, experienced plenty of give-and-take as they worked together. Conflict arose among the committee regarding the use of the land and the river. One of the steering committee members, Frank Fromherz, the director of the Office of Justice and Peace for the archdiocese of Portland, Oregon, identified the conflict that was evident around the meaning of "common good":

> I have been struck by the many ways the river is teaching us about the meaning of the common good. Some of the learning comes through an awareness of conflict. We have come to learn about many things: wheat farmers and their livelihoods, irrigation interests, sport and commercial fishing, tribal spirituality and cultural traditions, endangered species and

environmental regulations.... Conflicting interests and the legacy of past errors can make the idea of the common good appear remote. The disputes surrounding the river teach us about the common good partly by making us notice its absence."

Learning how to work with competing interests is a necessary part of the delicate work of bringing diverse, authoritative voices to the table. Facing these conflicts of interest is part of shaping our Catholic social tradition. Frank Fromherz was optimistic that the various expectations of the river will teach the community about the importance of the common good.

> The river and its watershed can teach us about the whole, for ultimately a watery epic in the Pacific Northwest flows into a great ocean and touches all of creation, and receives the generous returning dance of rain and snow, revealing the cyclical nature and seasonal character of the common good.
> Perhaps by the riverside we will hear, see, taste, smell and remember, then we might just decide to wade into the common good—an ancient and eloquent mentor—discovering that we have learned about how to live and how to think about how to live.[37]

A certain amount of humility is required as we discern our place in creation. Fromherz suggests learning from the river. Developing a little "species humility" may be necessary also in order to listen to the rest of creation.

Species Humility

Sister Elizabeth Johnson, in her presidential address to the Catholic Theological Society of America, posed a burning question: "What is humanity's place in the great scheme of things?" Previous theologies would have placed human beings with their rational souls as superior to the natural world. Such a ranking easily "gives rise to arrogance, one root of the present ecological crisis." But how is our "superiority" established?

> Consider for a moment, however, green plants. Predating the human race by millennia, green plants take in carbon dioxide and give off oxygen. Through this process of photosynthesis they created the atmosphere which makes life of land animals possible. Human beings could not exist without these plants that neither think nor move. They, on the other hand, get along fine without us. Wherein, then lies superiority?[38]

Sister Johnson wisely suggests that "with a kind of species humility we need to reimagine systematically the uniqueness of being human in the context of our profound kinship with the rest of nature." With reimagining our place in creation, a number of questions emerge, including:

- How to preach salvation as healing and rescue for the whole world rather than as solely an individual relationship with God?
- How to let go of contempt for matter, contempt for the body and sexuality, and how to revalue them as good and blessed?
- How to interpret human beings as primarily "earthlings" rather than as pilgrims or tourists whose real home is elsewhere?
- How to recognize the sacraments as symbols of divine graciousness in a universe that is itself a sacrament?
- What kinds of new spiritualities will emerge as we become creation-centered?[39]

Ecological spirituality will have a component of fasting and restraint in the consumption of food and other resources. Msgr. Charles Murphy reminds us that "Fasting is part of the Gospel. It helps us to focus on the nourishment that can only come from God. It encourages good health and enhances our enjoyment of the good things of life, freeing us from a certain deadness in spirit."[40]

For all living creatures, taking nourishment is a matter of survival. For human beings, eating is matter of survival, but it is also a moral act. What we eat affects our health, so the choices people make about what they eat can either promote or hinder health. The concern about how our food is produced has given rise to the organic food movement. In buying certain foods we are supporting the way the food is produced, the way the workers are treated, and indirectly the entire agribusiness. To focus attention on these concerns, the National Catholic Rural Life Conference (NCRLC) started the "Eating Is a Moral Act" campaign to stimulate thinking about issues of justice in the production of our food and the people who labor to produce it.

By raising questions about our current systems, this campaign invites us to become educated and moral consumers. This effort is presented, in part, in an "Eaters' Bill of Rights," which includes:

> Eaters have a right to food.
> Eaters have a right to safe food.
> Eaters have a right to nutritious food.
> Eaters have a right to food produced without harming air, water or land.
> Eaters have a right to food produced under socially just circumstances.
> Eaters have a right to know the conditions of their food production:
> - Is the environment harmed?
> - Are the animals treated with dignity and respect?
> - Are the farmers paid a just wage?
> - Is the food produced on farms by family farmers?

This campaign is putting into action the suggestion of the Catholic bishops in their 1989 statement, "Food Policy in a Hungry World," in which they said: "How do our food and agricultural policies enhance or diminish the life, dignity, and rights of the human person? What is their impact on human life, hungry people, farm families, and the land that sustains us? . . . We fear that the global food system often seems adrift without a moral compass."

The NCRLC turns to the principles of Catholic social teaching to provide a moral compass:

a. Human Dignity: Support fair wages, healthy working conditions for farmers, farmworkers, and food workers.

b. Human Dignity: Eaters have a right to nutritious food. Obesity is a public health issue.

c. Universal Destination of Goods: Support fair distribution of profits, not food cartel control.

d. Integrity of Creation: Support humane treatment of animals; restrict factory farms.

e. Integrity of Creation: Protect the environment by the food you eat.

f. Common Good: People around the world have a right to food security.

g. Common Good: Limit "food miles" and reduce greenhouse gas emissions.

h. Subsidiarity: Affirm local food production and local purchasing as a preference.

i. Solidarity: Encourage fair trade practices.

j. Option for the Poor: Provide nutritious food for those who are hungry.

The NCRLC is clear in placing human beings within the web of life, not above it. "The web of life is one. Creation has integrity and an inherent value beyond its usefulness to human beings. . . . Animals are to be treated with dignity and respect. The sin of species-ism is becoming more clearly acknowledged and recognized. We cannot do whatever we want with the created order. . . . The web of life is one. The way we treat animals is of moral significance. We cannot casually inflict pain on them or treat them as if they were inert beings or stones." To put those beliefs into effect, the National Catholic Rural Life Conference "supports the replacement of animal factories by sustainable and humane agricultural systems that are environmentally safe, economically viable, and socially just and species appropriate."[41]

The National Catholic Rural Life Conference focuses attention on many issues in rural America, as well as issues of agribusiness and treatment of animals and the environment. Bishops across the country have spoken out on agricultural and rural concerns, including the bishops of Minnesota, Illinois, Kansas, Nebraska, North Dakota, Indiana, Pennsylvania, Texas, Ohio, and New England. In November 2000, the Catholic bishops of the South released a pastoral letter on the poultry industry. These statements reveal the local church wrestling with its fidelity to the gospel values as they intersect with our complex issues of food production, the environment, and social justice. A quote from the bishops of Indiana celebrates the diversity of creation, which must be protected:

> The variety of forms of God's creatures—biodiversity—is one of the gifts of the Creator that we must cherish. The Fathers and theologians of the Church were convinced that the diversity of creatures is essential to show forth the glory of God: no creature can adequately reveal God to us, but the very great variety of created beings does better at this than any single species. Thus, if we cause the extinction of species, we are diminishing the glory of God.[42]

∞

We conclude with an insight from Native Americans in the Northeast. From the Six Nations Iroquois Confederacy, the people of the Longhouse, we hear:

> We who walk about on the Earth are to express a great respect, an affection, and a gratitude toward all the spirits which create and support life. We give a greeting and thanksgiving to the many supporters of our lives—the corn, beans, squash, the winds, the sun. When people cease to respect and express gratitude for these many things, then all life will be destroyed, and human life on this planet will come to an end.[43]

May we, with all people of the earth, continue to respect and give thanks for the gifts of creation.

∞

Prayer of St. Basil

O God, enlarge within us a sense of fellowship with all living things,
    our brothers and sisters the animals,
To whom you gave the earth as their home in common with us.
We remember with shame that in the past we have exercised high dominion
    with ruthless cruelty,
So that the voice of the earth, which should have gone up to you in song,
    has been a groan of travail.
May we realize that they live not for us alone but for themselves and for
    you,
    and that they love the sweetness of life.[44]

CHAPTER 3

Human Dignity:
Respect for Every Life

Arturo was an ornery, homeless man who slept under the pope's window, protected by the massive Bernini columns, in front of St. Peter's basilica in Rome. The Missionaries of Charity would visit him a few times a week around 11:00 p.m. as he was pulling his dirty blankets around his bearded face. While doing my doctoral studies in Rome, I helped the sisters once a week, making sandwiches and driving around Rome to visit the homeless. As we visited the street people of Rome in the late evening, I could see how precious each person was, even those who were ornery, like Arturo. Even though he was rather grumpy in exterior, he accepted our cheese sandwich and a cup of warm milk. Each time we stopped by, his disposition was the same. Sister Agnes explained that practically everything has been taken from Arturo; all he had left were his anger and gruff personality. His identity was one of his last possessions; he clung to it fiercely. His gruffness was one of his last possessions, perhaps his identity. Sister Agnes was able to appreciate his human dignity, despite the ornery exterior.

Often the poor themselves are the ones who teach about human greatness and dignity. On one especially cold December night in Rome—temperatures in the thirties—we were bringing blankets to people sleeping on the streets. Carmen slept in the portico of Sacra Cuore (Sacred Heart) Church near the central train station. She had a pile of plastic garbage bags that were her bed and covers. We offered her a woolen blanket to fend off the damp coolness of the night air. She declined the offer and said we should "give the blanket to someone who really needs it." She would manage on her bed of cardboard and plastic garbage bags. Even in her desperate state she thought of others who might be worse off than she! If I were in her shoes, I am sure I would have grabbed a couple of blankets.

As we unpack the meaning of human dignity as the central focus of the

47

church's social ethic, we examine the dignity of each person, especially the poor and vulnerable, including the unborn. Protecting the dignity of each person is set in the context of the consistent ethic of life and Pope John Paul II's gospel of life. We also offer a brief discussion about euthanasia and the death penalty.

SEEING THE DIGNITY OF EX-OFFENDERS

We easily see the value and dignity of innocent infants who pull at our heart-strings. Sometimes we see the human dignity of the poor. But seeing the sacred-ness of life of those in our prison systems is more difficult. I have had a number of opportunities to work with ex-convicts during our yearly trip to the state cap-ital, Albany, to meet with our legislators. Every year we invite residents from Freedom House, a drug and alcohol treatment program, to join us for the Albany Forum sponsored by the New York State Catholic Conference.

On this particular visit three Latino ex-convicts were part of my delegation of six as we visited our state assemblyman, Joseph Robach. My fellow delegates had two strikes against them, being ex-convicts and being minorities. The third strike against them was that they were all recovering drug addicts. Our cultural standards would not give them the time of day. By society's standards they were losers.

Each of them had found the inner strength to face their chemical addiction, to finish their prison terms, and to begin a new life. They were living in a residence for men who wanted to overcome their addiction. The house, known as Freedom House, is run by Catholic Charities in Rochester. Roberto, Carlos, and Luis broke through all of those stereotypes on that March afternoon. Dressed in suits and ties they spoke with honesty, eloquence, and conviction about their experience of prison and addiction. The legislator, a white, conservative, middle-class, Catholic male, sat with his mouth open in amazement as they shared their experience of addiction, prison, and recovery. Assemblyman Robach was surprised when they said that prison was not a deterrent for them when they were in the depths of their addiction. They saw prison as an improvement over their desperate lives on the street. Even death seemed an improvement to their suffering and misery as addicts.

We were urging the legislator to help revise the harsh drug-sentencing laws in New York State, known as the Rockefeller Drug Laws. The legislator needed to hear the reality of their experience to help craft new laws that would not only pro-mote public safety, but also truly address the problem of drug addiction. Harsh prison sentences were clearly not the answer. The dignity of these three men shone through in that forty-five-minute conversation. I was so impressed with their words. Despite all they had been through, their dignity as human beings was undeniable. The road ahead was not going to be easy, but they were working hard to move beyond their past and to help create a better future for themselves and others still caught in addiction and prison.

Every person—the child, the poor, the rich person, the addict, our irritating neighbor or relative—is precious. Every person deserves respect, even those who do not act respectfully to others. As Dorothy Day, the cofounder of the Catholic Worker movement, said, "To serve others, to give what we have is not enough unless we always show the utmost respect for each other and all we meet."[1] Sister Mary Scullion of Philadelphia was touched by the witness of Dorothy Day and picked up that radical respect for the dignity of every person.

"ALL HAVE THE SAME HUMAN DIGNITY"

In 1976 Sister Mary Scullion attended the Eucharistic Congress in Philadelphia and was inspired by the lives and words of Mother Teresa, Dorothy Day, Jesuit Fr. Pedro Arrupe, and Brazilian Bishop Dom Helder Camara who spoke at the Congress. Sister Mary came away with a new vision, beginning to see the hungry and homeless in her midst. "Before this, I would go to Mass and think I was fulfilling my obligation. But now, I began to see that there was hunger in our city and around the world, and I came to realize how much more needs to be done."

In her efforts to serve the poor she met Joan Dawson-McConnon, at the time a graduate student with a degree in accounting and soon to have a master's degree in taxation. Joan had the same impulses, having learned from her family that caring for others was the primary expression of faith. Joan understood that "faith was something you acted on." They brought together their unique gifts—Scullion, the out-front partner, and Dawson-McConnon, the behind-the-scenes finance person—to express their faith in protecting the dignity of Philadelphia's poor. Their basic conviction is that "People should not have to lay their bodies down on the street. That is just not acceptable. That's the working premise. People suffering in the streets should not be suffering."

Their conviction led to bold steps in finding places for the homeless. They eventually started Project Housing, Opportunities, Medical Care, Education (H.O.M.E.), a multilevel operation of services, residential space, and commerce. A small sampling of their efforts include:

- A new community center built from a converted, abandoned rectory.
- Thirty-nine units of new housing for women with children. These homes were rehabbed and sold to working poor people, but only after the women had months of education about home ownership, financing, and managing money.

- Permanent housing for men and women off the street with chronic mental illness.

Joan expresses the core conviction of these two women: "Whether she's [Mary] talking to extremely powerful and wealthy people or someone sitting on a vent, everyone gets talked about and thought about in the same way. *All have the same human dignity. It is something she really believes.*"[2] That is the Catholic view of human dignity in reality. That is the foundation of Catholic social teaching and social ministry.

CREATED IN GOD'S IMAGE

The sacredness of human life emerges from the first pages of the Bible:

> Then God said, "Let us make humankind in our image, according to our likeness; and let them have dominion over the fish of the sea, and over the birds of the air, and over the cattle, and over all the wild animals of the earth, and over every creeping thing that creeps upon the earth." So God created humankind in his image, in the image of God he created them; male and female he created them. (Gen. 1:26–27)

The *Catechism of the Catholic Church* echoes that biblical teaching by noting the equal dignity of all people.

> Created in the image of the one God and equally endowed with rational souls, all . . . have the same nature and the same origin. Redeemed by the sacrifice of Christ, all are called to participate in the same divine beatitude: all therefore enjoy an equal dignity." (no. 1934)

This teaching on the dignity of each person, which is the starting point and the foundation of all Catholic social teaching, means that

- Every person is precious.
- People are more important than things.
- Our efforts are to respect that dignity and help each person to flourish.

Genesis teaches that humanity is created in the image of God, which establishes the central dignity and sacredness of each person. "*As such every human being possesses an inalienable dignity that stamps human existence prior to any division into races or nations and prior to human labor and human achievement (Gen 4-11).*"[3]

The biblical vision calls on the community to protect the dignity of each person, especially those who are vulnerable and on the fringe of society: the widow, orphans, the weak, and the stranger (Exod. 23:9, Lev. 19:34).

The dignity of the human person is central in every aspect of the church's social teaching. For example, regarding the economy the U.S. bishops point out that "the basis for all that the Church believes about the moral dimensions of economic life is its vision of the transcendent worth—the sacredness—of human beings. The dignity of the human person, realized in community with others, is the criterion against which all aspects of economic life must be measured."[4] The dignity of the human person is the criterion for all of our social justice and pro-life activity in the church. Cardinal Joseph Bernardin came to that understanding of the centrality of human dignity as he worked on the church's teaching on war and pro-life issues.

CARDINAL BERNARDIN AND THE CONSISTENT ETHIC OF LIFE

In 1980, when he was the archbishop of Cincinnati, Joseph Bernardin was asked to chair the committee that was to draft the U.S. bishops' pastoral letter on war and nuclear weapons, *The Challenge of Peace*. When that work was finished in May 1983, he was asked to chair the bishops' Pro-Life Committee. Bernardin, now the archbishop of Chicago, saw connections between the issue of war and the issue of abortion. He committed himself to "shaping a position of linkage among the life issues."[5] He noted that "the central idea in the letter is the sacredness of human life and the responsibility we have, personally and socially, to protect and preserve the sanctity of life."[6] Cardinal Bernardin saw a linkage between Catholic social teaching about nuclear weapons and abortion, which led him to articulate a consistent ethic of life.

Bernardin named a few of the ways life was threatened:

- Nuclear weapons threaten life on a previously unimaginable scale.
- Abortion takes lives daily.
- Public executions are becoming weekly events in the most advanced technological society in history.
- Euthanasia is openly discussed and advocated.

The archbishop of Chicago recognized that "each of these assaults on life has its own meaning and morality; they cannot be collapsed into one problem." Yet he explained that "they must be confronted as pieces of a larger pattern. . . . I am persuaded by the interrelatedness of these diverse problems. . . ."[7] While others had made this connection before, Bernardin gave the notion a sustained focus and attracted national attention because of his visibility and leadership within the church.[8]

Some antiabortion groups argued that this "seamless garment" approach has diluted their political impact. Others argued that the principle of protecting innocent life distinguished the unborn child from the life of the convicted murderer. Still others argued that while nuclear war is a *threat* to life, "abortion involves the actual *taking* of life, here and now." Bernardin agreed with those distinctions, but countered that "I also find compelling the need to *relate* the cases while keeping them in distinct categories."[9]

The issues included in the consistent ethic of life (CEL) are not fixed. Usually the CEL includes abortion, euthanasia, capital punishment, poverty, and war. Some groups add the violence of racism and violence to creation. The pro-life umbrella includes these issues as well as cloning, and stem cell and embryonic research.

Responding with Integrity and Nonviolence

From all the external signs, Cardinal Bernardin was a successful cleric. He had risen quickly in ecclesiastical rank. By age thirty-eight he was a bishop; he was the first general secretary and later president of the National Conference of Catholic Bishops and then Cardinal Archbishop of Chicago at age fifty-four. But some of his closest priest friends confronted him on his priorities. They pointed out to him that his life was focused on the church and his career, rather than on Christ. This was "the beginning of a quiet process of conversion, marked by prayer and reflection on the cross that transformed a successful churchman into a man of God and prepared him for the trials that were to come."[10]

Cardinal Bernardin's last three years in Chicago were very tumultuous, and not because of opposition to his promoting the consistent ethic of life. The events that unfolded gave him the opportunity to put into practice his nonviolent ethic. The first challenge came in November 1993 when an ex-seminarian accused Bernardin of sexual molestation when the young man had been in the seminary in Cincinnati. The alleged victim claimed he remembered these events while under treatment by an unlicensed hypnotist. Bernardin vigorously denied the charges, but he did not mount a defensive counterattack, nor did he impugn the character of his alleged victim. He did not want to discourage other victims of abuse from coming forward. He insisted that this case be handled by the process of investigation that he had established for such allegations. The charges against Bernardin were widely publicized. Three months later, the accuser abruptly withdrew his charges, admitting that his memories were "unreliable." He apologized to Bernardin. Subsequently, Bernardin met with the young man privately and forgave him. The cardinal admitted publicly that the ordeal was very painful, but he insisted that his own experience of being falsely accused would not hinder his determination to reach out to the victims of abuse. Joseph Bernardin handled this painful time with courage and grace. When attacked, he did not respond aggressively, as is often a person's first impulse.

Within a few months of that ordeal, a second challenge emerged when Bernardin announced that he was suffering from cancer. He received aggressive treatment and resumed his pastoral duties. But now he added considerable time visiting others who were sick and dying. "He was determined to impart something of his abiding belief in the sacredness of life and his faith and hope in God's promises."[11] In September 1996, as he was coming to the end of his life, he lifted up his belief in the sacredness of life:

> As a bishop I have tried . . . to shape a moral message about the unique value of human life and our common responsibility for it. As my life slowly ebbs away, as my temporal destiny becomes clearer each hour and each day, I am not anxious, but rather reconfirmed in my conviction about the wonder of human life, a gift that flows from the very being of God and is entrusted to each of us. . . .
>
> The truth is that each life is of infinite value. . . . My final hope is that my efforts have been faithful to the truth of the gospel of life and that you . . . will find in this Gospel the vision and strength needed to promote and nurture the great gift of life God has shared with us.[12]

In the last weeks of his life, as he visibly declined, he received a great outpouring of affection, admiration, and prayerful support. His courage and his tranquility bore a powerful witness to his faith in God. He died on November 13, 1996.

Cardinal Bernardin taught the church about the consistent ethic of life in his speeches and leadership, but also by his living amid adversity and the way he faced his own death. He approached his own dying of cancer with a pro-life attitude and spirituality. The church's pro-life stance teaches that, while physical life is a value, it is not an ultimate value. Union with God is the ultimate value. Eventually, we all must let go of physical life. Our belief in the resurrection means that we trust in God's mercy and look forward to union with God.

In the Catholic tradition, we take care of our health and seek medical intervention when it provides a reasonable benefit without being excessively burdensome. The tradition teaches us not to use futile means to prolong life or to use excessively painful or costly treatments without a reasonable hope of success. On the other end of the spectrum, our tradition guides us not to hasten our dying or the dying of another through "mercy killing" (euthanasia) or physician-assisted suicide.[13] These decisions at the end of life are difficult and, at times, complicated by family dynamics. Our Catholic tradition is a commonsense approach that is pro-life without turning physical life into an ultimate value. Bernardin's example reinforced this tradition.

ENDORSING THE CONSISTENT ETHIC OF LIFE

The U.S. bishops followed the lead of Cardinal Bernardin and in 1985 endorsed the consistent ethic of life in their *Pastoral Plan for Pro-Life Activities*. Pope John

Paul II joined the chorus in his 1995 encyclical *The Gospel of Life*: "Where life is involved, the service of charity must be profoundly consistent. It cannot tolerate bias and discrimination, for human life is sacred and inviolable at every stage and in every situation; it is an indivisible good" (no. 87). In 2001 the revised Pastoral Plan reaffirmed the bishops' commitment to the consistent ethic of life, noting that "A wide spectrum of issues touches on the protection of human life and the promotion of human dignity." In that document the bishops also took into account some of the criticisms that the consistent ethic of life may have diluted the political focus on abortion.

The U.S. bishops' documents, along with the emphasis from the Vatican, stress the importance of the abortion issue among the "spectrum of issues."

> Among important issues involving the dignity of human life . . . , abortion necessarily plays a central role. Abortion, the direct killing of an innocent human being, is *always* gravely immoral (*The Gospel of Life*, no. 57); its victims are the most vulnerable and defenseless members of the human family. It is imperative that those who are called to serve the least among us give urgent attention and priority to this issue of justice.[14]

The U.S. bishops, in their 2001 *Pastoral Plan for Pro-Life Activities*, state their belief that the dual foci on abortion along with the consistent ethic of life are complementary: "A consistent ethic of life, which explains the Church's teaching at the level of moral principle—far from diminishing concern for abortion and euthanasia or equating all issues touching on the dignity of human life—recognizes instead the distinctive character of each issue while giving each its proper place within a coherent moral vision."

The document continues by listing the range of pastoral letters on war and peace, economic justice, and other social questions affecting the dignity of human life. They also point to the church witnessing to the consistent ethic of life through its parishes, schools, health care, and Catholic Charities' services. "Taken together, these diverse pastoral statements and practical programs constitute . . . a consistent strategy in support of all human life in its various stages and circumstance."

Quoting the *Gospel of Life*, the bishops note that opposing abortion and euthanasia "does not excuse indifference to those who suffer from poverty, violence, and injustice. Any politics of human life must work to resist the violence of war and the scandal of capital punishment. Any politics of human dignity must seriously address issues of racism, poverty, hunger, employment, education, housing and health care" (*The Gospel of Life*, no. 23).

The bishops repeat their commitment to the consistent ethic of life from their 1985 document:

> In this pastoral plan, then, we are guided by a key insight regarding the linkage between abortion and these other important issues: Precisely

because all issues involving human life are interdependent, a society which destroys human life by abortion under the mantle of law unavoidably undermines respect for life in all other contexts. Likewise, protection in law and practice of unborn human life will benefit all life, not only the lives of the unborn.[15]

THE GOSPEL OF LIFE

Pope John Paul II was a tireless advocate of the consistent ethic of life, even though he did not explicitly use that phrase. He was

- A critic of war, especially the two wars in the Persian Gulf
- A critic of the death penalty
- A critic of economic injustice and the violence of poverty
- A defender of workers' rights
- A critic of abortion and euthanasia
- A critic of the ecological crisis
- An apostle of the "Gospel of Life"

The centerpiece of his pro-life message is the encyclical which the U.S. Bishops quote from so abundantly: *The Gospel of Life*, released on March 25, 1995. In this letter he defined life as sacred from the "very beginning until its end." Physical life is not an absolute value, but is a "primary good respected to the highest degree. Upon the recognition of this right, every human community and the political community itself are founded." The pope sees "the value of every human life and the right to have each life respected" as the church's "good news," an essential part of the gospel.

Pope John Paul II taught that the incarnation reveals not only God's love for humanity, but also the "incomparable value of every human person ... The Gospel of God's love for man, the Gospel of the dignity of this person and the Gospel of life are a single and indivisible Gospel" (no. 2). The pope linked the good news of salvation with the good news of the value of every person—linking inseparably the church's religious message with its social agenda.

The Gospel of Life made an urgent appeal, the goal of which is to be

A precise and vigorous reaffirmation of the value of human life and its inviolability, and at the same time a pressing appeal in the name of God: Respect, protect, love and serve life, every human life! Only in this direction will you find justice, development, true freedom, peace and happiness. (no. 5)

While the encyclical covered a wide assortment of threats against human life, its primary concerns are abortion and euthanasia, which are defined as "a grave moral disorder" and a "violation of the law of God," respectively (nos. 57, 65).

The encyclical identified diverse sources of violence against life, including:

- Threats from nature that are made worse by the indifference and negligence of those who could help
- Hatred that leads to murder, war, and genocide
- Violence against children in the form of poverty, malnutrition, and hunger
- War and the arms trade
- The criminal drug culture
- Attacks against life in its earliest stages and in its final stages

The pope was not pointing to isolated attacks against the sacredness of life, but rather a "culture of death" and a "conspiracy against life." These threats to life he sees as "a war of the powerful against the weak." He sees cultural attitudes of "efficiency" that may lead to a disdain for the weak, handicapped, or sick. The culture of death "is actively fostered by powerful cultural, economic, and political currents which encourage an ideal of society excessively concerned with efficiency." He continues: "A life which would require greater acceptance, love, and care is considered useless or held to be an intolerable burden, and is therefore rejected in one way or another." He named an attitude in the culture wherein people with greater needs are seen as a threat to others' well-being. "A person who, because of illness, handicap or, simply, just by existing, compromises the well-being or lifestyle of those who are more favored tends to be looked upon as an enemy to be resisted or eliminated. In this way a kind of 'conspiracy against life' is unleashed" (no. 12).

Eighteen years later Pope John Paul II added his concern that life is being perceived as an "object" to be controlled through abortion, euthanasia, and cloning. He urged world leaders and all people to say "yes to life!" He went on to say,

> Respect life itself and individual lives: Everything starts here, for the most fundamental of human rights is certainly the right to life. Abortion, euthanasia, human cloning, for example, risk reducing the human person to a mere object: life and death to order, as it were!

He encouraged people and their leaders to have the courage to say no to attacks on life.

> No to death! That is to say, no to all that attacks the incomparable dignity of every human being, beginning with that of unborn children. If life is truly a treasure, we need to be able to preserve it and to make it bear fruit without distorting it. No to all that weakens the family, the basic cell of society. No to all that destroys in children the sense of striving, their respect for themselves and others, the sense of service.[16]

The pope's pro-life agenda included a concern for the dignity of each person and their own sense of value and self-esteem. It is a delicate balance to promote a sense of striving in the poor and to assist them when they are not able to earn a living wage. I wonder if our sense of service has suffered in the United States during the last decades of welfare reform. While encouraging and requiring those who are able to work is good, a mean-spirited attack on those who are in poverty has emerged in some quarters.[17] This is not in keeping with the respect that is due every person. Defending the dignity of the poor and developing a sense of service are virtues that the saints lived out in their lives. One of my favorite pro-life saints is a Spanish Dominican priest from the sixteenth century, Bartolomé de Las Casas (1484–1566), known as the "defender of the Indians."

DEFENDER OF INDIAN DIGNITY

As an eight-year-old, Bartolomé watched as Columbus returned to Seville from his first voyage to the New World. Bartolomé served in the military for some time before completing his university studies and being ordained a priest. In 1502 he arrived in Santo Domingo, Hispaniola (today, the Dominican Republic). As part of the conquering Spanish army he was awarded a plantation, known as an *encomienda*, complete with Indians as indentured laborers. He enjoyed the life of the colonial gentry as an *encomendero*, ignoring the spiritual care of the Indians charged to him. But something wasn't right for Las Casas; he was aware of the exploitation of the indigenous people. He brought his concerns to his confessor, Padre Pedro de Córdoba, who reminded him of the text from the Hebrew Scriptures: "A man murders his neighbor if he robs him of his livelihood, sheds blood if he withholds an employee's wages" (Sir. 34:22). Padre de Córdoba refused him absolution, which was a drastic step, done only when the penitent has no intention of changing his or her sinful ways. These words from the Bible stayed with Las Casas, leading to his conversion in 1514. He gave up his *encomienda* and began speaking out against the Spaniards' exploitation of the Indians. He joined the Dominican order, the religious community which included de Córdoba and other critics of the Spanish exploitation.

Gold was the main attraction for the Spanish in the New World. But the conquest of the Indian lands was ostensibly justified by the desire to preach the gospel. The pope had authorized the subjugation of the Indian populations for the purpose of spreading the gospel and their salvation. The assumption of many Spanish was their superiority over the pagan peoples, which allowed Spaniards to exploit them and the resources of the land. Las Casas cut through the rhetoric and noted the true religion of the conquistadors:

In order to gild a very cruel and harsh tyranny that destroys so many villages and people, solely for the sake of satisfying the greed of men and giving them gold, the latter, who themselves do not know the faith, use the pretext of teaching it to others and thereby deliver up the innocent in order to extract from their blood the wealth which these men regard as their god.[18]

With Pedro de Córdoba's support, Las Casas returned to Spain to plead the cause of the Indians before the Spanish crown. He was able to gather support from humanists and religious leaders in the court of Charles V. In his treatise, *The Indians Are Free Men and Must Be Treated as Such*, he argued for:

- Eliminating forced labor
- Dismantling the *encomienda* system and putting in its place
  - Peaceful settlement by farmers
  - Protection of the native populations
  - Land and animals given to the Indians
  - Health care, basic education, and food supplies
  - Legal rights and representation

The court of Charles V agreed with the plan and named Las Casas "Protector of the Indians," with the responsibility of carrying out these reforms. His plan was to establish a number of conversion centers in South America, intended to win over the Indians by peaceful means. He planned to bring farmers and skilled workers to introduce silk, spice, wine, wheat, and sugar production. Peaceful settlers would receive free passage, lands, animals, seeds, and tax abatements. They would work alongside free Indians. In 1520 the experiment began in Venezuela, but opposition from colonial authorities and the armed intervention of conquistadors against the Indian population caused the downfall of the community in 1521.

While this experiment was resisted Las Casas did have many victories in his fifty-two years of defending the rights and dignity of the Indians. While others claimed that Indians were a lesser race, he affirmed their full humanity and their entitlement to all human rights. His position was taken up by Pope Paul III, who declared the equality of Indians and Europeans in his 1537 papal bull, *Sublimus Deus*.

In 1544 Las Casas was named bishop of Chiapas in southern Mexico. He was shocked that the colonists were not respecting the rights of Indians as had been declared in the New Laws. He forbade his priest from giving absolution to any *encomendero* who would not free his Indian slaves. This stance aroused hatred among the ruling class who denounced him as a "lunatic." Receiving numerous death threats and eventually expelled from the province, Las Casas returned to Spain but made another trip to the New World in 1546 with additional authority.

At the first synod of bishops of Latin America he won support for *The Declaration of the Rights of the Indians*. This document established the rights of all people:

> All unbelievers, whatever their sect or religion and whatever their state of sin, by Natural and Divine Law and by the birthright of all peoples, properly possess and hold domain over the things they have acquired without detriment to others, and with equal right they are entitled to their principalities, realms, states, honors, jurisdictions, and dominions.[19]

In 1547 he returned to Spain for the last time, where he confronted the writing and teaching of Juan Gines de Sepulveda, who maintained, using Aristotle, that the Indians were naturally inferior and thus natural slaves. Las Casas confronted Sepulveda in a series of debates before King Charles and a royal commission. The crown sided with Las Casas. By the time Las Casas died in 1566, major changes had taken place in the Spanish royal policy regarding the rights of Indians. Las Casas truly deserved the title of "protector of the Indians."

Las Casas had helped shape Spain's attitude toward the equality of all people—notions that the American Declaration of Independence would intensify 240 years later. Las Casas also articulated a vision of the poor as reflecting the sufferings of Jesus. He wrote, "I leave in the Indies Jesus Christ, our God, scourged and afflicted and beaten and crucified not once, but thousands of times."

For Bartolomé de Las Casas there could be no salvation in Jesus Christ apart from social justice. Thus, the question was not whether the Indians were to be "saved"; rather, could the Spanish Christians who were persecuting Christ in the poor be saved?[20]

As Americans we are proud of our founding fathers' wisdom and courage in drafting the Declaration of Independence, which proclaims the dignity of every person, with the right to life, liberty, and the pursuit of happiness. As Roman Catholics, we can also be proud of the tradition of Bishop Las Casas and his supporters who approved another historic declaration, *The Declaration of the Rights of the Indians*, in 1546. These Catholic activists and moralists in the sixteenth century made a great contribution to the emerging understanding of human rights and the role of the state in protecting those rights. Their work and witness tried to establish a culture of life and respect for the indigenous peoples of the Americas, just as Pope John Paul II urged us to build a culture of life in our time.

CULTURAL TRANSFORMATION

To challenge the "culture of death" the pope urged building "a new culture of life." This culture of life would be new because it would have to address "today's unprecedented problems affecting human life," such as cloning and stem cell

Cloning not a real threat now

research. The culture of life would be new in its scope, which would be ecumenical and interfaith (*The Gospel of Life*, no. 95).

The starting point of this cultural transformation would be "in forming conscience with regard to the incomparable and inviolable worth of every human life." The culture of life would include "the courage to adopt a new lifestyle consisting in making practical choices—at the personal, family, social, and international level—on the basis of a correct scale of values: the primacy of being over having, of person over things" (no. 98). This is a tall order for a materialistic culture.

We addressed this distortion of having over being in chapter 1, and it emerges in this chapter as well in analyzing the underlying assumptions of the culture of death. Accumulation of possessions does not lead to life. In fact, that attitude can lead to death, as Amy's parents discovered.

* * *

Amy, a fifteen-year-old, had always earned straight A's in school, and her parents were extremely upset when a B appeared on her report card. "If I fail in what I do," Amy wrote to her parents in her suicide note, "I fail in what I am." Dr. Darold Treffert of the Winnebago Mental Health Institute in Wisconsin explained Amy's behavior and attitude with his theory called "the American Fairy Tale." This theory is based on two principles: first, more possessions mean more happiness, and second, a person who does or produces more is more important.[21] In Amy's framework, her life was of less value because she had not produced enough.

This attitude distorts the thinking not only of our teens, but of all ages in the society. It is part of the reason that millionaire George Eastman put a bullet through his heart at age seventy-eight. He believed his productive days were over and he was ill, so life had lost its value. Mr. Eastman was not an idiosyncratic exception to the rule. The highest suicide rates are among males who are eighty to eighty-five years old. These men no longer feel valued and find it difficult to face the dependency of old age.

ASSIMILATED AND DIGESTED?

The U.S. Catholic bishops have noted that, too often, Christians have been transformed by the culture rather than the other way around. In their 1998 statement *Living the Gospel of Life*, the bishops wrote:

> American Catholics have long sought to assimilate into U.S. cultural life. But in assimilating, we have too often been digested. We have been *changed* by our culture too much, and we have *changed it not enough*. If we are leaven, we must bring to our culture the whole Gospel, which is a *Gospel of life and joy*. That is our vocation as believers. And there is no

better place to start than promoting the beauty and sanctity of human life. Those who would claim to promote the cause of life through violence or the threat of violence contradict this Gospel at its core.[22]

"We have too often been digested." That is a graphic image to describe the fact that Catholics have been absorbed and assimilated into the cultural attitudes and practices rather than being absorbed into the values of the gospel. This is true in many areas of biblical values, not just in the pro-life area.

A FIRM FOUNDATION

A recent document from the New York State Catholic Conference, *Pursuing Justice*, points out how the dignity of the human person becomes the basis for the Catholic involvement in the spectrum of social issues:

> Our belief in the sanctity of human life and the inherent dignity of the human person is the foundation for all of the principles of our social teaching. We believe that every person is precious, from the moment of conception to the moment of natural death; that people are more important than things; and that the measure of every institution or policy is whether it enhances the life and dignity of the human person.
>
> - It is this firm foundation that solidifies the Church's opposition to abortion, euthanasia, assisted suicide and other direct attacks on human life.
> - It is the reason we work toward the abolition of capital punishment.
> - It is the impetus behind our advocacy for adequate health care for poor mothers, children, people with HIV/AIDS and the elderly.
> - And it is why we reject embryonic stem cell research and human cloning, procedures which destroy developing human lives and reduce the creation of human life to manufacture of a product.
> - The sacredness and dignity of human life is shared by all, regardless of sex, race, ethnicity, religious belief, disability, economic status, age or sexual orientation.
> - Thus respect for human life lies at the heart of the Church's opposition to racism, discrimination and violence of all kinds.
> - It is likewise the basis for our support for adequate food, shelter and clothing for the poor, just wages with decent working conditions, and health care and education for immigrants.

The New York bishops point out the important alternatives and positive action that Catholics are taking to witness to their respect for life:

> In addition to rejecting unjust policies that threaten human life, the Church works proactively to enhance human life by supporting alternatives to

abortion such as subsidized prenatal care and adoption; alternatives to assisted suicide such as palliative care and hospice options for the terminally ill; and measures to reduce gun violence, prevent drug abuse and rehabilitate prisoners.[23]

But how are we to influence cultural attitudes and social policy to become more respectful of life? How are we to approach the task of shaping public policy?

FROM MORAL VISION TO PUBLIC POLICY

While Bernardin and others hoped the Catholic community would also adopt the vision of the consistent ethic of life, the ethic was also intended for society as a whole. Bernardin offered some guidelines for shaping social policy. He suggested that the church must work gradually to transform the culture and society's policies, by taking steps that are feasible and realistic. Cardinal Bernardin believed that proponents of the consistent ethic of life must keep the following four points in mind as they work to move from moral vision to public policy:

1. Civil discourse in the United States is influenced and shaped by religious pluralism.
2. There is a legitimate secularity of the political process.
3. All participants in the political process must face the reality that these discussions are based on empirical evidence about which there is disagreement and complexity.
4. Some issues are questions of public morality and others of private morality. A persuasive case has to be evident that an action violates the rights of another or that the consequences are so important that the civil law ought to be invoked to be deemed "public morality."

Bernardin recognized that in a religiously pluralistic society moving from our religious convictions to public policy is a complex process. "But we have been able to do it—by a process of debate, decision-making, then review our decisions." The civil rights movement is an example of moral vision becoming public policy as "philosophers, activists, politicians, preachers, judges, and ordinary citizens had to state a case, shape a consensus, and then find a way to give the consensus public standing in the life of the nation."[24] Bernardin believed the same kind of messy process is needed to translate the moral vision of the consistent ethic of life into effective public policy.

The process requires courage and willingness to stand up for one's beliefs and values, but it also means being wise enough in the political arena to know when to accept a compromise rather than end up with nothing. Small steps in the right direction may be the best that can be accomplished.

The U.S. bishops and the Vatican do not buy the argument, adopted by some Catholic politicians, that while they "personally oppose evils like abortion, they cannot force their religious views onto the wider society." The bishops argue that this type of thinking does not hold up: "Most Americans would recognize the contradiction in the statement, 'While I am personally opposed to slavery or racism or sexism I cannot force my personal view on the rest of society.'" People of conviction must express their beliefs "by every ethical and legal means at their disposal."[25]

SOME HOPEFUL SIGNS

There is some good news to report on the human dignity front. There are hopeful signs that the U.S. population is becoming more respectful of the life of the pre-born. In preparation for the thirtieth anniversary of *Roe v. Wade* on January 22, 2003, the bishops noted some hopeful signs:

- Today fewer abortions are being done each year, and fewer doctors are willing to be involved in abortion. *Because of violence*
- More Americans identify themselves as pro-life, while the numbers of those saying they are "pro-choice" have declined significantly.
- Ultrasound and other medical advances have made possible a greater appreciation of the humanity of the unborn child.
- In these three decades thousands of pro-life groups, individual parishes, Catholic social service agencies, and pregnancy resource centers have provided practical assistance and support to thousands of women facing difficult pregnancies.
- Most state legislatures have enacted measures to restrict or regulate the practice of abortion and reduce its incidence.
- Above all, the pro-life movement is brimming with the vibrancy of youth.[26]

I had the grace of experiencing some of that "vibrancy of youth" when I traveled from Rochester, New York, to Washington, D.C., to participate in the March for Life on the thirtieth anniversary of *Roe v. Wade*.

As we marched down Constitution Avenue in the nation's capital in the cold January air, you could hear the shouts of high school students as they chanted, "Hey, hey! Ho, ho! *Roe v. Wade* has got to go!" These chants drowned out the middle-school children who were walking arm-in-arm a few feet away singing, "Jesus loves the little children, all the children of the world." Their song blended with the group that was praying the rosary and following the statue of Our Lady of Fatima and the gold-plated, processional cross. All of these Christians were expressing their spirituality, their convictions, and their hopes.

The day began with a 7:30 a.m. Mass at the Basilica of the National Shrine of the Immaculate Conception, which rooted the activism and witness in a sacramental and spiritual framework of carrying on God's concern for the weak and vulnerable. This liturgy was the highlight of the day for John, who brought his four teenage children to the March for Life. The liturgy connected the advocacy efforts with his faith. "When it comes right down to it, what makes it all meaningful is that life is a gift from God. The Mass really elevates the issue from the human to the divine."[27] A few hours after the Mass our contingent from Rochester, New York, was at Senator Charles Schumer's office writing down our concerns about the senator's pro-choice stance. Later in the afternoon, Senators Clinton and Schumer held an open forum to hear the opinions of our delegation. Both senators expressed their respect for the group by listening, even though they did not agree with the marchers' desire to overturn Roe v. Wade.

While this was my first March for Life in D.C., many of the young people in our group had been here many times before. Sarah, whose birthday is January 22, has spent many of her fifteen birthdays marching to the Supreme Court with brothers, sisters, and parents. Sarah said she didn't mind spending her birthdays in Washington because it is a cause she believes in. "I don't think anybody has the right to end the life of any child."[28] The issue of abortion is very clear for Sarah and her friends in the march. Their conviction is obviously shared by the beliefs of their parents, but it also may be rooted in their understanding of the value of embryonic life. The teens of today are the "ultrasound kids." Many of them have seen the ultrasound pictures of themselves in their mother's uterus. Some of them have those ultrasound pictures in their baby photo album, right next to the pictures of their birth and their baptism. Technology has helped them understand that human life is a continuum that does not begin at birth, but at the moment of conception. They have a concrete image of their own prebirth existence, and they want all unborn children to have the right to life.

Sarah, John, and the three hundred from the Rochester Diocese have internalized the church's teaching about the sacredness and dignity of life, and they are witnessing to that faith in the public arena, both in the streets and in the congressional offices.

I had lunch with John, a committed pro-life parishioner, in the cafeteria of the Senate Office Building after our stop at Senator Schumer's office. Our conversation found its way to the possible war with Iraq. John was more supportive than I of President Bush invading Iraq. I had many misgivings and felt the invasion would not be a just war. In fact, I had been in Washington, D.C., the week before marching in an antiwar rally. We did not discuss other issues of the CEL as our conversation moved to what our children were doing. It is not uncommon for pro-life people to be pro–death penalty and more open to supporting war. This is especially true among pro-life, evangelical Protestants.

On the other side, some people committed to social justice are weak in their opposition to abortion. This inconsistency is where the moral vision of the CEL cuts both ways. In his 1983 address Bernardin linked the pro-life agenda with the social justice agenda: "Those who defend the right to life of the weakest among us must be equally visible in support of the quality of life of the powerless among us: the old and the young, the hungry and the homeless, the undocumented immigrant and the unemployed worker." He went on to say:

> The consequences of a consistent ethic is [sic] to bring under review the positions of every group in the Church which sees the moral meaning in one place but not the other. The ethic cuts *two* ways, not one: It challenges pro-life groups, and it challenges justice and peace groups. The meaning of a consistent ethic is to say in the Catholic community that our moral tradition calls us beyond the split so evident in the wider society between moral witness to life before and after birth.[29]

The dignity of life means advocacy for the value of every life, even those who have taken the life of another person. Many American Catholics have difficulty accepting this teaching.

THE DEATH PENALTY

According to James Megivern, an expert on the history and theology of the death penalty, Pope John Paul II "had more to say about capital punishment than any previous pope in a comparably authoritative document. His spirited repudiation of death as a punishment was all but total, to the consternation of many."[30] In the *Gospel of Life* Pope John Paul II teaches that "not even a murderer loses his personal dignity, and God himself pledges to guarantee this," as can be seen by God's protection of the murderer Cain (no. 9). Later in the letter, after quoting from the 1992 version of the *Catechism of the Catholic Church*, he all but closes the door on capital punishment, stating that "punishment . . . ought not to go to the extreme of executing the offender except in cases of absolute necessity . . . such cases are very rare if not practically nonexistent" (no. 52).

The pope's argument is that if there are bloodless ways in which society can protect itself from violent criminals, then those methods such as lifetime sentences without the possibility of parole must be used. The exceptional case where capital punishment could be justified is if a society does not have a way of protecting itself from a violent criminal; then capital punishment may be a necessary option. For example, if a murderer is stalking a nomadic community, that society may be justified in using the death penalty to protect its members. But as the pope suggests, this is not the case in the United States.

Pope John Paul II brought this message directly to the United States when he visited St. Louis, Missouri, on January 27, 1999:

> The new evangelization calls for followers of Christ who are uncondi-
> tionally pro-life: who will proclaim, celebrate and serve the Gospel of life
> in every situation. A sign of hope is the increasing recognition that the
> dignity of human life must never be taken away, even in the case of some-
> one who has done great evil. Modern society has the means of protecting
> itself, without definitively denying criminals the chance to reform. I
> renew the appeal I made most recently at Christmas for a consensus to
> end the death penalty, which is both cruel and unnecessary.[31]

The U.S. bishops have weighed in on this topic a number of times. The Catholic bishops from the state of Texas spoke strongly against the death penalty on October 27, 1997. Among their reasons against the death penalty, they point to "strong evidence of its ineffectiveness, its racially biased applica-tion, and its staggering costs, both materially and emotionally":

- It is not a deterrent to crime.
- It is racially biased—of those executed nearly 90 percent were con-victed of killing whites, although people of color are more than half of all homicide victims.
- In Texas, it costs $2.3 million to prosecute and execute each capital case as compared to $400,000 for life imprisonment.
- Innocent people have been put to death. In 350 capital conviction cases over the last twenty years, it was late proven that the convicted person had not committed the crime. Of these cases, 25 people were executed before their innocence was discovered.

The bishops quote from the prophet Ezekiel: "As I live, says the Lord God, I swear I take no pleasure in the death of the wicked man, but rather in the wicked man's conversion, that he may live. Turn, turn from your evil ways!" "The words of Ezekiel are a powerful reminder that repentance not revenge, conversion not death are better guides for public policy on the death penalty than the current pol-icy of violence for violence, death for death."[32]

The church is closing the door on state-sanctioned killing, whether that be abortion, war, euthanasia, or the death penalty. This moral position is rooted in the sacredness and dignity of human life and the belief that people do not have the right to take life—others or their own. In subsequent chapters we discuss war and the violence of poverty. The church also argues in death penalty cases that a possi-bility of conversion and repentance always exists. We believe that God's grace can penetrate the most hardhearted criminal. Who are we to give up hope on our fel-low human beings? An execution may hinder that process.

Recent surveys reveal that American Catholics are less supportive of the death penalty than they were ten years ago. Pope John Paul II, the U.S. bishops, and the leaders of the growing anti-death penalty movement can take some of the credit for this transition. The message that the dignity of every human life deserves protection is seeping into the Catholic consciousness.

∞

Prayer for Life

Eternal God,
creator and sustainer of life,
bless us with the courage to defend all life
from conception to natural death.
Bless us with the strength to respect
all peoples from east to west, from north to south,
so that we may truly follow
the call of Jesus
to be neighbor.
We ask this in the name of Jesus,
who lives and reigns
With you and the Holy Spirit.
Amen.[33]

CHAPTER 4

Community, Family, Participation

As a young man Thomas Merton was a product of his times. Born in 1915, he fathered a child when he was a student at Cambridge. He "wantonly loved books, women, ideas, art, jazz, hard drink, cigarettes, argument, and having his opinions heard." Merton was on a fast track to becoming a wild man, high on drugs, perpetually on the road, writing in rebellion against the society of squares and men in gray suits. But God was not finished with him. Although Merton "came into the world, like everyone else, captive to a tainted ancestry of human selfishness, greed and violence," conversion was possible. At age twenty-three he was baptized a Roman Catholic; three years later he decided to become a Trappist monk, to the consternation of his friends.

> By a committed life of prayer and work he would learn the right means to root out the thicket of Western culture's materialism lodged within him. He would discover for himself and for others reading over his shoulder a traditional road toward selflessness, generosity, and nonviolence.... Merton would become another witness for his generation of the way out of self-defeating individualism by tracking anew the boundaries of that ancient other country whose citizens recognize a hidden ground of unity and love among all living beings.[1]

God invites all people to live in that "ancient other country whose citizens recognize a hidden ground of unity and love among all living beings." Merton was able to find his way, with God's help, to this "ancient other country," a place that we are all invited to as well.

As a Trappist monk Merton withdrew from the cares and confusion of modern life. He focused his heart and mind on God. But his contemplation and solitude led him back to the world, back to God's people. Merton scholar William

Shannon explains: "Finding God in his solitude, he found God's people, who are inseparable from God and who, at the deepest level of their being (the level that only contemplation can reach) are at one with one another in God, the Hidden Ground of Love of all that is."[2] As he stood on the corner of Fourth and Walnut, in the center of the shopping district in Louisville, in spring 1958, Merton had an overwhelming sense of being part of humanity, and that his love of God and a search for holiness led him right back to humanity: "I was suddenly overwhelmed with the realization that I love all those people, that they were mine and I theirs, that we could not be alien to one another even though we were total strangers." He realized that he had been living under an illusion. "It was like waking from a dream of separateness, of spurious self-isolation in a special world, the world of renunciation and supposed holiness." He explained,

> The whole illusion of a separate holy existence is a dream. Not that I question the reality of my vocation, or of my monastic life: but the conception of "separation from the world" that we have in the monastery too easily presents itself as a complete illusion: the illusion that by making vows we become a different species of being, pseudo-angels, "spiritual men," men of interior life, what have you.

Merton went on to express his delight at his discovery of the obvious.

> This sense of liberation from an illusory difference was such a relief and such a joy to me that I almost laughed out loud. And I suppose my happiness could have taken form in the words: "Thank God, thank God that I am like other men, that I am only a man among others." To think that for sixteen or seventeen years I have been taking seriously this pure illusion that is implicit in so much of our monastic thinking.

He realized that even in his solitude the rest of humanity would be with him. "It is because I am one with them that I owe it to them to be alone, and when I am alone they are not 'they' but my own self. There are no strangers!"[3]

Thomas Merton's commitment to social issues flowed from a deep contemplative vision. Shannon points out that "we shall only learn to deal effectively with violence when we discover (or recover, for it is really always there) in ourselves that contemplative awareness that enables us, as it had enabled Merton, to see the oneness we share with all God's people—indeed with the whole of God's creation."[4]

This chapter begins with a reflection on God as the reason for our communal identity and how God's work has been that of forming a covenantal community, through Moses and the prophets, through Jesus and the early church. Family is also examined as a complex and, at times, ambivalent symbol of the importance of the domestic church. The chapter concludes with a focus on the importance of participation as an expression of basic justice and as a way to prevent violence and establish peace.

GOD AS EMINENTLY COMMUNAL

As Thomas Merton discovered and the bishops have articulated, "our experience of the Triune God is also a basis for Catholic social thought." Catholic social thought is not some theological afterthought; it flows from the core understanding of the very nature of God. "In the coming of Jesus Christ, we understand the Trinitarian nature of God's own inner life. Jesus reveals God as Father and sends the Holy Spirit as his gift to us to dwell in our hearts and to form us into community." The bishops continue, "God's nature is communal and social; therefore our nature, created in his image, is communal and social as well. We are communal and social because of the way we have been created and because of the One who has redeemed us." This is a very solid foundation for our Catholic social tradition—rooted in God's community of the Trinity and in our very nature, as created in God's image. For this reason the Task Force on Catholic Social Teaching and Catholic Education concludes, "We cannot call ourselves Catholic unless we hear and heed the Church's teaching to serve those in need, to protect human life and dignity, and to pursue justice and peace."[5]

Community goes to the heart of God, and to God's creative activity in the world, and community is at the heart of what it means to be human. As mentioned above, we believe in a God who lives in community: the community of the Trinity. We also believe, as John Coleman puts it, that God's "work" as revealed in the Bible is creating, restoring when broken, and completing in the end time a covenant community whose main characteristics are peace and justice.[6] That work was begun in the covenants with the Hebrew community—through Noah, Abraham, and Moses. The prophets called the community back to the requirements of justice when greed and idolatry led them to disregard the requirements of the covenant. Jesus stood on the shoulders of the prophets and announced a new covenant that would be open to all people. The Spirit of God pushes the church to be faithful to the covenant of Jesus in every age and in every circumstance. The church's understanding of the centrality of covenant has always been strong, which is the reason the early church spread. One author suggests that "the radical sense of Christian community—open to all, insistent on absolute and exclusive loyalty, and concerned for every aspect of the believer's life" is the single, overriding reason that Christianity spread throughout the Roman Empire. "From the very beginning, the one distinctive gift of Christianity was this sense of community. . . . Christian congregations provided a unique opportunity for masses of people to discover a sense of security and self-respect."[7]

As the church is passed on from generation to generation, the meaning of the covenant has been reworked and reinterpreted, sometimes losing its original meaning. Scripture scholars like Walter Brueggemann, D. N. Premnath, Jorge Pixley, and William Herzog III, to name only a few, are helping us to rediscover the powerful message of God's covenant through Moses and the meaning of Jesus' preaching the reign of God as the new covenant.

Moses Forms a Countercommunity

God calls Moses and the Hebrews to break with the imperial reality of Egypt. Moses exposes the Pharaoh's false gods, and he leads his community out of the economics of exploitation and the politics of oppression. The slavery of the Hebrews was a denial of their human dignity as they had no voice and were forced to make the bricks and build the cities of the oppressive and exploitative regime. Moses declares that this is not God's will. A new reality, a new community is brought into being: a community that does not worship the false gods of Egypt, is not exploited economically, and where the community has a voice in the political process. "Moses dismantles the politics of oppression and exploitation by countering it with a *politics of justice and compassion*. The reality emerging out of the Exodus is . . . a new social community in history." The Hebrews "found themselves, undoubtedly surprisingly to them, involved in the intentional formation of a *new social community* to match the vision of *God's freedom*. That new social reality, which is utterly discontinuous with Egypt, lasted in its alternative way for 250 years. . . . The ministry of Moses . . . represents a radical break with the social reality of Pharaoh's Egypt. The newness and radical innovations of Moses and Israel in this period can hardly be overstated." Brueggemann explains why we don't see that newness: "Most of us are probably so used to these narratives that we have become insensitive to the radical and revolutionary social reality that emerged because of Moses."[8]

Moses confronts the three central institutions of Egypt:

1. The static religion of the Pharaoh
2. The economics of exploitation
3. The politics of oppression

The static religion of the Pharaoh legitimated the social order as it was established. The gods of Egypt are the immovable lords of order. They call for, sanction, and legitimate a society of order, which was the order established by the Pharaoh. The religion of Egypt served the interests of the people in charge, the people who benefited from its exploitation and oppression. The functioning of the Egyptian society seemed to testify to the rightness of their religion because the Pharaoh prospered and the bricks made by the Hebrew slaves built up the imperial cities.

The marvel of prophetic faith is that the imperial religion, the imperial economics, and imperial politics could be broken. Moses reveals a new god, a God who is free—free to challenge the gods of Egypt and free to hear the cries of those who are exploited. This God is not a god of the "haves" but of the "have nots." This God that Moses announces is a God of freedom, a God who does not serve the interests of those in control of society, but those on the margins, those who are voiceless. Brueggemann reflects, "And perhaps we have no more important theological investigations than to discern in whose image we have been made."[9] The image of God we worship shapes our social vision: "if we gather around a static god of order who only guards the interests of the 'haves,' oppression cannot be far behind." If, on the other hand, we worship a God who is free, free even to go against the regime, "free to hear and even answer slave cries, free from all proper godness as defined by the empire," we will envision a new social reality. This God of the Hebrews is present in the brickyards, hearing their cries and leading them out with justice and compassion. The narrative of liberation for Israel begins with their groaning for liberation—not unlike the groans for liberation of the American slaves.

> And the people of Israel groaned under their bondage, and cried out for help, and their cry under bondage came up to God. And God heard their groaning, and God remembered his covenant. . . . And God saw the people of Israel, and God knew their condition. (Exod 2:23–25)

Moses, through the experience of the Exodus, forms a countercommunity with a counterconsciousness. Israel would not follow the Egyptian model. It would be a community with a religion that did not interpret God as blessing the unjust economic and political system.

As the community settled in the land of Caanan, they lost the radical religion of the desert. Their economic system and political order began to reflect the patterns of their neighboring countries. Israel experienced economic prosperity and affluence which was not democratically shared. The entire program of Solomon was a self-serving attempt to secure his wealth and control. Solomon brought in the trappings of empires, including centralizing control, a standing army, central taxation, and forced labor.[10]

- The *economics of equality* was replaced with the *economics of affluence.*
- The *religion of God's freedom* was replaced with a *religion of order and control.*
- The *politics of justice* was replaced with the *politics of oppression.*

By the time of King Solomon, 250 years after the Exodus, the state of Israel is beginning to reflect on the sinful policies and practices of Pharaoh's Egypt.

> Solomon managed what one would think is not possible, for he had taken the Mosaic innovation and rendered it null and void. In tenth-century

Jerusalem it is as though the whole revolution and social experiment had not happened. The long sequence of imperial history went on as though it had not been interrupted by this revelation of the liberating God. Solomon managed a remarkable continuity with the very Egyptian reality that Moses had sought to counter.[11]

Solomon had undermined the world of Moses' community of liberation. "He had traded a vision of freedom for the reality of security. He had banished the neighbor for the sake of reducing everyone to servants. He had replaced covenanting with consuming, and all promises had been reduced to tradable commodities."[12] The task of the prophet is call people back to the covenant community envisioned by Moses.

PROPHETIC IMAGINATION

Another task of the prophet is to imagine a different kind of a future than the empire proposes. "The prophet does not ask if the vision can be implemented, for questions of implementation are of no consequence until the vision can be imagined. The *imagination* must come before the *implementation*." The creative energy of the prophet is to call the community to a new vision of reality. "It is the vocation of the prophet to keep alive the ministry of imagination, to keep on conjuring and proposing future alternatives to the single one the king wants to urge as the only thinkable one."[13]

The prophet has two roles: to criticize the present order and in that criticism to grieve for the community, and second to energize the community. Regarding the first task of grieving for the community, the words of the prophet Jeremiah come to mind:

> A voice is heard in Ramah,
> Lamentation and bitter weeping.
> Rachel is weeping for her children;
> She refuses to be comforted for her children,
> Because they are not.

(Jer. 31:15)

Grief and tears are an expression of solidarity in pain when no other form of solidarity remains. Tears can break barriers like no harshness or anger can. We know that Jesus, in keeping with this dimension of prophecy, wept over Jerusalem (Luke 19:41). He also taught that only those who mourn will be comforted (Matt. 5:4). Jesus knew that weeping permits the reign of God to begin. Such weeping is a radical criticism, a dismantling of the old order and the old relationships, and the beginning of new relationships.

We know this is true from our own experiences of loss and death. Through grieving and tears we weep over what was lost, but our grief opens the door to something new. We weep over being fired, a broken marriage, and the death of a loved one, but that painful experience may open us up to new job possibilities, a more selfless way of loving, or a new relationship "in the spirit" with our deceased loved one.

The prophetic vision is often the boldest when the situation seems utterly hopeless. "The deeper the crisis, the bolder the vision."[14] When the community faces difficult times it needs a vision of hope and justice.

The second task of the prophet is to energize the community. In the face of injustice and oppression, the royal consciousness leads to despair. The prophetic consciousness, on the other hand, speaks and acts a message of hope. "Hope is the decision to which God invites Israel, a decision against despair, against permanent consignment to chaos (Isa 45:18), oppression, barrenness, and exile."[15] This is hope rooted in the assurance that God does not quit even when the evidence is not hopeful.

"The hope-filled language of prophecy, in cutting through the royal despair and hopelessness, engages the community in new discernments and celebrations just when it had nearly given up and had nothing to celebrate." One powerful expression of hope is to give praise to God and to utter thanksgiving even when all is not well—just as Jesus did at the Last Supper, before being betrayed and executed. Doxology, the act of giving praise, makes us aware of God's presence even in the places that seem godless.[16] Through offering hope the prophet energizes the community, and in turn the community becomes a prophetic community.

JESUS AS PROPHET

Jesus clearly identified with the prophetic tradition and the new consciousness the prophets announced. In his teaching and in his very presence, Jesus presented the ultimate criticism of the royal consciousness. Jesus "has, in fact dismantled the royal consciousness and nullified its claims."[17] The royal consciousness said the Jews must submit to Roman authority and oppression or face extinction. The religious and political leaders saw Jesus as a threat to the survival of the order that Rome had imposed. The High Priest Caiaphas realized that Jesus had to die to protect the status quo. By his decisive solidarity with marginal people, Jesus criticized the injustice of the current order. While he announced good news to the poor, his message was bad news for those who benefit from the unjust situation.

Jesus announced in Luke 4:18–19 that a new age was beginning, but that announcement carried within it a harsh criticism of all those agents who benefit from the present order.

His message was to the poor, but others kept them poor and benefited from their poverty. He addressed the captives (which means bonded slaves), but others surely wanted that arrangement unchanged. He named the oppressed, but there are never oppressed without oppressors.[18]

His solidarity was expressed in compassion—a compassion that announced that the hurt of the marginal and powerless is taken seriously. Compassion is the one virtue that the empire does not permit. "Empires are never built or maintained on the basis of compassion. The norms of law (social control) are never accommodated to persons, but persons are accommodated to the norms."[19] Jesus' response of compassion is both personal for individuals and on whole populations who were "harassed and helpless":

> And Jesus went about all the cities and villages, teaching in their synagogues and preaching the gospel of the kingdom, and healing every disease and every infirmity. When he saw the crowds, he had compassion for them because they were harassed and helpless, like sheep without a shepherd. (Matt 9:35–36)

These words point out that the crowds had been rendered helpless and were being harassed. If someone is harassed, someone else is the harasser. Jesus' words are directed at both those who are harassed and those who are harassing them. In Jesus' time and in our time, the one thing the dominant culture cannot tolerate is compassion. Compassion is the ability to stand with the victims of the present order. The dominant culture can tolerate charity and good intentions, but it has no way to resist solidarity with the marginal, which is subversive of the present unjust order.[20] Archbishop Oscar Romero stood with the poor; the four American women who were martyred were in solidarity with the poor of El Salvador. Suffering made audible is the beginning of hope and a new reality, the reality of a new reign—not a reign of exploitation, but the reign of a compassionate God. This truly is good news for the poor and release for the captives.

The church is charged with preaching the good news to the poor and exhibiting the same compassion and justice of the prophets, a compassion that opens the door for hope and a new beginning. As we know, the early church struggled to be the compassion of Jesus and to continue God's work of building a covenant community whose characteristics are right relationships—the basis of biblical justice and peace.

The church's attitude toward the Roman Empire is a complex and shifting story. The early church challenged the idolatry of Rome and struggled to live the alternative consciousness where the economics of equality and the politics of justice were expressed in a religion that celebrated God's freedom. But as the church gained acceptance by the Roman emperor Constantine, it gradually shifted its stance. When Rome "fell" in 467, church leaders became more responsible for the social order. The church itself took on some of the cultural trappings of power and authority of Rome as it developed its hierarchical structure.

The radical voice of the gospel echoed still in the monastic traditions and in vigilant church leaders. St. Basil is an example of a leader who continued to respond to God's call for compassion and justice.

ST. BASIL FOCUSES ON COMMUNITY

Basil (329–379) came from a family of rich landowners in Caesarea in Cappadocia (modern-day Kayseri, Turkey). After his studies, he distributed all his possessions among the poor, influenced by the radical asceticism of the monks of Egypt. Basil had visited different monasteries before he joined one near his home city. He drew up a rule that had a revolutionary influence on the development of monasticism. Unlike the early monks whose spirituality focused on individual feats of asceticism, Basil stressed the importance of community.

The monastery for Basil was to model the ideal community, a community where the love of God and the love of neighbor could be cultivated side by side. He believed that the monastery should be integrated into the life of the church and society. Rather than existing in isolation, the monastery should welcome guests; it should include orphanages and schools; it should be a center of service and a center for the works of mercy. "For Basil the monastery did not exist for the sanctification of its members alone, but for the entire wider community."[21] Basil was making the connection between love of God and love of neighbor as the unified vision of contemplative life—a tradition that Thomas Merton would echo sixteen hundred years later. In seeking the isolation of the monastery the monk is led back to the service of God's people in the world.

As bishop of Caesarea in Cappadocia, Basil translated the social demands of the gospel into action by setting up a large welfare center at the gates of the city for the poor, the old, and the sick, together with a hospice for penniless travelers. Welfare centers of this kind also came into being in other cities in his diocese.

Although a famous preacher, Basil was better known for his emphasis on the social aspects of the gospel. He organized soup kitchens, personally donning an apron to wait on the hungry. He established a hospital for the sick poor that was described as one of the wonders of the church. Basil went beyond the traditional exhortation to charity. He called for a basic redistribution of wealth as a requirement of justice. In effect, he taught that the needs of the poor held a social mortgage on the surplus holdings of the rich; he challenged the well-to-do in his community with blunt language: "You refuse to give on the pretext that you haven't got enough for your own needs. But while your tongue makes excuses, your hand convicts you—that ring shining on your finger silently declares you to be a liar! How many debtors could be released from prison with one of those rings?"[22]

He preached a famous sermon on the rich farmer (Luke 12:18) in which he called the man who could help the needy but keeps his possessions to himself a "robber and a thief":

> Are you not a robber, you who consider your own that which has been given you solely to distribute to others? This bread which you have set aside is the bread of the hungry; this garment you have locked away is the clothing of the naked; those shoes which you let rot are the shoes of him who is barefoot; those riches you have hoarded are the riches of the poor.[23]

Basil took the Stoic thinking of the day which defended private property and turned it around. The Stoic Chrysippus had used the example that the first one to arrive at the theater has a right to choose his seat. Basil took up that image:

> Tell me, what is yours? Where did you get it and bring it into the world? It is as if one has taken a seat in the theatre and then drives out all who come later, thinking that what is for everyone is only for him. Rich people are like that. For having pre-empted what is common to all, they make it their own by virtue of this prior possession. If only each one would take as much as he requires to satisfy his immediate needs, and leave the rest to others who equally needed it, no one would be rich—and no one would be poor.[24]

Basil left a lasting legacy in the Eastern church. To this day monastic life in the East is based on the ideals he set forth in his monastic Rule. His emphasis on community in monastic life, his preaching, and his direct action to serve the needy shaped the early church's understanding of its mission to build community. The early church realized that all of God's people had a right to participate in the resources of the earth. That message still challenges us today.

We know that it is often in the family that our attitudes about compassion and justice are shaped. That certainly was true in the case of Basil, who came from a family renowned for its virtue. Basil's grandmother Macrina the Elder, his parents Basil the Elder and Emmelia, his older sister Macrina, and two younger brothers, Gregory of Nyssa and Peter of Sebaste, are all canonized saints. This "acorn" did not fall far from the tree.

FAMILY IN THE "NEW ERA"

While the church has unflinchingly taught the importance of community as essential for Christian life, it has a mixed history on stressing the importance of being part of a biological family. While the church recalls the importance of the Holy Family—and every family, as a vehicle of God's grace—it has also held up not having a family and remaining celibate as an effective form of discipleship. This ambivalence about family is found in the very words of Jesus. Luke's account records: "Then his mother and his brothers came to see him, but they could not reach him because of the crowd. And he was told, 'Your mother and brothers are standing outside, wanting to see you.' But he said to them, 'My mother and my brothers are those who hear the word of God and do it'" (Luke 8:19–21). On another occasion his relatives and family tried to restrain Jesus because they were "convinced he was out of his mind" (Mark 3:21).[25]

The Christian message was a "sword of division" setting family members against one another:

> I have not come to bring peace, but a sword. For I have come to set a man against his father, and a daughter against her mother, and a daughter-in-law against her mother-in-law; and one's foes will be members of one's own household. (Matt. 10:34–36)

The radical edge of Jesus' message is that we are to love him more than our family members: "Whoever loves father or mother more than me is not worthy of me; and whoever loves son or daughter more than me is not worthy of me" (Matt. 10:37). Jesus preached a "new age" that would exclude marrying: "Jesus said to them, 'Those who belong to this age marry and are given in marriage; but those who are considered worthy of a place in that age and in the resurrection from the dead neither marry nor are given in marriage" (Luke 20:34–35). As ethicist Margaret Farley notes, "All family bonds and responsibilities were relativized in favor of an imminent realm of God in which the unity with God and all persons would transcend the special human relations that were in place before its coming."[26]

God's "new era" relativized all other human institutions, including marriage and family. At the same time, the followers of Jesus became the new family for those without a family—the poor, the orphan, and the widows. "If any believing woman has relatives who are really widows, let her assist them; let the church not be burdened, so that it can assist those who are real widows" (1 Tim. 5:16). For those who had to leave their birth families because of the gospel, the church became their new community of brothers and sisters—their new family. This new family of the church offered a membership that abolished all barriers of nation, gender, or economic status. Here there "is neither Jew nor Greek, there is neither slave nor free, there is neither male nor female; for you all are one in Christ Jesus" (Gal. 3:28). While this was the framework of the age to come, it also could be experienced in the here and now.

In its response to "family" the church rejected family ties as the highest bond and substituted the church as the new family. But, in time, the church reaffirmed family ties as important, so as not to appear too radical in the Greco-Roman world. While we have the radical "egalitarian" statement of Galatians stated above, a few years later we find in Ephesians the traditional hierarchical framework wherein wives are instructed to be "subject to your husbands as you are to the Lord" (Eph. 5:22). The radical teaching of Jesus on family ties was softened so that the church was seen in a more positive light by the surrounding cultures. "The socially disruptive antifamily trends in the Christian community were thus moderated."[27] These later writings in the New Testament tried to adhere to the spirit of Jesus even as it affirmed traditional relationships. A new spirit was brought to the relationships within the family, even if the external (patriarchal) structures remained in place.

The same could be said of the relationship of servant and master. Paul sent the runaway slave, Onesimus, back to his master Philemon, with the instruction that the latter should treat his slave as a brother. Paul addressed Philemon, saying, "Perhaps this is the reason he was separated from you for a while, so that you might have him back forever, no longer as a slave but more than a slave, a beloved brother" (Phlm. 15–16). The social institutions were not overturned but were challenged to be transformed by the love and equality of God's realm. A remnant of the radical vision of equality remains, even as the church accepted traditional hierarchical relationships of males over females, masters over slaves. There is a hint in Paul's advice to the Corinthians of overturning the societal norms that tolerated inequality in marriage: "the husband rules over his wife's body and that the wife rules over her husband's body" (1 Cor. 7:4).

The early church's teaching on family remained ambiguous. In the third century the church rejected the extreme antifamily, antimarriage teaching of some Gnostic sects. "Marriage was affirmed as good by the Christian church, as part of creation, though celibacy was considered better."[28]

This view of marriage and family continued through the centuries, more or less in place until the fourteenth century when the humanists in the Renaissance proposed a change from otherworldliness to social responsibility, from renunciation and withdrawal to self-discipline and achievement in a world where family and productive labor were combined. The Protestant Reformation in the sixteenth century built on these new orientations and shifted the focus away from the monastery and the sanctuary to the marketplace. The Christian vocation "in the marketplace, behind the plow, and in front of the stove" was extolled.[29]

FAMILY SINCE VATICAN II

The Roman Catholic tradition resisted the "this worldly" focus until the Second Vatican Council, which Professor Farley calls "a quantum leap in the church's positive affirmation of the family."[30] In Vatican II and subsequent documents the family has been hailed as

- The foundation of society
- The "first cell of the church"
- The "domestic sanctuary" of the church[31]

Alongside this positive view of family, some segments of the church still preferred the celibate vocation. In his 1980 encyclical, *Familiaris Consortio*, Pope John Paul II reaffirmed the church's defense "throughout her history" of the "superiority of this charism [of celibacy] to that of marriage, by reason on the wholly singular link which it has with the kingdom of God" (no. 16).[32]

Today, Catholic theology and spirituality does not view the love of another human being as distracting from our love of God. In fact, love of a spouse and child is viewed as participation in divine love. Sexuality is viewed in more positive terms as a gift of God to be enjoyed and celebrated within committed love and not only tolerated for the sake of procreation. These positive themes provide the starting points for a reinterpretation of marriage and family within the Catholic tradition. This revisioning is only in beginning stages. Catholicism and other Christian denominations are still working on understanding the role of women in the church and society and the meaning of committed homosexual relationships.

Some ongoing issues remain, namely, how to understand the equal dignity and responsibility of men and women in marriage and family. Pope John Paul II preferred to speak of the "complementarity" of men and women. While this is an improvement over the overt inequality of past thinking, Sister Farley fears that this means that "the gendered hierarchy of roles and separation of spheres [public and private] remains entrenched in the tradition."[33]

On the positive side, Pope John Paul II's insistence on the value of the stay-at-home mom has resonated well with those who believe society undervalues the importance of parents who stay at home to nurture their children.

Pope John Paul II's most distinctive contribution was his teaching that the Christian family is the "domestic church." This characterization was used in Vatican II's *Lumen Gentium*: "The family is, so to speak, the domestic Church. In it parents should, by their word and example, be the first preachers of faith to their children" (no. 11). Earlier references to the family as the "church in miniature," the "small church," or the "church of the home" can be found in patristic theologians, including John Chrysostom and Augustine as well as Protestant theologians.[34] In a church that had often emphasized the primacy of discipleship through celibacy, this concept of family as the domestic church helped to highlight "the notion that the Christian couple and their children participate in an ongoing sacramental reality through which they are sanctified and invited to participate actively in the outward mission of the church, especially through service and hospitality."[35]

The understanding of family as the domestic church fits well with the church's principle of subsidiarity wherein smaller, local associations are linked with the larger institutions, but are also relatively independent. This is true for the family as it relates both to the larger church and to the state. The family is a sacrament of God's love when parents and children imitate Christ's self-giving love. The family is "a saving community" (*Familiaris Consortio*, no. 49) as it reflects and communicates Christ's love to others. The love between husband and wife and among family members participates in "the prophetic, priestly, and kingly mission" of Christ and the church. In this way the Christian family is a gospel community, a community in relation to God, and a community of service to others (nos. 50, 63). According to Pope John Paul II, the family also plays a vital role in society:

> It is from the family that citizens come to birth, and it is within the family that they find the first school of the social virtues that are the animating principle of the existence and development of society. Thus, far from being closed in on itself, the family is by nature and vocation open to other families and to society, and undertakes its social role.[36]

The family is "the most effective means of humanizing and personalizing society"; it is "the first and irreplaceable school of social life, and example and stimulus for the broader community of relationships marked by respect, justice, dialogue and love."[37]

The pope encouraged family to work for structural reform, claiming that the Christian family "is not closed in on itself, but remains open to the community, moved by a sense of justice and concern for others, as well as by a consciousness of its responsibility toward the whole of society." The family's commitment to the hungry, the poor, the old, the sick, the disabled, drug victims, ex-prisoners, and those without families, especially abandoned children and orphans, lead it to social action, and "active and responsible involvement in the authentically human growth of society and its institutions," extending even to the international level.[38] Our Catholic tradition is sprinkled with socially conscious families who lived out those social virtues that help our society develop. I met the mother of one of those families who taught by her example. Her name was Esperanza.

The Grandmothers from Waukegan

Esperanza, who could not speak much English, slept at our house just one night, but she made a big impression. Esperanza is a short Mexican American widow from Waukegan, Illinois, where she raised eleven children. All of her children graduated from college. Now at seventy years old, it's time to relax, right?

Not for Esperanza and the eleven other members from her parish and small Christian community in northern Illinois. They climbed onto the buses in Chicago as part of a nine-day journey to Washington, D.C., and New York City to demonstrate on behalf of recent immigrants whose rights and dignity are not being recognized.

Esperanza was part of a national campaign, Immigrant Workers' Freedom Ride—Legalization and a Road to Citizenship, which brought seventeen buses full of immigrant workers and their supporters from nine cities across the country. Esperanza was one of 142 riders on the three buses from Chicago. Fifty-two of the riders stayed in homes while the others stayed in a Super 8 motel. Esperanza and her friends, Juanita and Alicia, stayed at the Mich home. The night before, they had slept on camping pads and blankets on the floor of a church basement. They were so appreciative to be able to sleep in a bed.

Esperanza and her 141 companions embody the theme of this chapter. Here is a Catholic woman who raised her family and is deeply concerned about her community of immigrants, new and old, who are trying to participate in the U.S. economy. She continues to participate to build up the community, to make it more just and welcoming. She participates as a member of a small Christian community that nourishes her faith and encourages her to work for a more just society. I was humbled, honored, and energized by the witness of her life. She is one of the unnamed heroines of our church who has a sense of justice and lives it out with her other grandmother-friends in Waukegan.

FAMILIES AS "THE SALT OF THE EARTH"

"The most challenging work for justice is not done in Church committees, but in the secular world of *work, family life and citizenship*."[39] This is the conclusion of the bishops' reflection on bringing the gospel to our families, our work, and our civic places. Those of us in social justice ministry acknowledge this, but we are often not sure how to support it. We are so geared to getting parents, teens, and volunteers to join us in our projects and campaigns. At the same time we need to develop an attitude that reaffirms and supports the task of living the gospel at home, at work, in the neighborhood, and as we vote and participate in the public arenas. The parish as a whole—through its worship and preaching, through its faith formation programs, through its sacramental life—helps us to be agents of gospel values at home, at work, and in the community. But those identified with parish social ministry or the social justice efforts of the diocese must also evaluate their work in how it helps all of us to translate social justice into the everyday venues of school, home life, and work. My experience suggests that we activists are amazingly embarrassed and silent when that question is lifted up. We are so geared to getting people involved in our projects that we don't know how to think about our role in promoting that attitude in our parishes.

Justice in Everyday Life

"Our parishes are clearly called to help people live their faith in the world, helping them understand and act on the social dimensions of the Gospel in their everyday lives." "Living our faith in the world" is the challenge for all Christians. The bishops continue: "parish committees can be useful, but they are no substitute for everyday choices and commitments of believers—acting as parents, workers, students, owners, investors, advocates, policy makers and citizens."[40] Living the faith begins in our homes, carries forth into the workplace, and is visible in our interactions in the marketplace and government places. It is as simple as honesty and fairness. Parents need to live with integrity and honesty; our children are always watching. What lesson does a parent communicate who says to a fourteen-year-old child at the box office, "Don't say anything because I am going to try to get you in as a child"? Or the parent who is upset when the son's pencil is stolen at school, but who has no problem taking pens and pencils from work?

Our daughter, who was about to begin her second year of college, took me (and my credit card) shopping for clothes on the Labor Day weekend before she headed back to school. While at J.C. Penney's she picked up a belt, slippers, and a purse. I bought a pair of shoes. We paid our bill and wandered down the mall to another clothing store. I started thinking about the bill. I knew everything was on sale and that there was no sales tax on clothing that week, but how could we get everything for seventy-one dollars? I looked at the receipt. The clerk had forgotten to include my shoes, but had scanned the purse twice. I said that I needed to go back. My daughter thought we should just keep going, that it was the clerk's mistake. I said that once we realized the mistake it is comparable to stealing, and I needed to go back. When I returned to the store the sales clerk was very appreciative and said that a lot of people do not come back. She rang up the shoes and gave me an additional 10 percent discount for coming back. I am sure my nineteen-year-old daughter was watching my actions. I hope she learned something about the Seventh Commandment during our shopping excursion.[41]

The document *Communities of Salt and Light* offers eight concrete ways in which parishes can help their members to live the gospel in the world of family, work, and citizenship:

1. Building and sustaining marriages of quality, fidelity, equality, and permanence in an age that does not value commitment or hard work in relationships.

2. Raising families with Gospel values in a culture where materialism, selfishness, and prejudice still shape so much of our lives.

3. Being a good neighbor, welcoming newcomers and immigrants, treating people of different races, ethnic groups, and nationalities with respect and kindness.

4. Seeing themselves as evangelizers who recognize the unbreakable link between spreading the Gospel and work for social justice.

5. Bringing Christian values and virtues into the marketplaces.

6. Treating coworkers, customers, and competitors with respect and fairness, demonstrating economic initiative, and practicing justice.

7. Bringing integrity and excellence to public service and community responsibilities seeking the common good, respecting human life, and promoting human dignity.

8. Providing leadership in unions, community groups, professional associations, and political organizations at a time of rising cynicism and indifference.[42]

Supporting Those in the Workplace

In a later chapter we discuss the dignity of work and the rights of workers. In the context of this chapter, we lift up a few ideas of how parishes can be creative about how to support their members in living out the gospel at work. A few examples are offered just to get our wheels turning.

- One parish in the Milwaukee Archdiocese sends its permanent deacon and other volunteers to visit with truck drivers at the truck stop. They provide a listening set of ears and people willing to pray with those on the road.

- A suburban parish in Pittsford, New York, in the Rochester metropolitan area has a group called "Eye of the Needle" that brings together people in the parish who have monetary resources to reflect on what the gospel means for them. It recalls the words of Jesus when he said it is easier for a camel to pass through the eye of a needle than for a rich person to be saved (Luke 18:24–25). Eye of the Needle tries to be a place where Catholics wrestle— with honesty and challenging discussion—with the meaning of being wealthy and Christian.

- St. Martha's parish in Akron, Ohio, has eighteen Vocation Reflection Groups organized by occupation: educators, lawyers, journalists, and so on. They meet monthly to reflect on their work and to discuss how they can apply their beliefs and values in their workplaces. The pastor helps the lay facilitators from each group plan their monthly meetings. The Sunday liturgies are also used to recognize the different professions and bless them during the liturgy when the readings focus on a specific profession.[43]

- A downtown parish in Rochester, New York, has sponsored a forum for the discussion of public issues in the community known as the Downtown Community Forum. It offers monthly noontime or evening presentations and discussions on a wide range of topics, most of which are not religious but are issues in the community, for example, access to health care, city-suburban-rural planning, dealing with grief during the holidays, and the church as employer. These sessions are meant to promote the common good of the community without an explicit religious overlay.

- Catholic colleges or justice and peace centers offer discussions on topics for the business community at a breakfast meeting on a Friday morning where business leaders have the space to raise concerns about the issues they face in downsizing their workforce or other pertinent topics.

These few examples only begin to scratch the surface of what is possible for parishes and other Catholic institutions as they try to support their members in living their Christian faith in the world. The goal is to bring our Christian faith into our workplace, into the civic arenas to enable us to participate as Christians in the public arena as well as living our faith in our homes. The doorways into participation are many; sometimes even a natural disaster like a hurricane opens the way to new forms of participation, as the Christians of Central America discovered after Hurricane Mitch in 1998.

In the Wake of Hurricane Mitch

Ten thousand people died and hundreds of thousands of people lost their homes and their crops when Hurricane Mitch hit Central America on October 27, 1998. In the midst of such devastating losses a new approach to grassroots participation in the cleanup and rebuilding emerged. A new, church-sponsored experiment in participation and building democracy in the context of grinding poverty and pervasive political corruption took root. "We're trying hard to change this history of ours where the poor always get ignored, marginalized, or crushed," said Lorenzo Crux, a church leader who works with a new community organization in Aguán Valley of Honduras.[44]

In the wake of Hurricane Mitch, the social ministry of the diocese of Trujillo, Honduras, helped urban residents and rural villagers in the Aguán Valley to develop new forms of participation called Codels. The Codels were local emergency committees that took charge of the cleanup and reconstruction work. Citizens had to organize these committees if they wanted to receive supplies from the food-for-work program supported by Catholic Relief Services and managed by the diocese. The insight of this new approach was to help the poor become subjects of change and not simply the objects of someone else's largesse. Throughout the region Catholic Relief Services sponsored forums for migrants and their families to lobby government for their own needs rather than waiting for charity organizations and government elites sitting down over lunch to work things out.

One secret of the Codels' success was that half the participants had to be women, which was a radical departure from the traditional organizing efforts in the area. Mariana Ortiz was one participant who helped clean up after the hurricane and build a new system for drinking water. She noted that "Thanks to God, Hurricane Mitch did us a favor. We had big losses of people and property, but we gained consciousness. Through this experience we learned we have strength when we work together." The local committees organized the fair distribution of food and relief supplies.

As they did they began to transform local politics, which had long been dominated by corrupt and paternalistic political bosses. In confronting corrupt political systems, church leaders and aid workers have come to realize that assisting the poor is not simply a technical problem about how to develop a source of potable water, but it is also a political problem, namely, an imbalance of power. Development aid and technical assistance are necessary, but they must be complemented by organizing political power to change unjust policies.

It is not enough, according to the old adage, to teach a hungry person how to fish. The water where the fish are to be found may be fenced off, polluted, or fished out by a foreign company. Rick Jones, the Catholic Relief Service director in El Salvador, explains: "You can have the best agricultural project and teach small farmers how to grow tomatoes, but if public policies don't favor growing small tomatoes for the national market, then that project is bound to fail. No matter how successful, it won't be sustainable. So you need to have a policy environment that favors incorporating these people into the economy and society." He explains why aid programs are coming to realize the need for advocacy work and political participation. "Although they have great projects, when the projects are finished they haven't changed anything. They've come to realize that advocacy and public policy work are an essential part of development."[45]

This insight—that aid and technical expertise must be complemented by advocacy work that changes economic and political policies—is a lesson for Christians in the North as well as in Central America. Catholic Relief Services is reengineering its appeal in Catholic parishes in the United States. No longer is the approach to go to parish potluck suppers just to ask for funds. Now they are suggesting using the influence of money and consumer buying power and political action. Catholic Relief Services urges parishes and individuals to purchase fairly traded coffee and pressuring apparel makers to enforce "sweat free" practices in their factories.

Participation in works of charity and the works of justice is required by Catholic social teaching, which tells us to address the *root causes* of poverty and violence, as well as the immediate needs. The way to address the root causes of poverty and violence is through advocacy and community organization. Catholics in both Latin America and North America are learning the importance of both forms of participation. As we discussed in chapter 1, the Catholic Church has a new understanding of its social mission, which includes addressing the institutional and structural sources of poverty and violence. This reveals the dynamic nature of the church's social teaching and develops understanding of the meaning of participation.

PARTICIPATION

While the early church preachers and bishops focused on the right to participate in the bounty of the earth, later church teaching added the right to participate in the political process, to be an active participant in community decision making. In 1971 Pope Paul VI noted that participation and equality were two fundamental aspirations of humanity. Participation and equality are another way of promoting human dignity and human freedom. Pope Paul VI recognized that people today expect "a greater sharing in responsibility and in decision making." He said that sharing in responsibility and in decision making in the social and political arenas "must be established and strengthened."[46]

The U.S. bishops picked up the theme of participation in their 1986 pastoral letter on the economy, *Economic Justice for All.* They moved beyond affirming it as a fundamental aspiration to calling it a demand of basic justice: "Basic justice demands the establishment of minimum levels of participation in the life of the human community for all persons." They explained that "the ultimate injustice is for a person or group to be treated actively or abandoned passively as if they were nonmembers of the human race." The bishops pointed out that the lack of participation or exclusion happens in the political and economic spheres in both wealthy and poor nations. "These patterns of exclusion are created by free human beings. In this sense they can be called forms of social sin." The bishops teach that it is a sinful situation when we do not change policies and practices that continue to exclude people, socially, politically, and economically. "Acquiescence in them or failure to correct them when it is possible to do so is a sinful dereliction of Christian duty" (no. 77).

I wonder how many Christians confess their dereliction of Christian duty when they refuse to remove exclusionary practices? In the next paragraph the bishops repeat their understanding of the importance of participation:

> Recent Catholic social thought regards the task of overcoming these patterns of exclusion and powerlessness as a most basic demand of justice. Stated positively, justice demands that social institutions be ordered in a way that guarantees all persons the ability to participate actively in the

economic, political, and cultural life of society. The level of participation may legitimately be greater for some persons than for others, but there is a basic level of access that must be made available for all. Such participation is an essential expression of the social nature of human beings and of their communitarian vocation. (no. 78)

These strong convictions are a judgment on the policies of society and church whenever they resist expanding the legitimate arenas of participation in decision making or economic opportunity.

In his annual World Day of Peace Message, Pope John Paul II has explained the importance of participation for every human being. He reminds us that violence and injustice are often rooted in the denial of participation. In 1985 he pointed out:

It is essential for every human being to have a sense of participating, of being part of the decisions and endeavors that shape the destiny of the world. Violence and injustice have often in the past found their root causes in people's sense of being deprived of the right to shape their own lives. Future violence and injustice cannot be avoided when the basic right to participate in the choices of society is denied.[47]

Promoting the right to participate is, therefore, a way to work for peace and the reduction of violence.

God is at work in the world, lifting up witnesses and prophets of God's covenant community, a community of justice and peace. They are, for example, the members of Esperanza's small Christian community in Waukegan who climb the buses and demonstrate for justice for immigrant workers. God is inviting all to hear the call to build a community of peace and justice. God is inviting all to participate economically, politically, and socially in the resources of creation and human community. One of the more complex questions is how Catholics should participate in political life, as voters and politicians, especially when social policy is not in accord with the Catholic moral tradition.

Faithful Citizenship

In 2004 a number of U.S. bishops took a strong stand against Catholic politicians who publicly take stands contrary to the church's teaching. The issue of abortion, euthanasia, and embryonic stem-cell research were issues that we highlighted. A few bishops announced that such politicians should not approach the altar to receive Holy Communion, because they were not in communion with the church's teaching. This approach by a few bishops ignited a fiery discussion within the church and in the media. This complex question touches on theology, canon law, our view of the church, judgments about the political process, and social theory, as well as questions of strategies and tactics.

This section offers a modest framework for approaching these questions. The foundational document on this question is *Faithful Citizenship: A Catholic Call to Political Responsibility*, which has been updated every four years since 1975 as an aid to Catholics as the country approaches each presidential election.

The bishops remind us that "One of our greatest blessings in the United States is our right and responsibility to participate in civic life. Everyone can and should participate. Even those who cannot vote have the right to have their voices heard on issues that affect their communities."[48] They note that "We need more, not less engagement in political life." They urge Catholics to live out Catholic principles by running for office, working within political parties, and contributing money or time to campaigns, among other ways. In fact, the bishops stated that "responsible citizenship is a virtue; participation in the political process is a moral obligation."[49]

How the church enters public life is a crucial question. The bishops note that the church does not impose a sectarian doctrine, but acts on our moral convictions, shares our experience of serving the poor and vulnerable, and participates in the dialogue over our nation's future.

The bishops recommend examining the full range of issues and relying on the consistent ethic of life as the moral framework when it comes time to vote:

> As bishops, we seek to form the consciences of our people. We do not wish to instruct persons on how they should vote by endorsing or opposing candidates. We hope that voters will examine the position of candidates on the full range of issues, as well as on their personal integrity, philosophy, and performance. We are convinced that a consistent ethic of life should be the moral framework from which to address issues in the political arena.[50]

In the above statement the bishops were echoing the advice from the Vatican's Congregation for the Doctrine of the Faith, which pointed out the year before that "a political commitment to a single isolated aspect of the Church's social doctrine does not exhaust one's responsibility towards the common good."[51]

The bishops then briefly address dozens of specific issues grouped under four major headings: protecting human life, promoting family life, pursuing social justice, and practicing global solidarity. This shows the breadth of concern that is needed when evaluating political parties and candidates for office, especially candidates for national office. Finally, the bishops offer some advice on how the church, as an institution and as individuals should participate in the political arena:

- We are called to be **political but not partisan**. The Church cannot be a chaplain for any one party or cheerleader for any candidate. Our cause is the protection of the weak and vulnerable and defense of human life and dignity, not a political party or candidate.

- The Church is called to be **principled but not ideological**. We cannot compromise our basic values or teaching, but we should be open to different ways to advance them.
- We are to be **clear but also civil**.
- The Church is called to be **engaged but not used**. We welcome dialogue with political leaders and candidates . . . but we must be sure that events and "photo-ops" are not substitutes for work on policies that reflect our values.[52]

These are wise guidelines for civic engagement, not only during the election cycle but during every season.

We are called to live in family and community and to participate in society and the church. These values shape our attitudes and actions in a society that places more emphasis on the individual and individual autonomy. In such a social context the wisdom of our tradition keeps us centered in family and community as we promote the equality and participation of every human being.

∞

Prayer for Community

Embracing God,

We praise you for the communities of life which sustain us:

creation, family, church, and the community of all people.

May we learn from your Son Jesus to love our neighbors more deeply,

so that we may continue your work of creating a community of justice and peace in our world.

May that same love of neighbor fill us with creative energy to overcome the obstacles of intolerance and indifference and to build inclusive communities in our neighborhoods, nations, and among all your children. Amen.[53]

CHAPTER 5

Option for the Poor

Donna Ecker was a model Catholic suburban parishioner. She was a lector, active in a Bible study group, and involved in the family ministry program. Despite her involvement, Donna sensed there was something more she could be doing. "I felt there was someplace else that I had to be that I hadn't gotten to yet."

In response to that yearning, she volunteered at Bethany House, a Catholic Worker home for homeless women and children—many who are victims of domestic violence. By the end of the second day she realized that this was "where I needed to be."[1]

That was in 1985. Since then Donna has been the full-time, unpaid codirector of Bethany House—a home that provides food, clothing, and temporary housing for women and children who suffer from unemployment, substance addiction, domestic abuse, and many other problems. "What we're trying to do here is create an atmosphere where everyone who comes here feels cared for and supported." The compassion is the one thing that makes Bethany House work: the compassion of the staff and volunteers, and the compassion of the residents. The eight-bed home is run with volunteer, around-the-clock, unpaid help. In the Catholic Worker approach, Bethany House is supported only by donations and not by any government funding. The house operates solely on private donations from individuals and parish tithing committees. Food and donations come in month by month, trusting that "God will provide."

With the decision to work for no pay, Donna and her husband Tom, who is a permanent deacon, had to simplify their lives. Tom, who fully supports and works with Donna, explained, "We don't life the high life or fast life. But I don't feel that we gave up anything." The Eckers have made an option for the poor, an option that is rich in human rewards. Donna believes that Bethany House has made her rich in ways

93

that can't be measured. The "assets" in her bank account include the many lives she has been able to touch and the little moments of joy that her guests experience in her presence. Sometimes, just having a birthday party for a guest who has never had a birthday party brings a deep joy.

In living out her option for the poor Donna is supported by her spouse and by a community of prayer. Tom and Donna minister as a married couple. Donna credits Tom for sustaining ministry. "There's no way this could have happened if he was not as supportive as he is." Tom has recently retired and is happy to be able to spend more time at Bethany House. He assists in many ways, including weekly prayer services. Donna sought out a community of prayerful women to be part of her spiritual and moral support, which led her to become a lay associate of the Mercy Sisters. Donna explained that the Mercy Sisters offer more than spiritual support; some of the sisters volunteer at the house. In December 2002 Donna was honored with the Mercy Action Cunningham Award, a national award that also included five-thousand-dollar donation to Bethany House. The Sisters of Mercy offer their prayers, their time, and their financial support.

Donna said that working with homeless women and children has changed her views about homelessness and success. In the beginning she thought homelessness would be eradicated by society in a few years, but she is far less optimistic now. These days, she takes delight in smaller successes. For some residents, success might mean three months of living free from drug use, while for others it might mean emotionally reconnecting with their children.

"What brings me back every day is the women and children. Watching them in their struggles to do better, to love their children, to get on their feet. It takes a lot of courage and tenacity. . . . That's something a lot of people don't get to see. . . . Why wouldn't I come back?" asks Donna Ecker.

This chapter examines the rich biblical evidence for the option for the poor, how the term is used in the Latin American context, its meaning in Catholic social thought, the stories of holy people who have opted for the poor, and how we in North America make a preferential option for the poor.

ANCIENT YET NEW

Although God's option for the poor is well established in the biblical record, the phrase "option for the poor" has appeared only recently in the lexicon of Catholic social teaching. This concept was given the clearest articulation by the church of Latin America, especially by the theological movement knows as liberation theology. We begin with the biblical witness.

The "preferential option for the poor" is a central theme in both the Hebrew and Christian Scriptures. The foundational event in the history of the Hebrew community was God's response to the cries of the oppressed in Egypt: "I have heard the cry of my people and I see how they are being oppressed" (Exod. 3:9). God instructs Moses, "Go to Pharoah and tell him that Yahweh says, 'Let my people go'" (Exod. 8:1). This event reveals what kind of God Yahweh is and what kind of people Israel is to become. As Jorge Pixley notes, "The correct referent [for God] is always that God who redeemed Israel from slavery in Egypt. Any god who is not the savior of the poor and oppressed cannot be the true God of Israel." He continues in language that could be applied to today's use of religion to justify slavery and oppression: "A god who legitimates the oppression of peasants, no matter how solemn its cult, is not the true God of Israel, for the true God is only that One who hears the cries of the oppressed and frees them from their oppressors."[2]

The Exodus experience of God liberating the oppressed is foundational to biblical faith. The very identity of Israel as a people was a community that had been liberated from slavery and oppression by Yahweh (Deut. 26:6–9).

> This awareness of being a poor and oppressed people who struggle for life with the help of Yahweh is basic. Yahweh is the true God who hears the cries of those who are oppressed and Israel is the people of Yahweh that depends on Yahweh for the success of its struggles for liberation.[3]

By Yahweh's power and intervention, Moses did indeed lead the Hebrew slaves of Pharaoh out of their captivity, through a time of testing in the desert and into a new land of their own.

For a few hundred years the covenantal vision of liberation, equality, and participation was partially implemented in the economic arrangements and the political and social structures of Israel. But before long, greed, injustice, and oppression were visible in the community. Now the oppressor was not the Egyptian Pharaoh but those who had emerged from the Hebrew community as the new elites, with power and resources. Through the prophets, God protested against the social injustices, the bribery, and the arrogance of the rich (see Amos 2:6; 4:1; 5:12; Isa. 3:14–15; 10:1–2; Jer. 22:3). Through the Torah, the Law of the land, God called for protection and justice for the poor, the indebted, the widows, the resident foreigners, the domestic and wild animals, and even the earth itself (Lev. 19:33; 25:10–16; Exod. 15:12–15; 22:21; Deut. 23:12; 25:4).

The Hebrew Scriptures contain a consistent and insistent message that God watches over the poor, especially widows and orphans. The people of Israel were to imitate God by treating the aliens, widows, and orphans as God had treated them (Exod. 22:20–22). Many of the psalms call out to the Lord from foreign lands where they were an oppressed people. They proclaim God as a "stronghold for the oppressed" (Ps. 9:9).

The prophets of Israel were powerful champions of the poor. "According to the prophets of Israel, the law of justice stands to serve all, middle-class merchant and farmer as well as the widow, orphan, and alien (1 Kings)."[4] The Hebrew Scriptures regarded the poor as favored by God because they were victims of injustice. The Hebrew faith community believed that God intervened on behalf of the poor. "It is Yahweh who makes a man poor or rich, who brings down or raises up, who lifts up the weak from the dust and raises the poor from the ash heap" (1 Sam. 2:7–8).

God's identification with the poor and the outcast is clearly evident in the Christian Scriptures when God chooses a poor, young, single woman to be the bearer of the Christ child. The message and action of Jesus continues the tradition of social justice proclaimed in the Hebrew Scriptures. Jesus stands on the shoulders of the prophets and the psalmist who proclaim God's love for the poor in many words and actions:

- Jesus came to bring good news to the poor, to proclaim liberty to captives. (Luke 4:18–21)
- Jesus proclaimed that the poor and the hungry are blessed by God. (Luke 6:20–21)
- Jesus has a special concern for the rejected and outcasts of society, including lepers, prostitutes, tax collectors, and those disturbed in mind and spirit.
- He did not endorse the idea that prosperity was a sign of God's favor, but spoke out on the dangers of riches. (Matt. 6:19, 24; 13:22; 19:24; Luke 6:24; 12:20; 16:22–23)
- Jesus reversed Cain's question as he teaches that not only are we our brother and sister's keepers, but also we are to love our enemies.
- Jesus identified with the poor and neglected: "Whatever you did to the least of these brethren, you did unto me." (Matt. 25:40)
- He taught that the rich man is condemned, not only for abusing the poor man, but for ignoring him.
- Jesus taught that women are not second-class members of the human family; they are examples of loyal and valued disciples, as we see in the case of Mary Magdalene, who is the apostle to the apostles.
- Children were not pushed aside by Jesus but were welcomed and set up as examples of open and trusting discipleship.
- Those ostracized because of illness are offered healing and inclusion in the community.
- Social pariahs, like tax collectors for the colonizing Roman government and prostitutes, are given a privileged place among his followers.
- In the end, Jesus was rejected and put to death by the authorities because they, rightly, perceived that his message was undermining their power.
- The followers of Jesus took seriously his word to care for the poor and the alienated.
- James chided his community when they offered only kind words to the poor with no action to lift a hand in help.

- Luke describes the Christian community in Jerusalem as a place where "there was no needy person among them, for those who owned property or houses would sell them, bring the proceeds of the sale, and put them at the feet of the apostles, and they distributed to each according to need." (Acts 4:34–35)
- The early Christian community took seriously the needs of the widows in their community, who had no other means of support. The Acts of the Apostles (6:1–7) tells us that food was distributed every day to the widows. But inequalities crept into the distribution, so the Greek-speaking widows needed advocates to receive the support they deserved. The community appointed Greek-speaking "ministers" to distribute the food to their needy sisters.[5]

Jesus was a creative religious genius. Steeped in the biblical and religious tradition of his faith community, he gave a personal interpretation of that tradition which often challenged the doctrinaire teaching of the religious leaders. His central conviction was the Creator's love of the poor. From this belief Jesus taught:

- Care of the poor takes precedence over the law and every form of tradition. For this reason, he rejected the religious leaders' obsession with proper ritual.
- It was more important to purify the heart than to perform ritual washings before eating.
- Sharing one's bread with the poor was more important than fasting.
- It was impossible to honor God while scorning one's sister or brother.
- Sin was an absence of love.
- The law could be summarized in love of God and love of neighbor.

Jesus' freedom from ritualism and his capacity to reach out to each person, no matter what their social or religious position, attracted many followers. As Matthew points out, "The crowds were astounded at his teaching, for he taught them as one having authority, and not as their scribes" (Matt. 7:28–29). People saw in Jesus the values of God's kingdom. The people were pulled into this vision. They experienced the freedom he offered. He removed from his disciples the yoke of suffocating religious traditions, social conventions, and the barriers of fear. Those who live in the Spirit of Jesus live in this radical freedom.[6]

MARTIN DE PORRES

Born out of wedlock in Lima, Peru, to a Spanish knight and a black, freed slave named Ana, Martin de Porres started out on the wrong side of the tracks. Because he inherited his mother's features and complexion, his father did not acknowledge his mulatto child until many years later. At his baptism, he was registered as the "son of an unknown father" and was considered illegitimate. This standing placed him at considerable social and economic disadvantage in sixteenth-century Lima. Martin was apprenticed to a barber, a profession that in those days included hair-cutting as well as surgical and medical skills. Martin excelled in these skills, and at the age of fifteen he applied for the lowliest position as a *donado*, or lay helper, at a Dominican monastery. His work included sweeping the cloister and cleaning latrines. The brothers recognized his medical skills, and he was put in charge of the monastery infirmary.

Martin did not confine his healing ministry to the Dominican community. He cared for the sick and injured, especially the wretched poor who lived in the streets of Lima. Martin was apt to carry them back to his cell and lay them in his own bed. His superior told Martin not to bring the sick into the monastery, but he did not follow those orders. When confronted again, Martin answered by saying, "Forgive my mistake, and please be kind enough to instruct me. I did not know that the precept of obedience took precedence over that of charity." After that humble response, Martin was given liberty to act according to his own instincts.

"Martin's charity was poured out on all those who were counted as nothing—Indians, the poor, the sick. He had a special ministry to African slaves, to whom he would deliver gifts of food and drink, healing their sick, consoling them in their miserable bondage."[7] While Martin was gentle with his charges he was very hard on himself. He subsisted on bread and water, slept on the ground, wore a hair shirt, and flagellated himself nightly. When asked about this excessive asceticism, Martin responded that he was atoning for the immensity of sins. For what sins he might be atoning? Perhaps the great evils of slavery, the scorn heaped on the poor and indigenous peoples, the great injustices perpetrated by Christians in the New World. Martin "did not set himself apart from the sins of his age, and he punished himself accordingly."[8]

Martin died on November 3, 1639, when he was sixty years old. Pope John XXIII canonized him in 1962 and named him the patron saint of race relations and those who work for social justice. Here was a simple man who lived the option for the poor before the Latin Americans had coined the phrase.

LATIN AMERICAN ROOTS

In 1968 the bishops of Latin America met in Medellín, Colombia, to examine the situation in their countries in light of the new approaches of the Second Vatican Council. The bishops came face-to-face with the growing poverty in Latin America. In their analysis they shifted their support to the poor: "It is necessary that small basic communities be developed in order to establish a balance with minority groups, which are the groups in power. . . . The church—the people of God—will lend its support to the downtrodden of every social class so that they might come to know their rights and how to make use of them."[9]

The bishops confirmed a new direction in Latin America. As Father Alfred Hennelly noted, the Medellín documents "provided legitimation, inspiration, and pastoral plans for a continent-wide preferential option for the poor, encouraging those who were already engaged in the struggle and exhorting the entire church, both rich and poor, to become involved."[10]

Curt Cadorette, a Maryknoll priest who spent many years in Peru, claims that the bishops who wrote the Medellín Documents "effectively redefined the church in their continent and set in motion historical events that they could not totally foresee."[11] While many Christians, lay and ordained, identified with the poor and tried to reshape their societies, others in the church and society in Latin America attacked this new identification with the poor. "Some members of the upper classes, convinced that the church had been infiltrated by Marxists and furious at what they perceived to be the treason of an old ally, lashed out at progressive elements in the church." This lashing out led to persecution and martyrdom of Latin American Christians, beginning in the late 1960s through the present. This persecution against fellow Christians was unprecedented in their continent. Many Christians were singled out as dangerous subversives who paid with their lives for their adherence to the gospel.

Archbishop Dom Helder Camara of northeastern Brazil has been one of those accused. He ironically quipped: "When I feed the poor they call me a 'saint.' When I ask 'why' the poor are hungry, they called me a 'Communist.'" While in the United States in 1976 for the Eucharistic Congress in Philadelphia he added, "I don't need communism, I have the gospel." Taking up the preferential option for the poor has led to tension and conflict in Latin America. The same may happen in the United States when Christians begin to ask "why" the poor are poor.

The Latin American bishops met again eleven years later in 1979 in Puebla, Mexico. There were serious differences of opinion at the meeting, but the bishops did not step back from their commitment made at Medellín. While there were some caveats and nuances, "the bishops' teaching on the centrality of social reform and the church's preferential option for the poor remain central."[12] Tension remains in the Latin American church regarding social reform, the role of the church in the society, and how the church is to live out its preferential option for the poor.

Liberation Theologian: Gustavo Gutiérrez

Peruvian theologian Gustavo Gutiérrez points out that while the term "preferential option for the poor" comes from the Latin American church, "the content, the underlying intuition, is entirely biblical. Liberation theology tries to deepen our understanding of this core biblical conviction." According to Gutiérrez the preferential option for the poor "has gradually become a central tenet of the church's teaching." Father Gutiérrez examines each word in this controversial phrase:

The Poor

"The term *poverty* refers to the real poor. This is not a preferential option for the spiritually poor. After all, such an option would be very easy, if for no other reason that there are so few of them! The spiritually poor are the saints! The poverty to which the option refers is material poverty. Material poverty means premature and unjust death. The poor person is someone who is treated as a non-person, someone who is considered insignificant from an economic, political, and cultural point of view. The poor count as statistics; they are the nameless. But even though the poor remain insignificant within society, they are never insignificant before God."

Preferential

"God's love has two dimensions, the universal and the particular; and while there is a tension between the two, there is no contradiction. God's love excludes no one. Nevertheless, God demonstrates a special predilection toward those who have been excluded from the banquet of life. The word *preference* recalls the other dimension of the gratuitous love of God—the universality."

Option

"In some ways, option is perhaps the weakest word in the sentence. In English, the word merely connotes a choice between two things. In Spanish, however, it evokes the sense of commitment [*compromiso*]. The option for the poor is not optional, but is incumbent upon every Christian. It is not something that a Christian can either take or leave. As understood by Medellín, the option for the poor is twofold: it involves standing in solidarity *with* the poor, but it also entails a stance *against* inhumane poverty."[13]

This twofold stance of being against inhumane poverty and standing in solidarity with the poor is often filled with conflict. Such a stance is resisted by those who benefit from the present unjust and oppressive order. This solidarity with the poor unfortunately comes for some at a great price: the price of martyrdom.

Maura, Ita, Dorothy, and Jean

The history of the church is written in the blood of martyrs. But these four women represented a different kind of martyrdom, increasingly common in our time. Their murderers dared to call themselves Christian, indeed defenders of Christian values. And they died not simply clinging to the true faith but for clinging, like Jesus, to the poor.[14]

The "four women" Robert Ellsberg refers to are the four American women who were murdered in El Salvador in 1980: Maura Clarke and Ita Ford, two Maryknoll Sisters; Dorothy Kazel, an Ursuline Sister; and Jean Donovan, a lay missionary from Cleveland. Maura and Ita had spent many years as missionaries in Nicaragua and Chile. Sister Dorothy Kazel had worked the longest in El Salvador. Jean Donovan, at twenty-seven, was the youngest of the four.

Jean came from a background of privilege and had earned a degree in business. She contemplated the possibility of marriage and a lucrative career. The Donovan family had asked Jean to come home when the situation became more dangerous in El Salvador. Archbishop Oscar Romero had been assassinated while celebrating Mass just nine months earlier. Two weeks before her death, Jean wrote of her decision to stay in El Salvador:

> Several times I have decided to leave—I almost could except for the children, the poor bruised victims of adult lunacy. Who would care for them? Whose heart would be so staunch as to favor the reasonable thing in a sea of their tears and loneliness? Not mine, dear, not mine.

Their work was to support the church of El Salvador. It involved ministering to the needs of the refugees caused by the civil war. They delivered supplies and comforted terrified religious leaders and catechists in the rural areas. "The women's work confronted them with scenes from hell." They saw villages where the Salvadoran Army had committed massacres and then refused to allow the survivors to bury the dead. Sister Maura wrote, "The other day, passing a small lake in the jeep I saw a buzzard standing on top of a floating body. We did nothing but pray and feel." Each of these women had made a preferential option for the poor, "believing that the effective witness to the gospel was inseparable from the witness to life and solidarity with the oppressed. In El Salvador this was enough to label one a subversive."[15]

These four saw the hope and the spirit of the El Salvadoran people, even in those horrendous times. They had a reason for living, for sacrificing, and for dying. Sister Ita Clarke captured something of the spirit of the people in a letter she wrote to her niece.

> This is a terrible time in El Salvador for youth. A lot of idealism and commitment are getting snuffed out here and now. The reasons why so many people are being killed are quite complicated, yet there are some clear, simple strands. One is that people have found a meaning to life, to sacrifice, struggle, and even to die. And whether their life spans sixteen years,

sixty or ninety, for them their life has had a purpose. In many ways, they are fortunate people.

Brooklyn is not passing through the drama of El Salvador, but some things hold true wherever one is, and at whatever age. What I'm saying is that I hope you can come to find that which gives life a deep meaning for you, something that energizes you, enthuses you, enables you to keep moving ahead.[16]

Ita knew the risk they faced by keeping their commitment to the poor. On the night before their death, she quoted their deceased and much-loved Archbishop Romero. "One who is committed to the poor must risk the same fate as the poor. And in El Salvador we know what the fate of the poor signifies: to disappear, to be tortured, to be captive, and to be found dead."[17]

On December 2, 1980, Dorothy and Jean went to the airport to pick up Maura and Ita, who were returning from a meeting in Nicaragua. The four never made it home. Two days later a few peasants alerted church leaders and led them to the shallow grave in a cow pasture. Two had been raped and each shot in the head at close range.

The death of the four women had an enormous effect on the North American church. It helped to galvanize opposition to U.S. funding for the Salvadoran government. Their deaths also brought a defensive backlash by those who defended the U.S. policy in Central America. One American official shot back that "the nuns were not just nuns, the nuns were also political activists . . . on behalf of the Frente [the insurgents]."[18] In truth, the women were not "political activists on behalf of the Frente," except that standing with the poor put one in opposition to those who defended the current political oppression.

You say you don't want anything to happen to me. I'd prefer it that way myself—but I don't see that we have control over the forces of madness, and if you choose to enter into other peoples' suffering, or love others, you at least have to consent in some way to the possible consequences.[19]

Articulated in Catholic Social Teaching

Writing three years after Medellín, Pope Paul VI in 1971 picked up the language of the Latin American bishops in his Apostolic Letter, *Octogesima Adveniens* (A Call to Action), when he said: "in teaching us charity, the Gospel instructs us in the preferential respect due to the poor and the special situation they have in society: the more fortunate should renounce some of their rights so as to place their goods more generously at the service of others" (no. 23).

The U.S. bishops agreed with their counterparts to the south that we must make an option for poor. In their 1986 pastoral letter on the economy, *Economic Justice for All*, they taught:

> Such perspectives provide a basis today for what is called the "preferential option for the poor." Though in the Gospels and the New Testament as a whole the offer of salvation is extended to all peoples, Jesus takes the side of those most in need, physically and spiritually. The example of Jesus poses a number of challenges to the contemporary Church.
>
> - It imposes a prophetic mandate to speak for those who have no one to speak for them, to be a defender of the defenseless, who in biblical terms are the poor.
> - It also demands a compassionate vision that enables the Church to see things from the side of the poor and powerless, and to assess lifestyle, policies, and social institutions in terms of their impact on the poor.
> - It summons the Church also to be an instrument in assisting people to experience the liberating power of God in their lives, so that they may respond to the Gospel in freedom and dignity.
> - Finally, and most radically, it calls for an emptying of self, both individually and corporately, that allows the Church to experience the power of God in the midst of poverty and powerlessness.[20]

Again and again the U.S. bishops returned to the central theme of "option for the poor" in their letter on the economy:

- Decisions must be judged in light of what they do *for* the poor, what they do *to* the poor, and what they enable the poor to do *for themselves.* (*Economic Justice for All*, no. 24)
- *The obligation to provide justice for all means that the poor have the single most urgent claim on the conscience of the nation.* (no. 86)
- As individuals and as a nation, therefore, we are called to make a fundamental "option for the poor." (no. 87)

They believe that this option for poor implies "the obligation to evaluate social and economic activity from the viewpoint of the poor and the powerless." This obligation "arises from the radical command to love one's neighbor as one's self.... The prime purpose of this special commitment to the poor is to enable them to become active participants in the life of society. It is to enable *all* persons to share in and contribute to the common good" (no. 88).

The needs of the poor are considered "the highest priority":

> The fulfillment of the basic needs of the poor is of the highest priority. Personal decisions, policies of private and public bodies, and power

relationships must all be evaluated by their effects on those who lack the minimum necessities of nutrition, housing, education, and health care. In particular, this principle recognizes that meeting fundamental human needs must come before the fulfillment of desires for luxury consumer goods, for profits not conducive to the common good, and for unnecessary military hardware. (no. 90)

In 1994 the U.S. bishops, in *Communities of Salt and Light*, restated the option for the poor and claimed it was the litmus test for the justice of the community. "At a time when the rich are getting richer and the poor are getting poorer, we insist the moral test of our society is how we treat and care for the weakest among us." Later in the document the bishops state unambiguously that "Our parish communities are measured by how they serve 'the least of these' in our parish and beyond its boundaries—the hungry, the homeless, the sick, those in prison, the stranger" (nos. 1, 2).

Pope John Paul II echoed the preferential option for the poor in his writing and speaking. He used the phrase "preferential love of the poor" and interpreted the prior one hundred years of Catholic social teaching as evidence of the church's option for the poor even before this phrase was coined. Pope John Paul II characterized the preferential option for the poor as a "call to have a special openness with the small and the weak, those who suffer and weep, those that are humiliated and left on the margin of society, so as to help them with their dignity as human persons and children of God."[21]

Penny Lernoux

Penny Lernoux was an American journalist who went to Latin America in 1962 at the age of twenty-two to write about the transformation of the Latin American church and the brutal dictatorships throughout the continent. Although she was raised as a Roman Catholic, she had drifted away from the church, disillusioned in part because of its conservatism and seeming irrelevance.

In the early 1970s, after the groundbreaking events of Vatican II and the Medellín Conference, she began meeting a new kind of priest and missionary. These religious leaders were living in solidarity with the poor. Her encounter with the church of the poor in Latin America renewed her faith life and, at the same time, gave a focus to her journalism. She recalled her conversion:

> It was through them that I became aware of and entered into another world—not that of the U.S. Embassy or upper class, which comprises the confines of most American journalists, but the suffering and hopeful world of the slums and peasant villages. The experience changed my life, giving me new faith and a commitment as a writer to tell the truth of the poor to the best of my ability.[22]

While other American journalists were covering the struggle in Latin America in terms of a war against communism, Lernoux told the story from the standpoint of the poor. Penny's writing was "rooted in something deeper than professional commitment; her writing was itself an expression of her faith. She became a witness, a voice for the voiceless, a hero to many who depended on her courage in reporting the truth."[23]

I was one of the many readers who looked for her reports in the *National Catholic Reporter* for a faith-filled understanding of what was happening in the church in Latin America. Like her, I had gone to Latin America in 1971 and 1972 to learn about this church of the poor. I read and used her book, *Cry of the People*, which was published in 1980. Her writing clarified the epic transformation that was taking place in the Latin American church as it wrestled with the meaning of the Second Vatican Council's call to make the "joys and the hopes, the griefs and the anxieties of the poor" become the concerns of the followers of Christ.

Penny's life did not end in martyrdom like many of the Christians she had covered. She was a martyr in the literal meaning of the Greek word; she was a "witness," not by her death, but by her life. In the late 1980s she returned to the United States and began writing a history of the Maryknoll Sisters. She viewed this work as a type of "repayment of a debt she felt to the sisters she had known in Latin America and through whom she had regained her faith." We do not know how our option for the poor affects not only those with whom we minister, but those who observe our witness. The gospel became "believable" to Penny through the faith and service of the religious sisters and priests in Latin America.

In September 1989 at the age of forty-nine, Ms. Lernoux was diagnosed with cancer. She moved in with the Maryknoll Sisters in their mother house in Ossining, New York. Now she faced the poverty of being helpless to stop the cancer. It was a different kind of powerlessness than the poor in Latin America face, but very real nonetheless. She brought her restored faith to this unexpected chapter in her life.

> I feel like I'm walking down a new path. It's not physical fear or fear of death, because the courageous poor in Latin America have taught me a theology of life that, through solidarity and our common struggle, transcends death. Rather, it is a sense of helplessness—that I, who always wanted to be the champion of the poor, am just as helpless—that I, too, must hold out my begging bowl; that I must learn—am learning—the ultimate powerless of Christ. It is a cleansing experience. So many things seem less important, or not at all, especially the ambitions.[24]

Penny Lernoux died in 1989. Her passing was mourned by many who only knew her by the witness of her writing and the integrity of her option for the poor.

OPTION FOR THE POOR BY THE POOR

When we speak of an option for the poor we usually mean a choice freely made by the nonpoor. It is a choice that can be made by individuals, by the local faith community, or even by the continent-wide church, as in the case of Latin America. When Christians become aware that they are relatively wealthy and privileged, they decide to relinquish some of their privilege and wealth to identify with those who do not have wealth and privilege.

The poor can also make an option for the poor: a choice to be in solidarity with other underprivileged people rather than trying to exploit them and join the aspirations of the materialistic culture. I witnessed a small example of the working poor giving expression to their option for the poor.

On Monday afternoon, September 30, 2003, three buses of immigrant workers from Chicago stopped in the parking lot of the Church of the Nativity in Brockport, a town in the heart of the apple orchards of western New York. The 142 riders were part of the Immigrant Workers' Freedom Ride, which was bringing immigrant workers and their supporters from nine major cities to Washington, D.C., and New York City to demonstrate and lobby for more humane and just policies toward immigrant workers. The riders were immigrant workers who had found jobs in the hotel industry as cleaners and low-income staff in retail chain stores such as Wal-Mart and Target. Many of the riders were from Latin America. As the rally in the parking lot unfolded, a group of farm workers arrived with their crew leader, driving the van straight from the fields. They had not cleaned up or put on their good clothes. As they greeted each other through the chants, flag waving, and speeches, the riders experienced a powerful sense of solidarity. The immigrant workers from Chicago and the immigrant workers from Brockport looked into each others' eyes and knew their common struggle. The workers from Chicago spontaneously took up a collection for their fellow workers in upstate New York. They shared of the little they had with those who were newer immigrants. The $150 collected was not so important as the powerful message this gave to all of us. There is solidarity in the struggle, and the poor often shame us by their generosity.

A RELIGIOUS AND POLITICAL OPTION

For Christians, the option for the poor is a deeply religious choice with serious political ramifications. The *religious* foundations sustain the option, while the *political* implications are the more controversial and conflictual. The option for the poor presupposes that one has become aware that, in society as a whole and in most organizations in society, people "at the top" have opportunities and power while others "at the bottom" have little or no power and few opportunities. "To make an option for the poor is to choose to disengage from serving the interests of the powerful and instead to take the side of those who are relatively powerless."[25]

The option for the poor links the religious insight of the Judeo-Christian tradition (that God has made an option for the poor) with the political arena as the space where this option becomes a reality. The linkage is between faith and politics, and it contradicts the liberal Western tradition that religion is to be relegated to the private, personal spheres of individual and family affairs. The option for the poor says that Christianity has direct political implications. (The word "political" in this context does not mean political parties, but how a society organizes its political power.) "Option for the poor" means that we acknowledge that faith has political implications. Even those who try to privatize religion and keep it out of the public arena are not really eliminating religion's political implications; rather they are making an option to continue the current arrangement of power. The option for the poor teaches that we cannot be neutral. Being neutral means opting for the current realities, which, from the perspective of the poor, are unjust.

Father Donal Dorr believes that the option for the poor involves an experiential aspect and a political aspect, and that both are important. The experiential dimension means a deliberate, personal choice to enter into the world of the powerless to some degree. It means to share in a significant way their experience of poverty, alienation, or mistreatment. This stance is rooted in compassion, which is a willingness to suffer with those who are on the margins of circles of wealth and power. "By entering the world of deprived people one begins to experience not only their pain and struggle but also their hopes and their joys."[26]

The option for the poor breaks through the "them" and "us" attitude toward the poor. Rather, we begin to identify with the poor in our very lifestyle and attitudes. The poor are not objects of sympathy or of our paternalistic help. Rather, we are one in solidarity working to change society and doing it in a way that everyone's gifts are valued and needed.

Our option must also be accepted by the poor. It is not in my power to be fully in solidarity with a particular group of marginal people. All I can do is *offer* to be in solidarity with them. This offer is not made in words, but in the attitude with which we see the group and relate to them. In response, the marginal ones may choose to offer me the gift of their solidarity, which takes time. The poor must accept our option for the poor.

The second aspect of our option for the poor is the *political* dimension, meaning the willingness to take action to overcome systemic injustice. Dorr suggests four steps in this process of taking action:

1. Careful analysis of the situation to understand the root causes of injustice.

2. Avoiding collusion with those groups or individuals benefiting from the current system. This may mean not accepting funding from certain sources.

3. Planning effective challenges to the unjust order.

4. Designing realistic alternatives.[27]

For example, in solidarity with those who work in sweatshops, we can:

1. Analyze the situation to understand the reasons for sweatshop exploitation.

2. Join boycotts of the most notorious sweatshop products.

3. Make our voices known to corporate leadership and government leaders, challenging current practices.

4. Support Third World and local alternatives to sweatshop clothing.

An option for the poor is a perspective that every Christian can make, in decisions large and small.

RHETORIC OR REALITY?

The pope, the bishops, and the rest of the church can proclaim that the church has "opted for the poor" or is "a church of the poor," but those words do not make it so in reality. One pastoral leader, Denis Murphy, who lives in Manila and works with Urban Poor Associates, believes that those phrases "have the appeal of a vision, though the realization of such an abstract vision seems impossible to anyone who considers it seriously."[28]

Although he is writing about the Philippines, the question applies to the whole church. He explains the reason for his somber remarks:

> There was a time during the years 1960 to 1980 when people believed Philippine society could accept a real church of the poor, that is, a church where the poor had pride of place, and social change was expected to come from the organized movements of the poor. It was in keeping with the national resistance to the tyranny of martial law. But now times are different.[29]

In most parishes in Manila there is a mix of well-off people and poor people, and the priests usually spend their time with the well-off parishioners. The church is linked to the upper classes by tradition, lifestyle, education, and many other cultural bonds that are centuries old. "Few priests have made any serious study of the social and religious problems of the poor, and most share the anti-poor prejudices of the upper classes."

The seminarians seem to follow that linkage to the upper classes. When Murphy asked a class at the major seminary about the church's commitment to become the church of the poor, of imitating the poor Christ, taking up his cross and finding Christ in the suffering poor, the seminarians were honest enough to say that those words no longer meant very much. Murphy claims that "a church of the poor has a chance when large sectors of the society are struggling for change and social justice. It has little chance in a society committed to the values of the marketplace."[30]

Even as Denis Murphy was lamenting the situation in the Philippines, he found reasons to be hopeful. Four parishes with their priests from Quezon City held a demonstration at the mayor's office, asking the mayor's help in getting government land for the poor. At first, the mayor resisted, but the parishioners would not leave. Eventually, he promised to help twenty thousand families get land. The people broke into song and dance to celebrate their achievement. Action like this aligns the church with the poor and not only with the interests of the well-off. Murphy concludes, "Such priests and poor people are enough to begin with. As the founder of the Highlander movement, Myles Horton, said, 'We make the road by walking.'"[31]

HOW DO WE MAKE AN OPTION FOR THE POOR?

How do North American Catholics who are not poor make an option for the poor? Jack Jezreel, a social justice educator, suggests the following six things we can do to make an option for the poor.[32] *[handwritten: What if we are?]*

1. Connect directly to the poor.
I didn't care about the world's poor until I cared about Arturo, or Scott or Linda. By visiting the homeless on the street, I connected with them. Spend time with an abandoned old person at a nursing home. Tutor a fifth-grader in an inner-city school who needs help with math or reading. Serve and eat lunch with the guests at a soup kitchen. Don't stay in the kitchen behind the protection of the pan of lasagna you are dishing out. Pull up a chair next to the guests.

2. Ask questions and search for answers.
Our face-to-face contact may stimulate questions and concerns. We may ask: Why are there so many people at the soup kitchen if we have reformed welfare and the economy is doing well? Read about social issues in our diocesan newspaper or magazines like *U.S. Catholic, America,* or *Sojourners.* Connect with the

diocesan social ministry office and talk with people who have been working in social ministry for a long time. Sign up for courses, workshops, or retreats that focus on social justice concerns.

3. Start to advocate.

At some point we may realize that feeding the hungry, while being an important work of mercy, does not stop the flow of needy to our door. We may want to get involved in addressing root causes by becoming an advocate for systemic change. It may be that the people we are serving are working poor who have jobs that do not pay enough to live on. We could become advocates for "living wage" legislation in our community so that workers have enough to buy their own food with dignity.

4. Work with the poor as they empower themselves.

As we become advocates for the poor we also want to help them find their own voice and not only depend on us as their "advocates." We may want to join our own community organization to give voice to our concerns for our community. We can connect with local Catholic Campaign for Human Development projects, which are working to empower people.

5. Watch your money.

A mature, well-considered dedication to the poor often leads to a simpler life, with fewer things and less preoccupation with money, status, and possessions. We may realize that we don't "need" another pair of shoes when we work with people who only have one pair.

6. Use your resources for others.

The early church wrestled with the question, "Can a rich person be saved?" After arduous debate they came to the conclusion that, yes, a rich person can be saved on two conditions—if he or she lives simply and shares resources with the poor. The same holds true for us today. We may want to support a variety of works of charity and justice—some for immediate needs, some for advocacy and community organizing.

HOW A PARISH LIVES OUT ITS
OPTION FOR THE POOR

A parish community can become a community that makes an option for the poor, in ways large and small:

- Tithing of parish income and investments is a good way to support efforts that provide both direct service and empowerment of the poor.

- Use the bulletin regularly to keep parishioners informed of the parish's outreach ministry. This action supports those involved and encourages others to join.

- Explore the possibility of establishing a "sister parish" within your diocese or in a Third World country.

- Find ways to involve a wide range of parish members. Some will serve as leaders; some will help out with specific activities. Homebound persons may commit to pray for specific individuals in need. Parents could take children to visit a nursing home. The aim is to have the parish's outreach effort be a ministry of the entire parish.

- Join a legislative network that acts on public policy issues. Organize a meeting between members of your parish and your local elected officials to discuss key public policy issues affecting the poor and the vulnerable.[33]

The biblical record and the life of Jesus clearly show that God chooses to stand with the poor. The church, if it is to be faithful to the God of the Bible, also has to choose to be with the poor, not only by its words, but by its deeds. According to the words of Jesus in Matthew's Gospel, our eternal destiny depends on this option.

A basic moral test is how our most vulnerable members are faring. In a society marred by deepening divisions between rich and poor, our tradition recalls the story of the Last Judgment (Matt 25:31–46) and instructs us to put the needs of the poor and vulnerable first.[34]

Prayer for the Poor

God of Justice,
Thank you for the gift of your Son Jesus who taught us:
To open our eyes
to see you in the face of the poor.
To open our ears
to hear you in the cries of the exploited.
To open our mouths
to defend you in the poor and vulnerable in the public squares
as well as in our private deeds.
May we always remember that we find you in "the least of these."
Amen.[35]

CHAPTER 6

Rights and Responsibilities

In the Catholic tradition protecting human rights and responding to our responsibilities are the roadmap to healthy individuals and communities. Respecting our rights and living out our responsibilities are the way human dignity is enhanced. When human rights are not protected and responsibilities to each other are ignored, human community is destroyed and our dignity is threatened. Philomena's story is an example of rights and responsibilities gone amok.

By the time Philomena was ten years old she had lived in thirty-five foster homes. She had two children by the time she was eighteen, little self-worth, and a long history of run-ins with the law. She left her hometown of Utica, New York, to escape "bad relationships." She ended up on the streets of Rochester and finally in the county jail for abusing drugs. While she was in jail she met Amy, who was sentenced to thirty days in the Monroe County jail for participating in an antiabortion "rescue" or blockade at a Rochester hospital. Somehow these two women from two different worlds became friends. When Amy left the jail she did not forget her new friend, and Philomena did not forget Amy.

Four years later, Philomena found herself in jail again. This time she was pregnant. She called Amy for assistance. Amy responded by helping her get into Bethany House, a Catholic Worker house for women and children, after her release. Philomena gave birth to her third child, a daughter, Bena, while staying at Bethany House. Eventually, the staff of Bethany House helped her find an apartment, and she got a job.

Philomena pointed out the priceless gift she received while at Bethany House.

"They gave me unconditional love. That to me was a basic need at that time because I'd never had it before."

This unconditional love led to friendship between three women: Amy, Philomena, and Donna, the codirector of Bethany House. Both Donna and Amy are godmothers to two of Philomena's children. Philomena has been clean and sober for a decade. She now works in a family support program for the mentally ill through Monroe County's Mental Health Office. She points to Donna, the staff, and the volunteers as instrumental in turning her life around.

"She just is very welcoming and nonjudgmental. Even if a resident relapses into bad habits, Donna still welcomes you, and looks at you with the same eyes."[1] Donna's look communicates her respect for Philomena, even when things are not going well. Philomena does not lose her dignity when she is in jail or has a relapse. She still is a child of God, with dignity, rights, and responsibilities. Donna's look of unconditional love communicates that message to all the desperate women of Bethany House.

Philomena's story is a story of hope and recovery. It is a story about the redemptive power of love.

The Catholic tradition teaches that "human dignity can be protected and a healthy community can be achieved only if human rights are protected and responsibilities are met." The bishops' 1998 document *Sharing Catholic Social Teaching* continues: "Therefore, every person has a fundamental right to life and a right to those things required for human decency. Corresponding to these rights are duties and responsibilities—to one another, to our families, and to the larger society."[2]

Philomena, like every human being, has "a right to those things required for human decency." Being loved by those who raise us is something required for human decency, yet Philomena claims she had never experienced that kind of love. She realized how essential it is for her healing. See how these Christians around Bethany House love one another. Human rights and responsibilities— abstract notions start with the very concrete experience of being loved.

This chapter examines what we mean by "rights and responsibilities" today by looking at biblical perspectives and justice, which is a biblical counterpart for our contemporary notion of human rights. As we shall see, the Catholic tradition has not always embraced the modern meaning of human rights. That happened only with Pope John XXIII. After presenting the Catholic understanding of human rights and responsibility we concretize the notions by looking at the absence of rights and responsibilities in issues of racism and poverty. Responding to racism and poverty are two important ways of addressing the challenge of "rights and responsibilities."

BIBLICAL PERSPECTIVES

The Bible is filled with teachings about rights and responsibilities even though our notion of individual human rights is not present. Scripture scholar Father John Donahue explains:

In contrast to modern individualism the Israelite is in a world where "to live" is to be united with others in a social context either by bonds of family or by covenant relationships. This web of relationships—king with people, judge with complainants, family with tribe and kinfolk, the community with the resident alien and suffering in their midst and all with the covenant God—constitutes the world in which life is played out.[3]

Rights and responsibilities were viewed in the context of these overlapping relationships in the community. Rights were not viewed as individual rights, but rather as duties and responsibilities that were lived out in relationships. The word that best describes "fidelity to the demands of a relationship" is the biblical notion of "justice." The biblical notion of rights and responsibilities is not identified as the inalienable rights of each person, as our Declaration of Independence put it; rather, rights and responsibilities flow from the relationships that are part of living in community. This is the heart of the covenant that God established with the Hebrews and all people. The Hebrew word that is used to express that aspect of the covenant is *sedaqah*, which is translated as justice or righteousness. Justice or righteousness is the dominant message of the Bible. "It can be said without exaggeration that the Bible, taken as a whole, has one theme: The history of the revelation of God's righteousness."[4] The highly regarded Old Testament scholar Gerhard von Rad writes, "There is absolutely no concept in the Old Testament with so central a significance for all relationships of human life as that of *sedaqah* [justice/righteousness]."[5]

A pivotal expression of the biblical vision of justice is the experience of the Exodus. Walter Brueggemann explains that "justice as hoped for by Israel, resisted by Pharaoh, and finally given by Yahweh is not simply a retributive arrangement whereby each receives what is 'deserved,' rather a radical notion of distributive practice that gives to each one what is needed—by way of legitimacy, dignity, power, and wherewithal—in order to live a life of well-being." In this new justice of God each person is a valued "end" of God, not a "means" to someone else's wealth. The Passover vision of justice presents God, the creator of heaven and earth, "as the active agent in the reshaping of human social power for the sake of human community and well-being."[6]

The Ten Commandments are given and interpreted throughout Jewish history as a way of living out the meaning of justice in the community. The most important relationship is with God; hence the first three commandments assert the absolute holiness of God. Thus, God cannot be used to reinforce any political or economic system. The Bible also points out the idolatry of making any political or economic system of ultimate value. "Thus to 'love God' means to refuse every other ultimate love or loyalty."[7]

The last six commandments focus on "love of neighbor." These commandments are realistic teachings that concern the protection of and respect for the basic needs of every neighbor, "including those who have no power to defend themselves or access to advocate their own interest." These guarantees "serve to protect the weak from the strong." Brueggemann notes the essential linkage between love of God and love of neighbor: "The juxtaposition of the first three commands on the holiness of God and the last six on justice for the neighbor show that God's holiness and neighbor love are of a piece in this revolutionary experiment in ancient Israel. Indeed, Israel has known from the beginning that love of God cannot be remote from love of neighbor (1 John 4:20), and that holiness and justice always come together."[8]

Israel did not perfectly enact the justice called for in the covenant and the Ten Commandments. While Torah called for a limit on debt-slavery, the protection of the "resident alien" and the poor of Israel, and a prohibition of bribes (which would bias justice toward the wealthy), Torah also makes compromises to serve the interests of the wealthy. For example, the same law that limits bondage for a debt (Exod. 21:2, 4), also permits the breakup of a family of the indebted for the sake of economic gain. The creditor shall retain control of the wife and children when the man in debt is freed. The text even refers to the slave as the "property" of the owner, showing that even the Chosen People picked up the attitudes of the Pharaoh, who treated the Hebrews as his property. The text reveals the struggle in ancient Israel between egalitarian justice and the power of those who had economic control of society—a struggle of interpretation that continues in Jewish and Christian communities.

The book of Deuteronomy also reveals Israel's ongoing struggle for radical justice. In Deuteronomy 15:1–11 the author envisions a time when the poor have been freed from poverty. The poor who had debts cancelled by the Sabbath and Jubilee precepts are not only returned to the "economy," but are also entitled to means to reenter the economy with dignity and the possibility of economic viability. Brueggemann concludes, "We may take this provision as the signature of Israel's notion of radical justice, advocating the responsibility of the creditor community for rehabilitation and restoration of those lost in the shuffle of economic transactions." The rules of economics are covered by the religious ethic. "Economics is understood as an instrument of a covenantal social fabric, and is not permitted to be a separate sphere with its own anti-neighbor procedures and laws."[9]

The social vision of Israel is rooted in its historical memory of a time when every family, clan, and tribe had its rightful place of power. Each family is to have enough to survive, access to public decisions, and fair treatment in court. When these relationships are honored there is justice. When these social arrangements are distorted or usurped there is injustice. Where there is injustice, the religious actions and pious practices are morally bankrupt. In such a situation, powerful intervention is needed to restore justice. The prophets are concrete and analytical. They knew that poverty and injustice were not accidents. As Scripture scholar Devadasan Premnath notes, "They knew exactly what the causes were and who was responsible. They did not speak in abstraction. They knew what the oppression/injustice was, and who the oppressors were."[10]

In the biblical perspective, "justice then is not a romantic social ideal for another world. It is the hard work of redeploying social power and the transformation of the social system."[11]

Jesus, Moral Outrage at Rights Denied

In Western cultures few concepts carry as much passion and moral gravity as the question of human rights, especially when human rights are denied or violated. Western cultures, including the United States, have commissions and watchdog groups that alert us to human rights abuses in our country and around the world. In Western democracies, we have learned to equate respect for human rights with respect for basic human dignity. Moral focus and passion for human rights are to be cherished and celebrated, both in civic and religious settings.

Jesus also expressed moral outrage when the rights of the poor and day workers were trampled upon. This is very clear in his reaction to the moneychangers in the temple and in his parable of the Workers in the Vineyard.[12]

Cleansing the Temple

Mark's account of the cleansing of the temple is a follows:

> Then they came to Jerusalem. And he entered the temple and began to drive out those who were selling and those who were buying in the temple, and he overturned the tables of the moneychangers and the seats of those who sold doves; and he would not allow anyone to carry anything through the temple. He was teaching, "Is it not written, 'My house shall be called a house of prayer for all the nations'? But you have made it a den of robbers. And when the chief priests and the scribes heard it, they kept looking for a way to kill him. . . ." (Mark 11:15–18)

Biblical scholars and preachers have a number of interpretations for Jesus' cleansing of the temple. A standard interpretation was that Jesus is angered over the cheating by the moneychangers. The people who come to offer sacrifice at the temple must exchange their coinage to use the temple money to buy their sacrifice. The uneducated peasantry could easily be taken advantage of by the unscrupulous moneychangers. As Taylor summarizes it, "The action of Jesus is a spirited protest against injustice and the abuse of the temple system. There is no doubt that pilgrims were fleeced by the traders."[13]

While this is a fair interpretation of the text, Jesus is challenging a deeper injustice. William Herzog, in *Jesus, Justice, and the Reign of God: A Ministry of*

Liberation, argues that we cannot appreciate the meaning of Jesus' charge against the temple unless we have some understanding of the economic role played by the temple in Jerusalem. "The temple cleansing cannot be divorced from the role of the temple as a bank."

The temple amassed great wealth because of the half-shekel temple tax assessed on each male. Historical evidence supports the fact that large amounts of money were stored in the temple. The temple then was able to make loans on behalf of the wealthy elites to the poor. If the poor were not able to pay their loans, they would lose their land. "The temple was, therefore, at the very heart of the system of economic exploitation made possible by monetizing the economy and the concentration of wealth made possible by investing the temple and its leaders with the powers and rewards of a collaborating aristocracy." As evidence of this role of the temple funds, Herzog notes, "It was no accident that one of the first acts of the First Jewish Revolt in 66 C.E. [Common Era or A.D.] was burning of the debt records in the archives in Jerusalem."

The high priests and the lay aristocrats, such as the Sadducees, benefited from this system of exploitation. The high priests controlled the temple and all its functions, including the tribute collecting. The temple was not only a religious and political institution; it was a major economic force, controlling massive amounts of money while continuing to accumulate more. The temple had a large staff to assist those coming to offer sacrifice: the moneychangers, the sellers who provided the unblemished sacrificial victims, and the oil, wine, and flour required for offering a sacrifice. The temple bureaucracy oversaw the temple's many functions, including its staggering payroll, and the goods and services that defined the economy of Judea.

"When Jesus took action against the temple, therefore, he touched a raw nerve. . . ." We have "the match set to the barrel of gasoline." In Herzog's interpretation "the chief priests, the very paradigm of rectitude, are the social bandits creating havoc in the land." The moneychangers were the street-level representatives of the banking interests and essential operatives in the collection of the temple tribute. Therefore, Jesus struck at the very heart of the sacrificial system itself. Jesus had taken on the role of being the agent of God's forgiveness as was seen in the healing of the paralytic and the forgiving of his sins. He believed that the temple was no longer necessary as the vehicle of forgiveness. Jesus rejected the temple and all it stood for, including the exploitation of the poor. Jesus made the temple a symbol of economic exploitation that was taking place and rightfully called it a "den of thieves." In this reading of the text, Jesus was not only upbraiding the injustice of the minor bureaucrats, but the entire economic system that impoverished the working classes. No wonder the text concludes with the observation, "And when the chief priests and the scribes heard it, they kept looking for a way to kill him. . . ."[14]

"You Always Have the Poor with You"

The background for the cleansing of the temple also helps explain the meaning of the text in Mark 14:7 where Jesus says, "for you always have the poor with you, and you can show kindness to them whenever you wish." Why are there always the poor? Because there is always the ruling class that takes advantage of the people of the land. It does not mean that there will always be poor because they are lazy, unemployed "welfare moms." Rather, Jesus offers a sad commentary on the persistence of greed and exploitation, with the resulting poverty. Jesus interprets the message of Deuteronomy, which looks for the day when "there will, however, be no poor among you, because the Lord is sure to bless you in the land that the Lord your God is giving you as a possession to occupy, if only you will obey the Lord your God by diligently observing this entire commandment that I command you today" (Deut. 15:4–6). The elites have not obeyed the covenant, and as a result there are poor in the land. This is not God's plan or intention; it is the result of sin and greed. The persistent presence of the poor violates the intention of God's covenant. God's plan is that "there will be no poor among you," but we have not kept God's covenant, resulting in injustice and the violence of poverty.[15]

Jesus expressed his outrage at rights denied and the disregard of covenantal justice. Rights and responsibilities served only the powerful elites, contrary to the demands of the covenant. When this happens, the disciples of Jesus should be outraged as he was.

Crystal

Some may believe that the rights of others come into play when our needs have been met. But the ethic of Jesus and the early Christian community suggest that we cannot postpone responding to the needs and rights of others after all our needs are met. Crystal is a disciple who does not put off responding to the needs of others.

Crystal is a seventy-five-year-old woman who is slightly mentally handicapped, though she is spiritually and emotionally gifted. Crystal lives at a Catholic Worker homeless shelter; in fact, she has been there so long that she is now considered part of the staff. Her job at the shelter is to answer the door, which she does with her honest charm. She is good with names and remembers if you haven't been around for some time. She contributes to the Catholic Worker community by doing what she can. Crystal lives a life of voluntary poverty, although it probably doesn't seem like poverty to her because she is surrounded by people who care for her and her life has meaning and dignity. She has one coat, one dress, and one blouse. She has given away the rest of her clothing.

When Crystal receives her Social Security check she immediately walks a mile and a half to her church to give her tithe to the parish. She doesn't wait until Sunday when she would be at church, but makes the monthly trip on whatever day of the week her check arrives. She gives of the little she has, like the parable of the Widow's Mite in the Gospel. Crystal takes seriously her responsibilities to her Catholic Worker family and to her own faith community. Even with her limited resources she has not forgotten her responsibility to others and is willing to tax herself to assist others.

THE CHURCH AND HUMAN RIGHTS

While the Catholic Church has always defended the dignity of the human person, it has not always been supportive of the "human rights" movement as it emerged in seventeenth-century Europe. Many of the secular movements promoting human rights had an anticlerical and anti–Catholic Church tenor. In France, Italy, Spain, Mexico, and other countries the Catholic Church was perceived as an enemy of individual rights and opposed to the autonomy of the secular realm. The Church of Rome reacted to these movements and in its response may have overreacted by condemning human rights.

The church's opposition to modern theories of rights as articulated by Hobbes, Locke, and Kant was also based on the secular understanding of rights as individualistic claims in competition: individual against individual claiming their rights. The social contract was perceived as a way of curbing these competing claims for some semblance of order. The Catholic tradition, on the other hand, stressed the essential solidarity of each person with the human community. This was not a conflictual model of competing claims but an ethics of rights based on people's social nature. The Catholic "ethics of solidarity defends human rights as required by any just and cooperative common good."[16]

It wasn't until the 1963 encyclical of Pope John XXIII, *Pacem in Terris*, that the church's position took a radical change of accepting the importance of individual human rights, while still keeping its communitarian framework. "While the nineteenth-century popes look on human rights with skepticism and rejection, John XXIII makes them the fundamental point of departure for his social and ethical argument."[17] With Pope John XXIII's writing, the implementation of human rights becomes a decisive criterion for evaluating the morality of a society. We read in *Pacem in Terris*:

> Any society, if it is to be well-ordered and productive, must lay down as a foundation this principle, namely, that every human being is a person, that is, his nature is endowed with intelligence and free will. By virtue of this, he has rights and duties, flowing directly and simultaneously from his very nature. These rights are therefore universal, inviolable and inalienable. (no. 9)

Human rights are not to be guaranteed only in theory, but a just society will work to actualize these rights. Pope John XXIII taught in *Pacem in Terris*:

> A well-ordered human society requires that men recognize and observe their mutual rights and duties. It also demands that each contribute generously to the establishment of a civic order in which rights and duties are progressively more sincerely and effectively acknowledged and fulfilled. It is not enough, for example, to acknowledge and respect every man's right to the means of subsistence. One must also strive to ensure that he actually has enough in the way of food and nourishment. (nos. 31–32)

The Second Vatican Council confirmed the new direction taken by Pope John, which signaled a consensus in the church on the importance of human rights. Any discussion of rights in the Catholic tradition has two reference points: reciprocal duties and the common good. As the *Declaration on Religious Freedom* of Vatican II in 1965 summarized it: "In the exercise of their rights individual men and social groups are bound by the moral law to have respect both for the rights of others and for their own duties toward others and for the common welfare of all" (no. 7). Historian R. Scott Appleby called this "a stunning development, in part because it was a stunning reversal. And it took place within a relatively short historical passage—the period from 1895 to 1965."[18]

Pope John Paul II offered this list of human rights when he spoke at the United Nations in 1979:

- The right to life, liberty, and security of person
- The right to food, clothing, housing, sufficient health care, rest, and leisure
- The right to freedom of thought, conscience, and religion
- The right to manifest one's religion either individually or in a community, in public or private
- The right to choose a state of life, to found a family, and to enjoy all conditions necessary for family life
- The right to property and work, to adequate working conditions and just wage
- The right to assembly and association
- The right to freedom of movement, to internal and external migration
- The right to nationality and residence
- The right to political participation
- The right to participation in the free choice of the political system of the people to which one belongs[19]

These rights form of web of expectations for every society, an international yardstick to measure the way a particular society protects the dignity of the human person in the political, economic, and social context. In the United States we are very attentive to civil and political rights, while we rely on market forces to address economic and social rights. One right that invites further reflection in the American context is the right of private property.

THE RIGHT OF PRIVATE PROPERTY

Pope John XXIII affirmed the right of private property in 1961: "The right of private property, including that pertaining to goods devoted to productive enterprises, is permanently valid."[20] The needs of survival and the right of subsistence may override the right of private property. Pope Paul VI explained a few years later that "Private ownership confers on no one a supreme and unconditional right. No one is allowed to set aside solely for his own advantage possessions which exceed his needs when others lack the necessities of life."[21]

Pope John Paul II reaffirmed the traditional teaching in 1981 in his encyclical *On Human Work*:

> Christian tradition has never upheld this right (to ownership) as absolute and untouchable. On the contrary, it has always understood this right within the broader context of the right common to all to use the goods of the whole creation: The right to private property is subordinate to the right to common use, to the fact that goods are meant for everyone. (no. 14)

As we see, the Catholic tradition holds that the basic needs of people supersede our right to private property. In this framework, the right to private property is not an absolute right. It is justified to the extent that it promotes the common good. At times it may be necessary to override this right for the demands of the common good. The Second Vatican Council put it very clearly: "If a person is in extreme necessity, he has the right to take from the riches of others what he himself needs."[22] The U.S. bishops explained that "whenever a person or a group is deprived of its basic necessities, expropriation is justified. In such an extreme case the poor have not chosen social warfare; it is imposed upon them by the injustices of the possessors."[23] These strong words jar us into remembering the long-standing teaching of the church that the resources of the earth are meant for all, even though we are stewards of them as property "owners."

The persistence of poverty and racism is evidence that we have not achieved a just balance of rights and responsibilities. We still have work to do in establishing basic human rights for all Americans and for our global neighbors. One woman who helped the American church see its responsibility to address poverty and racism had an unlikely background as a member of the Russian nobility that fled the Bolshevist revolution.

Baroness Catherine de Hueck Doherty

Catherine Kolyschkine was born in Russia in 1896; her father was a wealthy diplomat. By age fifteen she was married to Baron Boris de Hueck, which made her a baroness. This was not a good time to be part of the Russian aristocracy as the tsarist empire collapsed in the October Revolution of 1917. Boris and Catherine came close to starving before risking a hazardous journey crossing the Russian border into Finland. By 1920 they arrived with their newborn son in Canada. Eventually she was invited to speak about her harrowing escape from communism. She earned a good amount of money on the lecture circuit. Though her marriage had collapsed, she had a luxurious apartment, a fancy car, and a country house in Graymore—all the signs of successful life.

Her conscience was uneasy with her materialistic life. At the peak of her success she felt the pull of the words of Jesus, "Go, sell what you have and give to the poor. Then come follow me." So in 1930 she gave up her worldly goods, moved into an apartment in the slums of Toronto, and committed herself to living "the gospel without compromise."[24]

CIVIL RIGHTS, RESPONSIBILITIES, AND RACISM

In March 1997, a thirteen-year-old black boy from the south side of Chicago, Lenard Clark, wandered on his bicycle into a white neighborhood. He was savagely beaten by three white teenagers. He lingered in a coma, near death, for several days before making a gradual recovery.

On January 2, 1996, a black teenager, Cynthia Wiggins, from Buffalo, New York, was hit by a dump truck on a busy road as she struggled through the snow and cold. She was trying to get to her job as a cashier at the Walden Galleria Mall in suburban Cheektowaga. She died of her injuries. Cynthia was a serious and dedicated young person who had grown up poor but dreamed of becoming a doctor. This may seem like an unfortunate accident, unrelated to racism, but wait. Why was Cynthia trying to cross a dangerous street after getting off the bus from Buffalo? Why didn't the bus stop at the mall? The truth is that the mall owners, the Pyramid Corporation, had refused to let Buffalo city buses pick up or unload on mall property. This policy was established to make it as difficult as possible for inner-city blacks to reach the mall.

We are shocked by the news of the beating of the thirteen-year-old. This is an expression of "hot" racism of the overt racists—even though they were only children themselves. But the "cold" racism of the Pyramid Corporation is also partially responsible for the death of Cynthia. The mall tried to impose segregation on the residents from black neighborhoods in Buffalo. Cynthia died, in part, because of those racist policies.

Racism is a denial of human dignity and a denial of basic human rights. It is present in overt and covert ways in the actions and attitudes of individuals as well as the policies, practices, and patterns of our institutions and our culture. This is true for society and for our religious communities.

The history of American Catholics on the question of race is, in general, not exemplary. Religious orders and bishops had slaves in this country. The Jesuits had African slaves working on their four plantations in Maryland until 1837, and the Capuchins and Ursulines also used slaves on their plantations. The first bishop of Baltimore, John Carroll (1735–1815), had two black servants, one free and the other a slave.

An African American Catholic theologian, Jaime Phelps, described the racism of Catholic theologians: "The silence of U.S. Catholic theologians about racism is parallel to the silence of leading German theologians and intellectuals during the Nazi atrocities and the prosecution of the so-called 'final solution' against the Jewish people." The president of the Catholic Theological Society of America, Jon Nilson, responded to Dr. Phelps's charge: "If ever there were a sentence that seems to come right off the page and seize the white reader by the throat, it is this one." He continues, "An initial reaction might well be to dismiss Phelps' claim as rhetorical overkill, a tactic to get whites to pay more attention to issues that she thinks important." But Nilson doesn't buy that argument:

> But that is a reaction born of ignorance. Her comparison of white Catholic theologians to the German theologians is
> - more than justified by Basil Davidson's conclusion that the slave trade "cost Africa at least 50 million souls";
> - more than justified by the extremes of suffering endured by the kidnapped Africans and their descendants for the 244 years of legalized slavery;
> - more than justified by the 71 years of oppression and discrimination known as Jim Crow;
> - more than justified by the 51 of those same years during which one black person was lynched about every 2.5 days somewhere in the United States "at the hands of persons unknown";
> - and more than justified because racism continues to infect our country today.[25]

Our history also has the stories of African American Catholics who confronted the violation of their human rights and their efforts to exercise their responsibility as members of society and the church. One stellar example is Daniel Rudd, who had two strikes against him: he was an African American and he was a layperson.

Daniel Rudd (1854–1933)

Daniel Rudd, the son of slave parents, was born and buried in Bardstown, Kentucky. He was the editor of the *American Catholic Tribune*, a paper published by and for African American Catholics. Rudd did more than just write about the issues of interest to his fellow black Catholics; he organized a lay congress to bring the lay Catholic leadership together. In January 1889 Rudd convened the first of five Black Catholic Congresses in the basement of St. Augustine's Church in Washington, D.C. Other congresses followed in Cincinnati, Philadelphia, Chicago, and Baltimore in the four succeeding years.

These congresses served as forums "for black opinion, they voiced a desire for the spread of Catholicism within the African American community and sounded a clarion call to the American Church to change the racist policies so prevalent on the local level."[26] The participants at these lay congresses recognized that they shared the concerns of other immigrants in the Catholic community, especially the Irish, "who, like ourselves are struggling for justice." They asked for schools and societies for African Americans, as well as help in addressing racial discrimination by labor unions, employers, landlords, and real estate agents.

The lay leaders were addressing these issues because there were no black clergy at this time, because of the racism in the seminaries, which did not admit black candidates. The larger Catholic community was not ready for this strong leadership from the black community. The reaction from the hierarchy was based on a twofold concern: lay leadership and racism. The official church was concerned about the "militant" tone of these meetings and of the work of Daniel Rudd's paper. "That blacks were speaking for themselves, that they were calling the total Catholic community to just behavior, earned for them the epithet 'militant.'" Black historian Cyprian Davis notes that because of this label, "support dwindled. Rudd was pressured to move his paper to the East, where he could work under ecclesiastical supervision." When Rudd "tacitly refused to do so, another black Catholic paper was established." Both papers failed, and the embryonic movement died. But Davis notes that the movement started by Daniel Rudd "addressed critical issues and planted necessary seeds." These seeds would remain dormant for almost ninety-three years until the next National Black Catholic Congress was held in 1987.

According to Davis, "The black lay Catholic congresses were not a failure. In fact, they achieved what Rudd set out to do in calling the first congress." He believes that "They demonstrated beyond a doubt not only that a black Catholic community existed but that it was active, devoted, articulate and proud. It also demonstrated that given the opportunity, there was real leadership within the black community." As evidence of this leadership Davis points to the address of the IV Black Catholic Congress, published in the *Boston Pilot* on September 23, 1893, which he considers a "foundation of Black Catholic theology." They gave the black community and the larger church a sense of social mission, a focus on human rights, a theology of the priesthood of the faithful, and their rootedness in the African origins of the church.[27]

Church Teaching on Racism

The first step in addressing racism in society and in the church is to acknowledge its persistence in ourselves, in our institutions, and in cultural attitudes. "Racism is an evil which endures in our society and in our church." The U.S. bishops explain, "Racism is a radical sin: a sin that divides the human family and violates the fundamental dignity of those called to be children of the same father."[28]

The Catholic Church has admitted that racism exists within the church and within society. In both settings it is sinful:

> Racism is the sin that says some human beings are inherently superior and others essentially inferior because of race. It is the sin that makes racial characteristics the determining factor for the exercise of human rights. It mocks the words of Jesus: "Treat others the way you would have them treat you."[29]

Racism is contrary to the message of Jesus, as Archbishop Sean O'Malley explains:

> When asked for a definition of neighbor, our Lord answers with the parable of the good Samaritan. Jesus astonished his audience by making the Samaritan, the member of a despised minority group, the hero and protagonist of the story. In one fell swoop Jesus pops the bubble of ethnic superiority and at the same time challenges us to be a neighbor to all in need and to remove the barriers in our heart that prevent us from seeing our connectedness with every human being.[30]

Racism is not just a matter of personal attitudes; it is also cultural and institutional, as the bishops note: "Discriminatory practices in labor markets, in educational systems, and in electoral politics create major obstacles for blacks, Hispanics, Native Americans, and other racial minorities in their struggle to improve their economic status." Some progress has been made, with business and the military often taking the first steps in appreciating the value of promoting racial diversity.

Cultural attitudes are beginning to shift to respect the richness of the human family with a diversity of races. The media is beginning to reflect a multiracial face, even if the control of these corporations is far from diverse. Social attitudes are beginning to be more open to interracial dating and marriage. Yet, as filmmaker Michael Moore points out in his movie *Bowling for Columbine*, fear of crime by black males in our cities captivates our news reporting and instills new levels of subtle racism. Extreme talk radio hosts give expression to the latent and overt racism in society. The September 11 attack has also opened a new target of racial fear.

After acknowledging the presence of racism, we must ask for forgiveness from those who have been mistreated and from God. Bishop Dale Melczek of Gary, Indiana, has taken the step of asking for forgiveness for the sin of racism. In a pastoral letter dated September 7, 2003, he said: "We must express our sorrow for past sins of racism, whether committed personally or by the institution of the church and ritualize atonement for those sins." So he suggests, "In 2004, will ask the faithful of the Diocese of Gary to gather at the Holy Angels Cathedral to participate in an atonement service."[31]

Racism is a form of violence to the dignity and human rights of another human being. For too many people the violence of racism is linked with the violence of poverty, which is also a denial of basic human dignity and the right to the basic necessities of life. Father James Groppi, an activist priest in Milwaukee in the 1960s, pointed out the violence of poverty that he saw in the black community which he served:

> Violence is many things. It's watching little black children go to bed at night wondering whether or not the rats will come through the wall and bite them.
> It's sitting in the house for two weeks with overcoats on and wrapped in blankets trying to keep warm.
> Violence is watching the kids across the street walk out of the house without any shoes on.
> It's knowing they're wondering whether they'll get a next meal.[32]

Forty years later, the church still confronts the persistent problem of poverty, in this country and around the world. The reality of poverty, like racism, puts our beliefs about rights and responsibilities on the line. How can our rhetoric about rights and responsibilities be taken seriously in the face of enduring poverty and racism?

The reality of poverty and racism reveals how far we are from honoring the rights of each person and how far we are from honoring our responsibility to each other as members of the one human family.

ECONOMIC RIGHTS AND RESPONSIBILITIES AMID POVERTY

Every person has a right to sit at the table of life, where by our common labor the basic hungers and needs of each persons are met. It is a simple vision. As the

U.S. bishops say in their letter, *A Place at the Table*, "This is not about having a new car or about how fast you can get on the Internet; rather this is about having a decent place to live, enough to eat, clean water in your village, and clean air in your community."

The current realities reveal how far we are from the goal of protecting each person's dignity by having their basic needs met:

- In the United States 34 million people are not able to have their basic needs covered, and more than half of the world's population live on less than two dollars a day.
- Throughout the world, 1.2 billion people live on less than one dollar a day.
- Eight hundred million people, most of them children, live with hunger or malnutrition, which means "they die younger than they should, struggle with hunger and disease, and live with little hope and less opportunity for a life of dignity."[33]

The Catholic bishops offer the image of the table as a way to think about our response to poverty. "A table is where people come together for food. For many, there is not enough food and, in some cases, no table at all.

"A table is where people meet to make decisions—in neighborhoods, nations, and the global community. Many people have no place at the table. Their voices and needs are ignored or dismissed."[34]

For Catholics, the table recalls the Eucharistic table which expresses our new covenant with God and the community with whom we break bread. As we break bread at the table of the Lord, we are to break bread to feed the hungers in our world. As the *Catechism of the Catholic Church* insists, "The Eucharist commits us to the poor. To receive in truth the Body and Blood of Christ given up for us, we must recognize Christ in the poorest" (no. 1397).

The metaphor of the table also suggests the four institutions that must take up their unique responsibility in addressing poverty.

The table we seek for all rests on these four institutions, or legs:
(1) what families and individuals can do,
(2) what community and religious institutions can do,
(3) what the private sector can do, and
(4) what the government can do to work together to overcome poverty.[35]

By identifying these four institutions the bishops are spreading out the responsibilities to a diverse set of people and agencies, each bringing something different to the table.

The bishops explain that a first leg of the table comprises families and individuals:

- Every person has a responsibility to respect the dignity of others and to work to secure not only their own rights but also the rights of others.
- Public policy and all our institutions must reward, encourage, and support parents, including single parents, who make wise decisions for their children. Their hard work, their love and discipline, and their time and presence within their families are gifts not only to their children, but to our society and to the common good. They are also significant investments in avoiding or escaping poverty.

(2) A second leg of the table is the role and responsibility of community organizations and faith-based institutions.

- These institutions can confront structures of injustice and build community, and they can demand accountability from public officials.
- Faith is a religious commitment; it is also a community resource. On the toughest problems, in the toughest, most desperate neighborhoods and villages, religious and community institutions are present and making a difference.

(3) A third leg of the table is the marketplace and institutions of business, commerce, and labor.

- The private sector must be not only an engine of growth and productivity, but also a reflection of our values and priorities, a contributor to the common good.
- Employers and the labor movement must both help the poorest workers to have a voice and a place at the table where wages and working conditions are set.
- Parents need to be able to provide a life of dignity for their children by their work. Workers and farmers need living wages, access to health care, vacation time and family and medical leave, a voice and real participation in the workplace, and the prospect of a decent retirement.
- Work must offer an escape from poverty, not another version of it.
- The process of globalization must provide opportunities for the participation of the poorest people and economic development of the poorest nations.

(4) A fourth essential leg of the table is the role and responsibility of government—a means to do together what we cannot accomplish on our own.

- In the Catholic tradition, government has a positive role because of its responsibility to serve the common good, provide a safety net for the vulnerable, and help overcome discrimination and ensure equal opportunity for all.

- Government has inescapable responsibilities toward those who are poor and vulnerable, to ensure their rights and defend their dignity.
- Government action is necessary to help overcome structures of injustice and misuse of power and to address problems beyond the reach of individuals and community efforts.
- Government must act when these other institutions fall short in defending the weak and protecting human life and human rights.

The wisdom of the Catholic tradition is to recognize the essential role and complementary responsibilities of individuals, families, communities, the market, and government to work together to overcome poverty and advance human dignity.[36] This is a "thick" description of rights and responsibilities in contrast to "thin" descriptions, which only emphasize one of these domains. A thick description is multileveled, avoiding ideological debates that place all the blame and responsibility on the individual, or on the other hand, government and social structures. The Catholic tradition developed the principle of subsidiarity to maintain a proper balance between the responsibilities of the family, the community organization, business, and the various levels of government.

Subsidiarity

The responsibilities of the four layers of institutions, the four "legs of the table," together compose a complex network of interaction and assistance. For example, when confronting poverty and unemployment, the individual and family have their unique responsibility and realm of activity. But a family may not be able to pull itself up by the bootstraps. It may need "assistance" from the next layer of social institutions—the community organization, the faith community, business, or even the various levels of government. Providing the appropriate assistance to the lower level, or more basic unit of society, is what the church means by "the principle of subsidiarity." The word comes from the Latin *subsidium*, which means help or backup. "In Catholic usage the term means that larger organizational structures and higher authorities are by nature a backup form to supply what individuals and smaller or voluntary groupings cannot do."[37] This principle means that the larger institutions should not interfere on the local level when the local level can handle the need. Because of the complexity of life and social problems, the local unit may not be able to adequately address the need or issue at hand. As the Task Force on Catholic Social Teaching put it:

> The Church vigorously defends the unique roles of families, community associations, and other intermediate institutions and insists their roles cannot be ignored or absorbed by the state or other large institutions.

However, when the common good or the rights of individuals are harmed or threatened, society—including governmental institutions—has a responsibility to act to protect human dignity and rights.[38]

There is, of course, much debate about when the larger institutions should be involved. For instance, what is the role of the government in addressing the question of unemployment? Are we to rely on marketplace dynamics to resolve that problem? What role should the county, state, or federal governments play? Or, for example, regarding protecting our environment, when does the international level of governance need to be involved to address questions like global warming or the use of international waters? At times, even the national level of government may not be able to address international issues. Help may be needed from international organizations, but these organizations should not overpower national or local agencies that can adequately address local aspects of the problem. This principle guards against too much interference by government, but also against government not providing enough help to promote the common good.

HOW TO RESPOND AS A COMMUNITY

The bishops remind us that action is required for a Christian, as the Letter of James insists: "If a brother or sister has nothing to wear and has no food for the day, and one of you says to them, 'Go in peace, keep warm, and eat well,' but you do not give them the necessities of the body, what good is it? So also faith of itself, if it does not have works, is dead" (2:15–17).

Our action as a Christian community is multidimensional:

- A faith made visible by "works" needs to be rooted in prayer and worship.
- An activist faith is shaped by Christian education and formation; it is also nourished and challenged by preaching the liberating Word of God.
- We need to live out our faith in our everyday lives, as consumers, parents, workers, and active citizens.
- Our faith can lead us to serve those in need as "we house the homeless, feed the hungry, visit those in prison, welcome immigrants, and provide countless other services."
- "The Gospel and Catholic teaching require us to serve those in need and to work for a more just society and world." Through advocacy and community organizations, the Catholic community must work with others to shape a more just and peaceful world.

All of this action gives expression to the virtue of solidarity, which is the most challenging virtue of our time. This virtue calls us to "break through the boundaries of neighborhood and nation to recognize the web of life that connects all of us in this age of globalization."[39]

Although rights and responsibilities are abstract notions, they are filled with urgency when we connect with real people whose rights are denied. That is the implicit assumption of this theme of Catholic social teaching: to stay in direct contact with those, like Philomena, who are not at the table of nourishment, health, housing, and quality education, or the table of economic and political power and decision making. As we build relationships with those whose civil, economic, or political rights are denied, we will find a way to make room at the table so that all of God's people may feast at the banquet of life.

∞

Prayer for Basic Rights

God of freedom,

We praise you for the invitation to feast at your table,

both now and in the heavenly banquet.

With your grace, may we make room at all the tables in our lives

for those who have been excluded from the feast of full human life.

Strengthen with hope and creative action

all people denied their basic human rights and freedoms.

May we who follow your Son

be empowered by your Spirit to continue your work in the world.

Amen.

CHAPTER 7

Dignity of Work and Workers' Rights

Stanley works in Stone Construction Equipment Company, a manufacturing company that builds construction equipment, in a small town in upstate New York. He knows his company is up against a lot of competition, and many manufacturing jobs have left the United States in search of a labor force that will work for less money. Stanley is fortunate to work in a company that is trying to stay competitive and to keep good-paying jobs with benefits in the United States. He watched as the department that builds on-site cement mixers was challenged by a competitor that had moved to Mexico and now was underselling the Stone Company mixers.

The CEO of the company, Bob Fien, an active Catholic, was not just going to follow the trend of moving to a Third World country. He called together the workers who made the cement mixers to explain the situation and to ask for their input. Bob explained that under the current procedures it took them ten hours to produce a cement mixer. How could they become more productive so as to compete with the Mexican imports? The supervisors and workers took the challenge seriously, because they are not only employees of the company, but also stockholders. Each worker receives company stock on an annual basis, so if the company does well, their stock maintains its value. A worker with a high school education, such as a welder, who stays at Stone Construction for twenty-five years can have a nice nest egg available upon retirement—approximately five hundred thousand dollars. The workers are the owners; the company is 100 percent employee-owned. As Bob Fien notes, "When people feel like they are the owners, they react differently. They want to make sure they do things better, because it is their company."[1] The workers at Stone Equipment have a vested interest not only in keeping the shop open, but in the company's thriving. The workers rose to the challenge; they streamlined the process so that it took only four hours to produce each cement mixer. They are easily competing with the company that moved south of the border.

Stanley also knows that the company really respects the workers. The dignity of each worker and the work that they do are highly valued, from the janitors to the engineers. The company puts that respect and equal treatment into practice. To avoid giving the subtle message that the workers were not be trusted, the leadership of the company had a celebration to smash the time clocks with a sledgehammer. Stanley also knows that the CEO does not have a reserved parking spot near the building. There are no reserved spots. If you got to work early, you could park near the front of the lot. Stanley has seen all these changes through the years and is proud that the company is doing well, but he was astonished when he was asked to lead a team to improve the productivity of manufacturing the hoods for the equipment.

Although Stanley is a reliable and knowledgeable worker, he was not perceived as a leader. He could be found taking his breaks alone. He seemed isolated from the other workers because he stuttered. How could he lead this team; how would he communicate? The challenge before him and the team was to change the process of producing hundreds of hoods that then needed to be stored in a warehouse. Stone Construction needed to adopt just-in-time procedures, which meant that hoods would be produced just in time to be assembled.

Bob Fien had noticed Stanley; he knew his gifts and his limitations, and he believed that Stanley was the right man to lead the team. The team tackled the problem under Stanley's guidance. The company hadn't left the workers on their own; it had invested in a high-quality training course on just-in-time processes. Everyone had taken the course and passed; one worker had to take it a second time to complete it successfully. It wasn't easy, but with the training they had, and with the atmosphere of trust and joint ownership, they found ways to implement just-in-time production.

After the new procedures for producing hoods was working well, Bob thanked Stanley for his leadership. He gave Stanley a hug of appreciation, and Stanley started to cry on the boss's shoulder: tears of appreciation and pride. Stanley said it was he who was thankful for the invitation to lead the team. It was a powerful expression of mutual respect and appreciation, by the boss and the worker. And guess what? Stanley doesn't stutter anymore.

The story of Stone Construction Equipment Company is a story of financial success, national recognition, and treating workers with dignity and respect. It is very heartening to hear of companies like Stone, led by CEOs like Bob Fien. Bob is a nationally recognized advocate for a type of profit-sharing known as an Employee Stock Ownership Plan (ESOP). He travels around the country speaking to fellow CEOs about the advantages of treating workers with respect and giving them a share in the profits and ownership of the company.

These companies provide parables and examples of the principles of Catholic social teaching in reality. The concrete example of this manufacturing company takes us out of the realm of "wouldn't it be nice" if workers and owners shared in the wealth generated by their labor and were treated with respect. Stone Construction Equipment Company does more than profit sharing, as CEO Bob Fien explains:

> Profit sharing is nothing more than giving people a piece of the profits in any given year. In the course of a person's life that will end up being a relatively small sum. Wealth is generated when a portion of the profit is returned to the balance sheet. That strengthens the financial position of a company and increases the value of its stock. That is where the big bucks are, in owning stock. And that is the concept of ESOP: when you make the company profitable through your labor and a portion of that profit is returned to the balance sheet, you have generated wealth for the company by increasing the value of its stock. You should share in that wealth by owning stock yourself. It's the essence of *Rerum Novarum*.[2]

This example shows us that justice can be successful in the real world. It shows that respecting the dignity of workers and their rights can be rewarding and profitable. Unfortunately, not all workers work under these conditions. Many poultry workers and poultry farmers are not treated with the same respect and work in very difficult conditions.

Maria Montez is a senior citizen who has been working in a poultry processing plant for five years. She is friendly, though shy, and says a number of times that she is glad to have a job. She works hard using very sharp knives to cut up chicken carcasses as they whiz by at ninety chickens per minute. Señora Montez gets one bathroom break per shift and a short lunch break. She could get fired if she doesn't keep up with the frenetic pace without complaining. Maria speaks of the pain and injury to her arms and hands. She has numbness in her arms and hands from the motions she repeats hundreds of time during her long shifts. The pain often keeps her awake at night, and she treats her numbness by using rubbing alcohol on her skin. Yes, the company has health insurance, but it is of no use to her, because the deductible is several hundred dollars, which she cannot afford on her wages. She has asked to be rotated to other tasks with different motions, but her supervisor told her she is too dependable in her job to be transferred.[3] Señora Montez works hard, like Stanley, but she does not have the same benefits or voice at the workplace, even to protect her own health. The average wage for poultry workers in 2000 was six dollars an hour.

Life isn't that much better for the small farmers who raise the chickens. Because of vertical integration in the poultry industry, the company controls the production and profits by contracting with the thirty thousand small farmers who raise chickens. The company owns the chickens, supplies the feed, slaughters the birds, and markets the meat. "Through these contracts farmers nearly always come up short," Father John Rausch explains. "The contracts give full control of the process to the firms, but full responsibility for any problems to the farmer. The mortgage debt incurred by contract poultry farmers keeps them serfs on their own land and intimidates them from speaking out, fearful of bankruptcy if the company cancels their contracts and stops delivery of young chicks."

The Catholic bishops of the South called attention to these abuses of workers and farmers in their pastoral letter, *Voices and Choices*, released in November 2000. The letter recognizes the structural injustices in the industry, which tolerates low wages and allows only a meager return to farmers in order to maximize corporate profits and market cheap chicken. When workers are paid a poverty wage, the poultry industry is actually shifting certain costs to the public. These costs include health care, supplemental food stamps for the working poor, and pollution of the environment. As Bishop John McRaith of Owensboro, Kentucky, warns: "Somebody's paying the price, not only for bigness but for cheap food."[4]

The letter notes that 60 percent of poultry companies surveyed were in violation of the Fair Labor Standards Act by failing to pay workers for job-related tasks such as cleanup, or necessary breaks for restroom use, and charging workers for required protective gear. The bishops also pointed to the fact that poultry workers experienced repetitive-motion injuries at a rate five times higher than workers in general manufacturing. Studies also show that real average wages for poultry workers has declined from 1987 to 1997 while the "line speed" limit increased from seventy birds per minute in 1979 to ninety-one per minute in 1999. These factors produced very high profits for the chicken broiler industry, exceeding $1 billion in 1996. Such structural extremes need to be addressed.

As we review central issues concerning the dignity of work and workers' rights, we begin with a brief structural analysis which asks: who has the power in the workplace, and how do workers give voice to their collective power? The biblical material reveals the priority of people over profits, and the ten principles of economic justice spell out rights and responsibilities in the economic arena. The chapter concludes with a discussion of living wage and worker rights within the church.

IMBALANCE OF POWER

The bishops of the South recalled the pastoral letter of the U.S. bishops, *Economic Justice for All*, which spoke of the imbalance of economic power in the United States. "The way power is distributed in a free market economy frequently gives employers greater bargaining power over employees in the negotiation of labor contracts. Such unequal power may press workers into a choice between an inadequate wage and no wage at all" (par. 103). Pope Leo XIII, writing in 1891, could have been speaking of the situation of poultry workers and chicken farmers when he argued: "As a rule, workman and employer should make free agreements, and in particular should freely agree as to wages; nevertheless . . . if through necessity or fear of a worse evil, the workman accepts harder conditions because an employer or contractor will give him no better, he is a victim of force and injustice" (*Rerum Novarum*, par. 6).

The issue is often missed even by Catholic businesspeople and clergy, who tend to ignore or downplay the structural question of the imbalance of power. Instead, they translate the issue into a personal question of whether the individual boss or owner is fair. I know one pastor who believed that the struggle for better working conditions by low-wage workers in a nursing home should be handled like marriage counseling. He believed that if you put both parties in the room with a counselor, they could work out their differences. What he missed in the analogy to marriage was the imbalance of power between individual workers and management. A vocal worker does not have equal power in that situation and could easily find herself without a job.

While individuals have a personal responsibility to be just, it is important to reform the structures and policies so that workers have a voice. The issue is not only about wages and working conditions; it is a question about workers sharing in power and decision making. A benevolent boss or owner may be willing to keep his or her workers happy by paying decent wages and providing adequate benefits, but a question remains: is it still a paternalistic system in which the owners have all the power? A paternalistic business does not treat its workers as adults who are free to participate in the decisions that affect them. Paternalism says, "We know what is best for you." Paternalism, even generous paternalism, damages workers' dignity.

The bishops of the South realize how difficult it is for workers to organize, to bring their aggregate power to the bargaining table.

> Having a "voice" can lead to having a "choice" about wages, working conditions, job safety, medical care and other benefits. It is often difficult for workers to achieve this sharing of responsibility with owners and managers, which is why, for decades, the Church has supported the right of individuals to associate in groups organized to see that "voices and choices" become a reality.[5]

Organizing workers is never easy. In the poultry industry, like in migrant farm work, additional obstacles include a high turnover of the workforce, vulnerable status, and isolation of many of the workers. Juan Sanchez, a labor organizer, expresses the need to be organized: "People are tired, but they want to be organized. It's the only way to get the company's attention when they are abused by supervisors or overburdened with work. They want to protect themselves."[6]

Some people who work in the poultry industry have more power to influence corporate policy and make changes. The bishops point to a senior manager in a poultry company, John Stephens, who must keep his operations profitable in the competitive business. The biggest challenge he faces is employee turnover. As soon as people find another job they are gone, so he hires immigrants, sometimes with questionable documentation. "The poultry industry in the U.S. is not an employment of choice for people," Stephens admits. "The work is very hard physically and repetitious—that's part of the problem."[7] Keeping a trained staff would be easier for managers like Stephens if there were industry-wide safety and health standards, improved working conditions, and just wages. These improvements usually come from collective bargaining, where the workers coalesce their power. Changes can also be brought about by advocates outside the industry who bring their voice and power to bear when workers' rights and dignity are threatened. In both strategies, empowerment of workers and advocacy from outside voices, the church can play an important role.

GUIDING PRINCIPLES

The church can be true to its gospel mandate to bring good news to the poor if it keeps its priorities straight. The church's primary goal is not the survival of its institutions, but fidelity to the gospel message. The Second Vatican Council reminded us of that priority when it taught, "The social order and its development must constantly yield to the good of the person, since the order of things must be subordinate to the order of persons and not the other way around, as the Lord suggested when he said that the Sabbath was made for man and not man for the Sabbath" (*Gaudium et Spes*, no. 26).

Pope John Paul II spoke very clearly on the priorities of our faith tradition when he visited Toronto in 1984: "The needs of the poor take priority over the desires of the rich; the rights of workers over the maximization of profits; the preservation of the environment over uncontrolled industrial expansion; and production to meet social needs over production for military purposes."[8]

Teachings flow from our biblical heritage. The pages of the Bible are clearly attentive to the rights of workers and the dignity of work. Jesus spends more time addressing economic issues than any other issue in his preaching and teaching. Sometimes the message has been dulled or reinterpreted away from its original focus. One example of Jesus' teaching is the parable of the Laborers in the Vineyard in Matthew 20:1–16.

Parables as Subversive Speech

When we hear this familiar parable we immediately identify God as the "generous" owner of the vineyard who pays the laborers who worked only one hour the same wage as those who had "borne the burden of the day and the scorching heat." This interpretation conveys a truth about God's reign: that those who come into the vineyard late are given the same reward as those who have been in the vineyard from the first call. The parallel is to the Jewish community, which had been following God's invitation from the very beginning, and the Gentiles who only recently have been part of God's covenant community (vineyard). While this is the traditional reading of the parable, is it the only way Jesus intended for it to be read? Any parable lends itself to different interpretations.

To hear the words in a new way we need to know a little something about the economic reality of the day laborers of Jesus' time. In this interpretation, I am following the insights of Scripture scholar William Herzog, as developed in his text, *Parables as Subversive Speech*.[9] At the time, like today, small farmers were losing land to the large estates because of debt. When they lost the land they were forced to work as day laborers. All they had to sell was their animal energy. Others joined this growing pool of unemployed because they were the sons and daughters who did not inherit the land; only the eldest inherited the land. This class of peasants had a very grim existence. During the harvest they may find work; even at harvest time there seemed to be more workers than needed. The owners took advantage of this surplus of laborers. When there was no work the laborers were reduced to begging, malnutrition, and poverty. Many of them died within four to five years. The pay of a denarius a day was a subsistence wage that barely covered one person's daily needs. The worker could not feed his family with this subsistence wage.

With that background, we approach the parable a second time. Now, we realize how the owner of the vineyard tried to keep the workers in their place when they spoke up against the injustice. He mocked their labor in the hot sun all day by paying the ones who worked an hour the same rate. To the wealthy owner, their labor all day is only worth what he chooses to value it. He is not generous. The workers should react, for their labor has been devalued. Why are the workers complaining? Because they have been shamed. The landowner had aimed a deliberate insult at them, and they reacted to it. By reversing the order of payment so that the last hired received a wage equal to that of the first hired, the owner has told them in effect that he values their daylong effort in the scorching heat no more than the brief labor of the eleventh-hour workers. If the workers consent to his judgment that their labor is worthless, then they have nothing at all left to offer. All they have is their labor, which he mocks by his "generosity."

Rooted in human dignity, the workers must react. The owner responds, "Can't I be generous with what belongs to me?" Now, the owner mocks God, for in the

Jewish framework the land belongs to Yahweh. The earth and its resources are meant for all.

In this parable, Jesus gave voice to the oppressed worker who confronts the greed of the elites. Jesus unmasked the situation in which the oppressed are condemned for speaking out. When the workers confronted the injustice of the system the owner mocked them and blamed them for complaining, painting himself as the virtuous one.

We see a different story when we change our traditional interpretation of this parable. When we do not presume that we should identify God with the landowner we open ourselves to a new angle of understanding. We begin to see the world from the perspective of the oppressed day laborer, just as Jesus was giving voice to their complaint. The parable interpreted in this way again shows God on the side of the poor.

The church, if it is faithful to the words and actions of Jesus, will look for ways to give voice to workers who bear the heat of the day, but who are not treated with dignity or paid enough to meet their basic needs. The Bible is bursting with texts like this parable that address the rights of workers, especially when they are trampled upon by the aristocracy.[10]

Basic Principles for Reflection and Action

The Catholic Church has tried to keep the voice of Jesus alive in its social teachings. The parables of Jesus have been translated into principles to guide our reflection, our judgment, and our action. Like Jesus, the church has spent a lot of time and energy addressing issues of economic justice. In 1986 the U.S. bishops published *Economic Justice for All*, the product of five years of hearings, revisions, and debate. Ten years later, they decided to "keep it simple" so they put together a list of ten principles that can serve as the ten commandments of economic justice.[11]

1. *The economy exists for the person, not the person for the economy.* This teaching echoes the words of Jesus on getting our priorities straight: "The Sabbath was made for humanity, not humanity for the Sabbath."

2. *All economic life should be shaped by moral principles.* Economic choices and institutions must be judged by how they protect or undermine the life and dignity of the human person, support the family, and serve the common good.

3. *A fundamental moral measure of any economy is how the poor and vulnerable are faring.* The Judeo-Christian biblical tradition forcefully teaches that the justice of the community is judged by how the community treats its widows, orphans, and resident aliens.

4. *All people have a right to life and to secure the basic necessities of life (e.g., food,*

clothing, shelter, education, health care, safe environment, economic security).

5. *All people have the right to economic initiative, to productive work, to just wages and benefits, to decent working conditions, as well as to organize and join unions or other associations.*

6. *All people, to the extent they are able, have a corresponding duty to work, a responsibility to provide for the needs of their families, and an obligation to contribute to the broader society.* Yes, we have rights, but we also have duties and responsibilities. Pope John Paul II described our duty to work "both because the Creator has commanded it and because of his own humanity, which requires work in order to be maintained and developed." The pope elaborated that we have a duty to work "out of regard for others," especially one's own family, but for the whole human family. We work because we are part of the long history of human labor; we are heirs of the fruit of their labor, and we share in shaping future generations by our work today (*Laborem Exercens*, no. 16).

7. *In economic life, free markets have both clear advantages and limits; government has essential responsibilities and limitations; voluntary groups have irreplaceable roles, but cannot substitute for the proper working of the market and the just policies of the state.* This principle is very controversial. How do we find the proper role for the free market and the role of the state and international order? The principle of subsidiarity says "keep it as local as possible."

8. *Society has a moral obligation, including governmental action where necessary, to assure opportunity, meet basic human needs, and pursue justice in economic life.* This principle applies to providing an effective educational system. The church has recognized the need for governmental action to promote the common good when it is not achieved through market forces or intermediary institutions. In fact, the government loses its legitimacy when it does not promote the overall welfare of the community.

9. *Workers, owners, managers, stockholders, and consumers are moral agents in economic life. By our choices, initiative, creativity, and investment, we enhance or diminish economic opportunity, community life, and social justice.* In other words, it is not only the bottom line that matters. Bob Fien took seriously his moral agency at Stone Construction Equipment Company. While structural and systemic forces limit personal freedom, that is not the whole story. Individuals still are responsible and can make choices that promote the greater good, just as they can make choices that are short-sighted, immoral, and corrupt. Bob Fien commented to U.S. Secretary of Commerce Don Evans that CEOs in the United States don't have enough courage to resist the trend of exporting jobs. They "follow the flock" rather than deciding to make jobs competitive in the United States.

10. *The global economy has moral dimensions and human consequences. Decisions on investment, trade, aid, and development should protect human life and promote human rights, especially for those most in need wherever they might live on this globe.* The story of Salvador Solis illustrates the impact of trade in a globalized marketplace.

Salvador—Picking Apples

Salvador is a Mexican farmer who lost his land and is now picking apples on farms in upstate New York. As he recalls:

> I came to this country from Michoacán, Mexico, in 1984. I came here illegally, but I came out of necessity, because I could no longer support my family in Mexico.
>
> I was a farmer in Mexico. I raised corn and beans, and also grew some pine trees, which I grew for the resin that is used for making many things like medicine and clothing. In this way, I was able to sustain myself and my family: my wife Lucila, and our six children.
>
> In the 1980s, however, prices began to fall. Cheap corn and beans from huge company farms in the United States began to flood the market. In Mexico, seeds and fertilizer are very expensive, and the Mexican government does not give subsidies [like the U.S. government does to its agribusiness].
>
> All of the farmers in Mexico began to go downhill. By 1984, I could no longer sustain my family. I especially could not compete with the huge quantities of feed corn coming from America.
>
> So I crossed the border to California, and I was separated from everyone—my wife, my children, my parents. I made more money in the United States, but I was living in a cage of gold. I felt I could not go back to see my wife and children because I might not have been able to return. I could have been caught crossing the border. If I had been unable to return to the United States, how would my family have survived?
>
> Finally, after three years, I decided to take the risk to visit my family. I was caught a couple of times and was deported, but crossed the border again. But after a while, it began to wear me down.
>
> Later, I brought my wife, my oldest son and two youngest children, who were 2 and 3 at the time, across the border. The middle children—ages 13, 12, and 8—stayed with my mother. Daniela was only 3, and she nearly died of dehydration crossing the border in the desert.[12]

Salvador is one of the many undocumented workers who work in the fields, cleaning hotels, and as domestic help. Salvador would rather be in Mexico on his own land, in his own culture, growing beans and corn, but instead he is an undocumented worker because of "free trade" changes that were part of the North American Free Trade Agreement (NAFTA). Even though the U.S. leadership expects free trade, it also continues to support certain industries and sectors of agriculture. This is due, in part, to the fact that European nations subsidize their farmers; to be competitive, the United States subsidizes growers here. Unfortunately, Mexico cannot afford to subsidize its farmers, and Salvador could not compete with the cheap corn and beans that flowed into Mexico from the United States. He lost money trying to compete in the unfair "free market," and he ultimately lost his land. His choices were to work in the factories along the border with the United States, to become a migrant farm worker, or to starve. He chose to immigrate to the United States. Salvador is emphatic that while he appreciates the work he has in the United States, he would rather be working in Mexico, in his own culture, surrounded by his extended family.

Salvador's story can be repeated, with a few details changed, for millions of workers around the world. Structures are put in place that benefit the wealthy nations, especially regarding trade. Why are Africans buying canned tomatoes from Italy rather than growing their own tomatoes? Because the Italian government subsidizes the tomato industry. The same is true for cotton, olive oil, and many other commodities on the international market.

Workers' rights and other questions of economic justice must now be addressed on the international level. The bishops address this issue in their tenth commandment. The church as an institution has a role to play, as does the leadership of individual Christians in government, business, and nongovernmental agencies to change trade policies so that they serve the needs of the many and not only the interests of the richer nations.

These ten principles set up a foundation of economic justice for our more focused discussion of workers' rights and the dignity of work. If national and global economies were guided by these principles, workers' rights would be honored on all levels of economic activity. We begin our focused discussion with a summary of the theology and dignity of work.

THE DIGNITY OF WORK

The positive side of work recognizes that people who are made in the image and likeness of God also share God's creative power. Work through this lens is essential to our humanity, the means by which people reach out to bring fulfillment to the world, and in so doing bring fulfillment to themselves. The first component of this positive vision of work is to repeat that the right to work is a basic human right. Without work our dignity as human beings is threatened because work is a primary way that we participate in and contribute to the good of society. Human dignity is enhanced by participating in and contributing to the common good.

The Catholic vision also maintains three basic points about the dignity of the worker. First, the dignity of the worker is more important than the product that is produced or the service that is delivered. Second, work must be done in a way that builds up a sense of community among workers. Finally, the work must be done in a way that gives workers a voice in what they are doing. Workers are to have a voice in conditions affecting their work, not only through grievance procedures but in positive and constructive avenues as well. "This voice must not depend upon the willingness of superiors to listen but must be a structured means by which workers can make their voices heard."[13] Giving voice to workers' concerns in a structured way is the reason for unions, for this should not depend on the virtue or lack of virtue of the managers and owners.

Although a theology of work would emphasize the positive aspects of labor as continuing the creative work of God, work has a negative side. Work is also experienced and understood as drudgery. The book of Genesis has God instructing Adam and Eve, "By the sweat of your brow, you will earn your bread." This dimension of work is seen as a penalty, something to be avoided if possible, done only under close supervision and with the threat of dire consequences, such as starvation, if one fails to work. The Roman Catholic tradition, without denying that work too often is drudgery, promotes a positive understanding of work as the means to human fulfillment, both personal and communal.

Pope John Paul II was most articulate about the dignity of work, especially in his 1981 encyclical, *Laborem Exercens*. First, he connects human labor to God's creative "work." Humanity "ought to imitate God both in working and also in resting, since God himself wished to present his own creative activity under the form of work and rest" (no. 25). Then the pope pointed to the dignity of the worker as a person: "The basis for determining the value of human work is not primarily the kind of work being done, but the fact that the one who is doing it is a person" (no. 6). Third, the pope focused on the ethical meaning of work, namely, that work is a good thing for humanity, because through work we not only transform nature, adapting it to our needs, but we also achieve fulfillment as human beings (no. 9).

"Dirty Work"

While we may speak of the dignity of work, we have to be honest and admit that not all work has equal dignity in our culture. Feminist ethicists have focused on what we consider "dirty" work. There are many forms of dirty work: farmers, miners, and construction workers, who are generally male, get dirty from their work. The dirt associated with these types of dirty work is almost a badge of honor. Other kinds of dirty work are seen as less honorable. The dirt and work that is associated with our bodies, especially work that involves contact with bodily fluids or waste products, has been the domain of women, often located in the unpaid domestic household. Christine Firer Hinze summarizes our hierarchy of work as it relates to dirt:

> Dirty work carries connotations of work deemed distasteful, repugnant, and hence to be avoided whenever one has a choice in the matter. The less mediated by technology, by formal training and certification, or by controlled distance between the worker and others' bodily functions, fluids, and excreta, the more undesirable and dirty the work is apt to be considered. Comparing the work of a chef, professor, or surgeon on the one hand, to that of a dishwasher, custodian, or nurse's aide on the other hand illustrates the point. . . . People performing work deemed dirty may find the repugnance dirt elicits rubbing off on them, rendering their social status and self-esteem at least threatened, and often harmed.

In this framework, women who do unpaid domestic work are undervalued in the culture. Well-off women may choose to hire other women to take care of the dirty work. Barbara Ehrenreich notes that in 20 percent of U.S. households the family members do no domestic work at all. Many of our most influential political, cultural, academic, religious, and business leaders identify their status in light of, among other things, escaping dirty work. These leaders reinforce the cultural linkage between dirty work and disrespect. This disrespect is translated into less status, power, and economic compensation. Why are home health aides or nurse's aides, who often are women of color, not paid a living wage?

Dr. Firer Hinze challenges our thinking: "To the extent that Christians continue to acquiesce, however unwittingly, in our culture's systemic degradation and devaluation of dirty work, we undermine the commitment to social and economic justice that is at the heart of our social mission." She points out that by actively ignoring the moral and economic import of bodily related dirt, we fail to address people in the places where we really live. Our theology of work must correct this bias against "dirty work" by valuing all types of work and all workers, especially those who care for the needs of our children, sick, and elderly. "Correcting this omission will enhance the credibility and effectiveness of Christian ethical analysis and the churches' social ministry today."[14]

WORKERS' RIGHTS

Workers have a duty to work, but they also have rights as workers. The Roman Catholic tradition speaks of the right to employment, a right to participate in the economy, which is the way human dignity is concretized and made real. With the right to work comes the right to a just wage, the right to rest, the right to a safe workplace, the right to join worker associations, the right to strike, and the right to health care.[15]

Pope Leo XIII, in his 1891 encyclical, *Rerum Novarum*, recognized the right of workers to form unions or associations, which are vehicles to bargain collectively for fair wages and proper working conditions. As the bishops of the South recognized for poultry workers, unions can be an effective strategy in addressing the inequality of power that exists between management and employees. Unions are also a way to establish solidarity and community among workers and to give a voice to workers in their workplace. Unions also contribute to the good of workers and the common good by offering ongoing education and training of workers.

While unions are an effective means of achieving the above-mentioned goals, they are not the only means of accomplishing them. Each situation must be evaluated on its own, and the final decision rests with the workers to decide without duress or intimidation from either union organizers or management. The Catholic tradition maintains that efforts by government and business to break unions and prevent workers from joining unions are not ethical. The U.S. bishops note, "No one may deny the right to organize without attacking human dignity itself. Therefore, we firmly oppose organized efforts, such as those regrettably now seen in this country, to break existing unions and prevent workers from organizing."[16]

As a major social institution, unions have obligations to the society and must not only serve their own narrow self-interests. Unions must act in ways that benefit and empower workers and contribute to the common good.[17]

Unions are not always in adversarial relationships with management. Unions also work in collaborative ways with management and the leaders of their industry. Training and education of workers is one area of collaboration. Unions can also use their collective voice and power to help establish social policy and funding streams that benefit the industry or service in which they work, as well as the whole community. For example, unions that represent the staff in nursing homes and hospitals have lobbied with health care administrators to secure adequate funding for nursing homes and hospitals.

The U.S. bishops clearly summarize the Catholic tradition on the right of workers to form unions in their 1986 pastoral letter on the economy. "The Church fully supports the right of workers to form unions or other associations to secure their rights to fair wages and working conditions" (no. 104).

The Catholic tradition also recognizes that strikes may be used as a way to address labor grievances. Monsignor John Ryan sketched out the conditions for a justified strike in 1920: (1) if what is sought by the strike is just, (2) if all peaceful and less harmful means of bargaining have been exhausted, and (3) if the good to be attained outweighs the evil that may occur.[18]

Pope John Paul II outlined the teaching on the right to strike in *Laborem Exercens*:

> One method used by unions in pursuing the just rights of their members is the strike or work stoppage. . . . This method is recognized by Catholic social teaching as legitimate in the proper conditions and within just limits. In this connection workers should be assured the

right to strike, without being subjected to personal penal sanctions for taking part in a strike. While admitting that it is a legitimate means, we must at the same time emphasize that a strike remains, in a sense, an extreme means. It must not be abused; it must not be abused especially for "political" purposes. (no. 20)

Living Wage

Church leaders have been wrestling with the meaning of a just wage for more than 120 years. In Fribourg, Switzerland, lay leaders and clergy met for a month each year starting in 1885 to bring the best of the Catholic tradition to bear on the pressing economic issues of their day. This Fribourg Union was an early think tank of theologians and lay leaders who helped to give expression to emerging Catholic social thinking. Pope Leo XIII knew of their deliberations and asked for a full report as he prepared his 1891 encyclical, *Rerum Novarum* (On the Condition of the Workers). The Fribourg Union (1885–1891) set forth the basic principles on work and wages that have shaped official social teachings, including the principle that "a just wage is determined by the minimum necessary to maintain a family in ordinary circumstances."

Pope Leo XIII argued in *Rerum Novarum* that in justice the worker should "receive what will enable him, housed, clothed, and secure, to live his life without hardship" (par. 51). And again, "Hence arises necessarily the right of securing things to sustain life, and only a wage earned by his labor gives a poor man the means to acquire these things" (par. 62).

Msgr. John Ryan argued for the basic right to a living wage in the American context in his 1906 text, *A Living Wage: Its Ethical and Economic Aspects.* According to his calculations about 60 percent of America's industrial workers were not receiving a living wage in 1906. The struggle for a living wage is a tortured story both in European and American history. This struggle gave birth both to Marxist philosophy and to modern Catholic social teaching with the breakthrough encyclical of Pope Leo XIII, *Rerum Novarum.* American Catholic history recalls the leadership of men and women like Elizabeth Rogers, Leonora Barry, Mary Kenney O'Sullivan, Terrence Powderly, Dorothy Day, and Peter Maurin, and "labor priests" like Peter Yorke, Edward McGlynn, Peter Dietz, Raymond McGowan, Francis Haas, John O'Grady, and George Higgins. A unique figure in Catholic labor history in the United States is Mary Harris Jones, also known as "Mother Jones."

Mary Harris Jones

Mary Harris was born in County Cork, Ireland, in 1837. As a teenager she immigrated with her family to Toronto. Her younger brother became a priest and eventually the chancellor of the Archdiocese of Toronto. They did not agree on religion or politics and were estranged as adults. In 1860 she married a leader of workers in Memphis, George Jones. They were both active in their faith as founding members of St. Mary's Church on Market Street in Memphis. Tragedy struck her family seven years later. Her four children died of the yellow fever all within a week. She recalled, "One by one, my four little children sickened and died. I washed their little bodies and got them ready for burial. My husband caught the fever and died. I sat alone through nights of grief. No one came to me. No one could. Other homes were as stricken as mine. All day long, all night long, I heard the grating of the wheels of the death carts."[19] This tragedy gradually propelled Jones in a life of commitment with a special concern for the well-being of children and the working poor.

For nearly half a century, from 1877 (in the Pittsburgh labor riots) until 1923 when she was ninety-three years old (and working with the striking coal miners of West Virginia), Mother Jones appeared wherever labor troubles were acute. She was described as "a little old woman in a black bonnet, with a high falsetto voice and a handsome face framed in curly white hair and lighted by shrewd, kindly gray eyes which could flash defiance from behind their spectacles alike at distant capitalists and at near-by company guards and militia."[20] She organized not only the workers but also their wives, often armed with mops and brooms.

A biographer notes that "she had no consistent philosophy, except altruism and economic betterment. Though she weighed no more than 100 pounds, she didn't hesitate to fight violence with violence, or even incite some on her own." He goes on to say: "Her specialty, aside from violating injunctions and going to jail, was pageants of poverty, processions of the angry and the abused."[21] For example, on September 25, 1900, she assisted in organizing the coal miners' strike near Hazelton, Pennsylvania. She urged the women to "put on their kitchen clothes and bring their mops and brooms with them and a couple of tin pans. We marched over the mountains fifteen miles, beating on the tin pans as if they were cymbals." The all-night march, which included reporters, wagons, and American flags, was intended to elicit support from miners who had not yet joined the strike by catching them early in the morning before they went to work. It is not clear from the reports how much impact this midnight march had.[22]

On another occasion, July 7, 1903, she led a band of men, women, and children on a twenty-two-day hike through three states from Philadelphia to President Theodore Roosevelt's home at Oyster Bay on Long Island. The purpose of the march was to promote a reduction in the workweek from sixty hours to fifty-five and to protest the use of child labor, especially in the textile industry. (The textile industry was the largest user of child labor, employing eighty thousand children, most of them girls.) Jones considered child labor the worst of industrial sins and was disappointed that the news media did not address the plight of children.

When the small band reached Oyster Bay, the president was not at home. Jones had to put her requests in writing, to which Roosevelt responded that, while he sympathized with her cause, it was up to the states to deal with this issue. While Jones saw no immediate response to the plight of children, the march did have an impact in focusing attention on the issue. In 1909 a White House Conference on Children and Youth would be held, and other executive actions began to address the plight of working children. The three states through which they marched did enact stricter laws within a few years of the march. An effective federal child-labor law, however, would not be passed until 1941.[23]

From the late 1890s through the early 1920s she was an organizer for the United Mine Workers. She tirelessly rallied workers and their families in Pennsylvania, West Virginia, and anywhere she was needed. She amazingly received cooperation from Chinese, African American, Mexican, and Eastern European workers. During her time the UMW doubled the wages of miners and established an eight-hour workday. The UMW actually stabilized the coal industry by helping honest owners thrive while keeping less stable companies on the sidelines.

She scorned the church when it offered only relief in the next life and did little to lighten the workers' load in the here and now. The relative wealth of the church and its abandonment of what she considered the revolutionary thrust of the Gospel also raised her ire. "Jesus . . . took twelve men from among the laborers of his time (no college graduates among them) and with them founded an organization that revolutionized the society amid which it arose. Just so in our day the organization of workers must be the first step to the overthrow of capitalism." She believed that the Christian churches should play a liberating role in the here and now, and that with the labor movement the church should "go down and redeem the Israelites that were in bondage," and lead them from the land of bondage and plunder into the land of freedom. She urged workers to "pray for the dead and fight like hell for the living."[24]

Mother Jones returned to the Catholic Church, planned her own funeral, and received the last sacraments. Mother Jones was a controversial woman who stood up for the rights of workers. In this she was an activist daughter of the church.

Just Wage

Papal documents since *Rerum Novarum* have deepened the church's commitment to the basic right of a just wage. *The Catechism of the Catholic Church* summarizes this rich tradition by simply stating, "Everyone should be able to draw from work the means of providing for his life and that of his family, and of serving the human community" (no. 2428).

The Catechism then elaborates on this basic right by quoting from *Gaudium et Spes* (par. 67):

> A just wage is the legitimate fruit of work. To refuse or withhold it can be a grave injustice. In determining fair pay both the needs and the contributions of each person must be taken into account. Remuneration for work should guarantee man the opportunity to provide a dignified livelihood for himself and his family on the material, social, cultural, and spiritual level, taking into account the role and productivity of each, the state of the business, and the common good. (no. 2434)

U.S. bishops specify in *Economic Justice for All* that a just wage also includes benefits like health care coverage for workers and their dependents, life and disability insurance, a pension plan, and unemployment compensation. Related benefits include healthful working conditions, weekly rest, paid vacations, emergency leave time, and reasonable security against dismissal (no. 103).

The right to a just wage is not an optional right with Catholic social teaching. This right is rooted in the dignity of the human person which, while it is of eternal worth, is realized in the concrete here and now. Each person's dignity is lived out or denied within realities of life. If the lived experience of people does not reflect and enhance human dignity, then the social, economic, and political context must be changed to make it more humane and protective of the person's dignity.

Western cultures have come to believe that the best way to protect human dignity is to guarantee human rights. In the human rights tradition, each person, because of his or her dignity, has certain rights and duties that are universal, inviolable, and inalienable. Human rights form "a constellation of the conditions for the realization of human worth in action, in an ordered arrangement."[25] No one right can be singled out without recognizing its relationship to other rights. The full web of rights guarantees the full development of individuals and their communities.

Within this context of human rights, the just wage is connected to the individual's right to work. When workers receive a just wage they are able to carry out other rights, such as the right to shelter, food, health care, education, support of their families, and the building up of the common good.

The right to a just wage implies duties and responsibilities as well. Each worker is responsible to work a full day and to respect his or her fellow workers. For their part, employers have the responsibility to pay a just wage, to respect the human limitations of the workers, to allow workers' associations, to use all available technology prudently, and to make the company competitive and profitable.

In the Catholic tradition, the just wage is linked to support for workers and their families. "All heads of households, whether female or male, whether married or not, deserve a wage that enables them to provide sufficiently for themselves and their dependents." Frank Almade points out six practical implications of the commitment to a just wage:

1. There is no single just wage; it depends on the circumstances in each region.

2. A just wage is at least a minimum to cover the needs of the worker. *define?*

3. A just wage is a family wage.

4. There should be a public system of employee administration which includes workers' participation and consultation, wage scales, job evaluation, opportunities for promotion and further training and education, signed agreements, grievance procedures, and an annual review of the whole system.

5. A just wage means equal pay for equal work. There can be no discrimination based on race, sex, national origin, age, or marital status. Benefits may be adjusted to support dependent family members.

6. A just wage is conditioned by the employer's ability to pay the wage, market forces, and the common good. A just wage is linked to other sectors of the society, which Pope John Paul II calls the "indirect employers," such as governments, central banks, trade unions, and international trade agreements.[26]

Just Wage in Reality: St. Paul, Minnesota

One company that wrestled with the reality of paying its workers a living wage is Reell Precision Manufacturing in St. Paul, Minnesota, a producer of high-tech clutches and hinges for the office-machine and computer industries. The company's mission included promoting the "growth of people," which translated into the commitment to pay all its workers at least a living wage. In St. Paul a living wage was estimated at eleven dollars per hour or twenty-two thousand dollars per year in 1996. The actual market-rate wage for factory workers in that industry was seven dollars per hour or fourteen thousand dollars per year. How could Reell Precision be expected to pay four dollars above the market-rate wage?

The company did not shrink from the challenge by saying that "the market rate rules"; rather they saw themselves as moral agents in the marketplace, which meant rethinking how they were doing business and acting creatively. It wasn't as simple as giving a higher wage to the assembly workers. They did a deeper analysis and realized that the low wages were a symptom of a much larger problem of how the company worked. When work is designed to use seven dollars worth of talent, it is difficult to pay workers more than that amount. So they had to redesign the way the work is done to give the low-end workers greater responsibilities.

To pay a living wage the company designed a whole new way of doing work. Theologian Michael Naughton explains:

> Reell redesigned the assembly line from a Command-Direct-Control style management, in which management and engineers made all the decisions concerning the assembly area, to a Teach-Equip-Trust style management, in which employees were taught inspection procedures, equipped with quality instruments and trusted to do things right on

their own assembly line. By restructuring the work process according to the principles of participation and subsidiarity, employees decreased set-up times for new products, reduced the need for quality inspection, increased overall quality and required less supervision. By reducing these costs, the company not only was able to pay a living wage; it also created more humane work.[27]

The new living wage is given to workers who are able to handle the new responsibilities. For instance, when a new employee is hired with no experience and no skills, the company pays the worker the market rate of seven dollars, but it doesn't stop there. They make a commitment to move employees toward the living wage through training and skill development. As employees learn skills and gain experience, which Reell provides for employees, their pay goes up. On average, it takes a new employee a few years to reach the living wage.

While it was redesigning its work process and raising wages, Reell Precision did not have to lay anyone off. "The engineers who originally supervised the workers and inspected quality were freed to focus on things they were trained to do—create a better-designed product. With a better-quality product, Reell was able to gain a premium price for its product and also increase sales, all of which provided adequate revenue to support a living wage and avoid layoffs. While the moral and economic order do not always converge, we should take heed of those cases that do."[28]

Catholic social tradition is realistic about the living wage. It does not say that a company must pay employees in excess of a sustainable wage—that is, a wage consistent with sound financial management. The Catholic tradition does not expect a company to pay such high wages that it risks its economic viability. At the same time Catholic social tradition does emphasize the obligation in justice to create right relationships with employees and to work toward a living wage. Reell Precision's policy is in keeping with the principles of Catholic social tradition, even if it pays less than a living wage, as long as the company is working toward correcting the situation.

Living Wage in the Church

It is one thing to recommend a living wage in society, quite another to implement a living wage for church employees. The recommendation to pay a living wage would be seen as hypocritical if the church did not apply the same teaching to its own workers.

The church has stressed for some time the importance of paying a living wage to its employees. In 1917 the *Code of Canon Law* instructed administrators to give fair wages and decent working conditions to employees (Canon 1524). Unfortunately this canon wasn't automatically implemented. The *Revised Code of Canon Law* repeated and updated that teaching in 1983 (canons 231 and 1286). Vatican II had affirmed a just wage for church workers in two of its documents, the *Decree on the Missions* (no. 17) and the *Decree on the Apostolate of Lay People* (no. 22).

The most explicit statement on the church's responsibility to practice what it preaches is found in the 1971 document *Justice in the World* (par. 41): "While the Church is bound to give witness to justice, she recognizes that anyone who ventures to speak to people about justice must first be just in their eyes." The document notes that all who serve the church by their labor—laity, religious, and priests—are to receive just remuneration (par. 41). Pope John Paul II confirmed this point in *Centesimus Annus* when he wrote that only if the church does the works of justice *internally* will the call for justice in the world be authentic and credible (par. 57).

A Just and Fair Workplace

As we can see from the above descriptions of a just wage, justice in the workplace is more than a matter of adequate wages, although justice certainly includes wages. Leaders from Catholic health care and labor unions had candid and constructive dialogues about Catholic social teaching and the workplace. They produced a document called *A Fair and Just Workplace: Principles and Practices for Catholic Health Care*, released in November 1999. Although written with health care workers in mind, the document offers standards that apply to all workers: "Among the elements of a just and fair workplace are: fair wages, adequate benefits, safe and decent working conditions, and the right to participate in decisions which affect one's work, as well as opportunities for advancement, learning and growth." The document spells out these criteria of a just workplace by posing assessment questions, such as:

- Does the institution provide a safe and healthful working environment?
- Do the lowest-paid workers receive wages sufficient to sustain themselves and their families?
- Is health care insurance provided, or are wages sufficient for a worker to both sustain a family and purchase health care insurance?
- Are work hours flexible so as to permit adequate rest, leisure time, educational opportunities, and quality family time?
- Are training and educational opportunities available that will lead to advancement and promotions available to workers?
- What is the purpose of part-time or contract positions—to advance the institution and meet the needs of workers, or to avoid paying benefits?

- Do workers have easy access to written procedures that explain how to resolve disputes with supervisors or file a grievance to protect their rights or the rights of others?
- Do workers have avenues for meaningful input into decisions affecting the workplace?[29]

These are lofty goals that can be achieved in the workplace, within church institutions, and within society. One man who gave his life to protecting the dignity and the rights of workers was a farm worker from the fields of Arizona and California, Cesar Chavez.

Chavez—Family Man, Community Organizer

It is an old story: the young Chavez had to quit school to work in the fields full-time to help support his family because his father had lost the family farm during the Depression. He worked stooped over in the fields as his family followed the crops up and down the West Coast. As the son of migrant farm workers, Cesar Chavez had attended thirty-seven schools by the time he was in the eighth grade. Farm workers were (and are) notoriously the poorest and most exploited American workers. They were unorganized and deliberately excluded from the labor laws that helped other workers.

In 1949 at the age of twenty-two he was married and living in a barrio of San Jose, California, called Sal Si Puede (Leave, if you can), which seemed to signal the desperate hope of many migrant workers. That same year he met a priest who helped him and his community find a way out. In 1949 a priest from San Francisco, Donald McDonnell, was ministering to the farm workers. Father McDonnell told Chavez about the Catholic social tradition, as Chavez recalled: "He told me about social justice and the Church's stand on farm labor and reading from the encyclicals of Pope Leo XIII, in which he upheld labor unions." These teachings fascinated the young Chavez. "I would do anything to get the Father to tell me more about labor history. I began going to the Bracero camps with him to help with the Mass, to the city jail with him to talk to the prisoners, anything to be with him."[30]

Chavez learned about the world of Catholic social teaching, which proclaimed the dignity of his work and the rights of workers. Three years later Father McDonnell recommended Chavez as a potential leader to the community organizer, Fred Ross, who had come into the community to organize a local chapter of the Community Service Organization (CSO). Chavez eventually worked with Ross for ten years as they organized Mexican Americans in California. This community organization addressed police brutality, school and job discrimination, and inadequate housing. They also worked on citizenship classes and voter registration campaigns. Chavez hoped that the CSO would become a base from which to organize farm workers, but this did not happen. So in 1962, Chavez broke away from CSO because it "got pretty middle class, [and] didn't want to go into the fields. So I left."[31]

Chavez could have had a secure life as an organizer with CSO and enjoyed a middle-class existence, but he remembered his people in the fields and made an option for the least of these. As a family man with eight children, leaving CSO was a risk for him and his whole family. With his organizing skills and with a deep spirituality Chavez and Dolores Huerta founded the United Farm Workers Union (UFW). Chavez would often be babysitting his youngest children in the car as he drove through dozens of farm-worker towns trying to build up the membership of the new union.

Chavez brought together his charismatic leadership, keen organizing skills, and a solid Catholic spirituality rooted in his Mexican American culture, always with a nonviolent strategy. For the next thirty-one years Chavez worked to organize farm workers so that they might be able to participate more effectively as economic actors with better wages and health benefits and as a community whose collective voice and power would be taken seriously by growers and politicians. By the 1970s the UFW had about eighty thousand members; after a number of setbacks the number in 2003 was about twenty thousand. While not completely successful, Chavez brought the eyes of the church, the media, and politicians to focus on the plight of farm workers, who have a long struggle to achieve justice, with many powerful forces blocking their efforts.

Cesar Chavez stands as an example of a Christian laborer and family man who chose to work for the good of his community even at a great cost to himself and his family. His own words when he broke a long fast in 1968 summarize his spirituality and the kind of man he was:

> When we are really honest with ourselves we must admit that our lives are all that really belong to us. So it is how we use our lives that determines what kind of men we are. It is my deepest belief that only by giving our lives do we find life. I am convinced that the truest act of courage, the strongest act of manliness is to sacrifice ourselves for others in [the] totally nonviolent struggle for justice. To be a man is to suffer for others. God help us to be men![32]

Cesar Chavez found a way to participate in the economy as a farm worker and an organizer. He brought his faith to his work and truly was a minister of the Gospel in the marketplace and in the fields.

∞

United Farm Workers' Prayer

Written by Cesar Chavez (1927–1993), founder of United Farm Workers

Show me the suffering of the most miserable, so I may know my people's plight.

Free me to pray for others, for you are present in every person.

Help me to take responsibility for my own life, so that I can be free at last.

Grant me courage to serve others, for in service there is true life.

Give me honesty and patience, so that I can work with other workers.

Bring forth song and celebration, so that the Spirit will be alive among us.

Let the Spirit flourish and grow, so that we will never tire of the struggle.

Let us remember those who have died for justice, for they have given us life.

Help us love even those who hate us, so we can change the world.

Amen.[33]

CHAPTER 8

Solidarity:
War and Peace

Recognizing the solidarity of the human family is a matter of perspective. Astronauts are rewarded with a perspective of our planet that very few people have. From outer space the Earth is our fragile, blue marble of life in the universe. Divisions of war, race, religion, and wealth are invisible. Indian-born astronaut Kalpana Chawla, who flew on two space shuttle trips, including one that ended in tragedy, noted that she did not feel Indian in space. "When you look at the stars and the galaxy, you feel that you are not just from any particular piece of land, but from the solar system."[1]

Solidarity is the seventh "starting point" or basic principle of Catholic social thought. This chapter unfolds the meaning of this recent term and links it with the issue of war, as an expression of the failure of solidarity between nations. The theme of forgiveness is discussed as a dimension of solidarity and a requirement for building peace. The chapter also examines four responses to war, namely, the just war tradition, pacifism, active nonviolence, and preventive war. It concludes with the notion that our understanding of the ethics of war and peace is still developing within the Catholic tradition.

∞

A young German woman has just finished her master's of divinity degree and has a few months open before looking for a job teaching theology in a German high school. So what should Julia do with her open time? Take a long vacation to Spain, Italy, or the Greek islands? Those are great ideas, but Julia wants something with a little more depth and meaning. After checking out the Internet, she settles on a shelter for homeless women in a tough neighborhood in Rochester, New York. Sight unseen she arrives in January 2003 at the doorstep of Bethany House, a Catholic Worker house in one of the snowbelt cities of upstate New York. She has come five thousand miles to volunteer at a home for women and children who are homeless, often because of domestic violence or drug abuse.

About the same time in Washington State, Jessica is about to make a similar decision. She has decided to join another Catholic Worker house, St. Joseph House of Hospitality, which feeds the needy and houses homeless men. Jessica travels three thousand miles to live a life of voluntary poverty and serve the people most Americans try to avoid.

Katie and Matt are a retired couple living in small burg in Wisconsin. While doing all the things grandparents do to help out their grandkids, children, and great-grandchildren, they also make time to be involved in civic organizations and volunteer one day a week at the clothing and food cupboard in a nearby town.

Why do people do such things? Why do so many people make time to serve the needs of others, in their vocation, in their families, and as citizens? In the context of this chapter, I answer that people respond to the needs of others because of a sense of human solidarity. We know in some visceral way that, although our languages and skin color may be different, we are all connected as human beings. Julia, Jessica, Katie, and Matt are aware of their connectedness to those in need; they are mindful of the invitation of Jesus to serve their neighbor. That is what solidarity looks like in everyday life. And, of course, the concept of solidarity overlaps with all the other values of Catholic social teaching.

SOLIDARITY: ANCIENT CONCEPT, RECENT TERM

While the notion of solidarity is as ancient as the Hebrew covenants that God made with Abraham and Moses, the actual word "solidarity" appeared in English only in the middle of the nineteenth century.[2] Catholic thinkers lifted the term from the labor movements in France and Germany. The Catholic theologians needed a term to distinguish Roman Catholic communitarian thinking, and the word "solidarity" was called upon to serve in this mediating role. They tried to capture the Catholic vision of human beings as essentially social, in contrast to the individualistic tendencies of capitalism. The term was also intended to counter the subordination of individuals to "the collective will" of communism. "Solidarity" tried to communicate a vision of society as cooperative and harmonious.

Pope Pius XI utilized the term in his 1931 encyclical *Quadragesimo Anno* (After Forty Years) as a counterpoint to socialism. He emphasized (1) the God-gifted dignity of the human person, which government and economic policy should recognize; (2) the importance of subsidiarity, which establishes a role for family and local communal initiatives; and (3) that solidarity cannot be limited to one group but includes all of humanity created and redeemed by God.[3]

In his two encyclicals *Mater et Magistra* and *Pacem in Terris*, Pope John XXIII expanded the notion of solidarity from focusing on workers within a specific nation to global solidarity. Pope Paul VI stressed "the spirit of solidarity" that was essential for full human development of the whole person and every person. Pope John Paul II articulated the Catholic virtue of solidarity, which was the foundation for the Polish workers' struggle for a true union of their own in their communist country. The building of the union known as Solidarity in Poland was not without risk, as we see in the story of Father Jerzy Popieluszko.

Jerzy Popieluszko

Jerzy was born to a peasant family in Poland in 1947. His generation had grown up under communism. Like most Poles he shared a disdain for the communist system, but he had never been active in political resistance. Jerzy was a priest working as a chaplain to medical students at the university in Warsaw. Poland was on the verge of change in 1978 when the Polish cardinal, Karol Woytila, was elected pope. In June 1979 the pope made the first of four visits to Poland. He stirred millions of Poles to national pride and confidence as he urged them, "Do not be afraid to insist on your rights. Refuse a life based on lies and double thinking. Do not be afraid to suffer with Christ." Within a year of his visit the militant trade union movement Solidarity was born.

Father Popieluszko became involved in the Solidarity movement almost by chance. In August 1980 the shipworkers in Gdansk went on strike. The steelworkers in Warsaw expressed their solidarity with the shipworkers by going on strike as well. The steelworkers in Warsaw asked the chancery to send a priest who could celebrate Mass at the factory. Father Jerzy heard of the request and volunteered to go.

The Mass was celebrated in front of the factory when the workers had erected an enormous cross. For the thirty-three-year-old priest, this Mass was a turning point in his life. He saw with great clarity that the workers' struggle for justice and freedom was truly a spiritual struggle. With the bishop's support, Jerzy became the chaplain to the striking steelworkers.

The Polish government struck back by declaring martial law in December 1981, resulting in the arrest of thousands of Solidarity members and their supporters. As their chaplain, Jerzy visited the prisoners and organized support for their families. He also drew enormous crowds with his patriotic sermons, in which he highlighted the moral and spiritual aspects of the Solidarity movement. The movement affirmed the spiritual side of humanity and struggled against a foreign-imposed totalitarianism, rejecting a culture built on hatred, lies, and fear: "At this time, when we need so much strength to regain and uphold our freedom, let us pray to God to fill us with the power of His Spirit, to reawaken the spirit of true solidarity in our hearts."

As Father Jerzy's popularity grew, so did the government's efforts to silence him. He was subjected to much harassment. He was followed wherever he went, his Masses were often interrupted by provocateurs, and a bomb was hurled at his apartment. But he would not be silent or be paralyzed by fear: "The only thing we should fear is the betrayal of Christ for a few silver pieces of meaningless peace."[4]

By 1984 the pressure from the government had increased. Father Jerzy had been brought in for interrogation thirteen times, and in July he was charged with "abusing freedom of conscience and religion to the detriment of the Polish People's Republic." The indictment brought on a storm of protests, so the government offered him amnesty. The workers who were concerned for his safety asked the cardinal of Warsaw to send him abroad for study. But Father Popieluszko would not abandon the workers in their time of need:

> If we must die it is better to meet death while defending a worthwhile cause than sitting back and letting an injustice take place.... The priest is called to bear witness to the truth, to suffer for the truth, and if need be to give up his life for it. We have many such examples in Christianity. From them we should draw conclusions for ourselves.[5]

His death came on October 20, 1984, after being abducted by three men who stuffed him in the trunk of their car. Father Jerzy's driver managed to escape and reported the abduction. Masses were said throughout the country for the priest's safe release. The government buckled under the pressure and launched an immediate investigation. They arrested four members of the security police who led them to the priest's body. The abductors confessed that in the early morning hours of October 20, after savagely and repeatedly beating Father Jerzy, they tied him up, weighted his body with stones, and tossed him, still alive, into a reservoir.

The security forces had tried to silence his voice, but in death his voice only became louder. Father Jerzy helped to usher in a new day for Polish workers and the Polish people. Within five years of his death, the first free elections were held in postwar Poland. The people peacefully threw out the communist regime and elected a democratic government based on the principles of the Solidarity movement.

A THEOLOGY OF SOLIDARITY

Pope John Paul II viewed solidarity as both a gift and a challenge. He maintained in *Laborem Exercens* in 1981 that humanity is gifted by God in solidarity with each other by the very fact of our shared creation and shared redemption. Solidarity is also a challenge, inviting workers and all people to focus their activity on the common good. In his subsequent encyclical, *Sollicitudo Rei Socialis* (1983), he spoke of the "virtue of solidarity," which is not just a vague feeling of compassion, but "*a firm and preserving determination* to commit oneself to the *common good*" (no. 38).

Although the term has a special meaning in labor history in Poland and elsewhere, solidarity is not meant just for workers. All groups of people are invited to practice solidarity—namely between individuals, professions, classes, communities, and nations. The work of solidarity is to overcome the alienation and injustice that so many people experience.

Theologian Matthew Lamb asks,

> Given the massive injustices that sin causes in history, a human justice is inadequate. How can we render justice to the murdered and dead? Human solidarity breaks down in the cycles of violence and counter violence, as one grievance evokes another, as one war is followed by another.[6]

Human solidarity has broken down in the Mideast, as one attack follows another. The attack on September 11, 2001, led to war against Iraq. Human justice falls into silence and anger. But a theology of solidarity puts us on God's landscape, with divine points of reference. A theologically rooted solidarity insists that "the depths of human suffering can only be redeemed by God's loving solidarity with us. . . . We humans are enabled to forgive as God has forgiven, loving not only our friends but also our enemies, that is, being as universal in our solidarity as God." Such a divine solidarity can "end the cycles of violence, not by muting the cries of the victims, but by transforming, as only God can, those sufferings into new life."

In this theological solidarity, the church is the sacramental presence of human and divine solidarity. "As incarnating the presence of agapic love, the church proclaims the coming fullness of human solidarity with all the just, who are enfolded in the eternal life of the triune God."[7]

Unrestrained Conflict

Pope John Paul II knows that living the virtue of solidarity may entail conflict and struggle, as we saw in the life and death of Father Popieluszko. The pope has pointed out that conflict has a positive role "when it takes the form of a 'struggle for justice.'"[8] What the church has condemned as immoral is unrestrained conflict whether in class warfare or in military conflict. As John Paul II noted in the encyclical *Centesimus Annus*, "a conflict which set man against man, almost as if they were 'wolves' . . . a conflict all the more harsh and inhumane because it knew no rule or regulation" (no. 5). Such conflict is rejected by the Catholic tradition because it is unrestrained, not mitigated by the rights of others or the rule of law or reason. Moral theologian Patrick McCormick explains the immorality of unrestrained violence. "Such unrestrained violence, which intends the complete destruction of the adversary without any attention to moral limits, denies the very dignity of the self, the neighbor, and the covenantal relationship with God."⁹ Unrestrained violence leads to the evil of total warfare, as well as the arrogance of militarism, imperialism, totalitarianism, and all kinds of terrorism.

Pope John Paul II has consistently taught that conflict is part of life, such as in adversarial relationships or groups organizing to defend their common interests vis-à-vis other groups. He admits that struggle against economic and political systems is justified. He knows firsthand of the struggle of Polish workers against the communist system and leaders. For John Paul II the response to injustice cannot be unrestrained conflict. Instead, there must be a twofold approach of (1) addressing the "real and serious grievances" that lead to violence, and (2) relying on negotiation, arbitration, and compromise to achieve a just and peaceful resolution of the crisis. The goal is to address the root causes of conflict in nonviolent methods of diplomacy and compromise, rather than resorting to violence. Such an approach is called for in the various hot spots around the world, including the Mideast, Northern Ireland, and some African countries.

The Catholic tradition, as articulated by Pope John Paul II in *Centesimus Annus*, urges that humanity use "the weapons of truth and justice" rather than smart bombs or suicide attacks. He points to the nonviolent transformation in the Soviet Union and in Eastern Europe. The common "wisdom" of both the East and the West assumed that such drastic political and economic changes could only happen through another major war. The common wisdom about war as the only vehicle of change has been proven wrong. Rather, nonviolent means of "protest [which] tenaciously insisted on trying every avenue of negotiation, dialogue, and witness to the truth, appealing to the conscience of the adversary and seeking to reawaken in him a sense of shared human dignity" (no. 23) has been successful.

Pat McCormick notes that "just struggle does not gloss over wrongs but confronts sinful structures in a spirit of solidarity with the marginalized and with respect for the truth and the adversary."¹⁰ The pope believes that the moral stance of solidarity and nonviolence are the best hope for humanity. This moral vision must be translated into structural and institutional responses. First, oppressive economic and political structures must be replaced with effective systems that protect the full spectrum of personal and national rights, especially the rights to development and full participation in the new world order. Second, nations must develop international structures and channels of negotiation and arbitration. These structures would serve as a genuine alternative and counterweight to the almost automatic use of force, violence, and war.¹¹

For John Paul II the continued reliance upon war as a means for resolving international conflicts has become increasingly senseless in light of the growing interdependence and militarization of the globe. He made this very clear in the buildup to the Persian Gulf War in 1991, and he made it clear in the buildup to the second U.S. war with Iraq. Regarding the first Iraqi war he wrote:

> I myself, on the occasion of the recent tragic war in the Persian Gulf, repeated the cry "Never again war!" No, never again war, which destroys the lives of innocent people, teaches how to kill, throws into upheaval even the lives of those who do the killing and leaves behind a trail of resentment and hatred, thus making it all the more difficult to find a just solution of the very problems which provoked the war.[12]

FORGIVENESS AS A BUILDING BLOCK OF PEACE

Pope John Paul II has also offered the world another strategy for restoring relationships and building peace that is connected to solidarity: forgiveness. His 2002 World Day of Peace message was entitled, "No Peace without Forgiveness, No Justice without Forgiveness." In that document he asked,

> *How do we restore the moral and social order subjected to such horrific violence?* My reasoned conviction, confirmed in turn by biblical revelation, is that the shattered order cannot be fully restored except by a response that combines justice with forgiveness. *The pillars of true peace are justice and that form of love which is forgiveness.* (no. 2)

The pope admitted that talking about justice and forgiveness as the source of peace is not easy, because of the misconception that justice and forgiveness are irreconcilable. He believed that "forgiveness is the opposite of resentment and revenge, not justice." He explained the relationship of peace, justice, and forgiveness in these terms:

> True peace therefore is the fruit of justice, that moral virtue and legal guarantee which ensures full respect for rights and responsibilities, and the just distribution of benefits and burdens. But because human justice is always fragile and imperfect, subject as it is to the limitations and egoism of individuals and groups, it must include and, as it were, be completed by the *forgiveness which heals and rebuilds troubled human relations from their foundations.* This is true in circumstances great and small, at the personal level or on a wider, even international scale. Forgiveness is in no way opposed to justice, as if to forgive meant to overlook the need to right the wrong done. It is rather the fullness of justice, leading to that tranquility of order which is much more than a fragile and temporary cessation of hostilities, involving as it does the deepest healing of the wounds which fester in human hearts. Justice and forgiveness are both essential to such healing. (no. 3)

While forgiveness starts with individual people, it must eventually become a politics of forgiveness. "I would reaffirm that forgiveness inhabits people's hearts before it becomes a social reality. Only to the degree that an ethics and a culture of forgiveness prevail can we hope for a 'politics' of forgiveness, expressed in society's attitudes and laws. . . ." He explained that forgiveness starts with "a personal choice, a decision of the heart to go against the natural instinct to pay back evil with evil." He pointed out that all people want to be forgiven, so why not treat others as we would like to be treated? "All human beings cherish the hope of being able to start all over again, and not remain for ever shut up in their own mistakes and guilt" (no. 8).

As each individual hopes to be forgiven, so "*society too is absolutely in need of forgiveness*. Families, groups, societies, States and the international community itself need forgiveness in order to renew ties that have been sundered, [to] go beyond sterile situations of mutual condemnation...." In short, "*The ability to forgive lies at the very basis of the idea of a future society marked by justice and solidarity*" (no. 9).

John Paul II's thinking is very much in line with what Protestant theologian Paul Tillich describes as transforming or creative justice.[13] Creative justice is the ability to forgive in order to reunite. The example of the parable of the Prodigal Son comes to mind. The father forgives his wasteful and repentant son so that he is reunited with the family. This kind of justice seems offensive to the other son, who has been faithful and not run off with his inheritance.

The pope may also have been thinking of the international witness to the power of forgiveness given by Nelson Mandela, who after twenty-seven years as a political prisoner led people to reconciliation and forgiveness in South Africa. The newly elected President Mandela invited his white jailer as an honored guest at his 1994 presidential inauguration. Archbishop Desmond Tutu led the Truth and Reconciliation Commission, which allowed notorious violators of human rights a choice: tell the whole truth or face prosecution. The truth about the atrocities of apartheid was revealed, and many violators were forgiven. This national forgiveness averted a racial bloodbath in South Africa. Archbishop Tutu appropriately entitled his 1999 book, *No Future without Forgiveness*.

William Bole calls these and other examples of merciful acts by national leaders the "politics of forgiveness." The politics of forgiveness is not easy to swallow because it is new and unconventional. "The concept is foreign to most secular political philosophies and peripheral at best to Christian theories of just war and the common good." Pope John Paul II clearly brought a new dimension to the Catholic approach to war, and the pope was not alone. Among twentieth-century philosophers, the German-Jewish refugee Hannah Arendt stands out for her thinking on forgiveness. Writing after the Holocaust, she described forgiveness as one of two human capacities, along with the ability to enter into covenants, that make it possible to alter the political future to save it from determinism.

Forgiveness does not mean forgetting, but it is about remembering in a certain way. Christian ethicist Donald Shriver Jr. defined forgiveness as "an act that joins moral truth, forbearance, empathy, and commitment to repair a fractured human relation."[14] This is not just an academic definition, as Bole points out; it has been tried in the real world:

> Moral truth, in particular the social catharsis of truth-telling and public confession, is what South Africa pursued in setting up the Tutu commission. Forbearance is what President Mandela and Kim [of South Korea] signaled at their respective inaugurations. Empathy is what the late King Hussein of Jordan had for eight Israeli families whose children were gunned down by a rogue Jordanian soldier six years ago. Hussein went to their homes and knelt before the parents, begging forgiveness.[15]

Forgiveness is a new reality on the international scene, it has been tried in limited settings. To gain in acceptance it will first have to become part of the lived experience of people in many lands, in many homes, from Northern Ireland to Palestine and New York City. But what choice do we have? According to Archbishop Tutu and Pope John Paul II there is no future without forgiveness.

PRO-LIFE: THE WAY TO PEACE

As Pope John Paul II addressed the diplomatic corps accredited to the Vatican on January 13, 2003, he noted the fear that is prevalent in many hearts: "I have been personally struck by the feeling of fear which often dwells in the hearts of our contemporaries. An insidious terrorism capable of striking at any time and anywhere." The pope went on to suggest three things that are needed to save humanity from "sinking into the abyss." "First, a yes to life! Respect life itself and individual lives. . . . Next, respect for law . . . [and] finally, the duty of solidarity."

John Paul, who made solidarity one of the central values and themes of his papacy, went on to explain in very concrete terms why a commitment to human solidarity is so important.

> In a world with a superabundance of information but which paradoxically finds it so difficult to communicate, and where living conditions are scandalously unequal, it is important to spare no effort to ensure that everyone feels responsible for the growth and happiness of all. Our future is at stake. An unemployed young person, a handicapped person who is marginalized, elderly people who are uncared for, countries which are captives of hunger and poverty: These situations all too often make people despair and fall prey to the temptation either of closing in on themselves or of resorting to violence.[16]

Pope John Paul II spoke out against war, urging leaders to have the courage to say no. "No to death! . . . No to all that attacks the incomparable dignity of every human being, beginning with that of unborn children. . . . No to war! War is not always inevitable. It is always a defeat for humanity. . . . War itself is an attack on human life, since it brings in its wake suffering and death. The battle for peace is always a battle for life!"[17]

THE SCRIPTURES: THE WITNESS OF JESUS

As mentioned earlier, while the word "solidarity" entered the English language in the nineteenth century, the concept of solidarity as "a unity that produces community" has been present in the Judeo-Christian tradition since its beginning. The initial solidarity is God's unity with us, which includes all of humanity and all of the created order. The one-word synopsis of God's revelation is "Emmanuel," "God with us." This divine-human solidarity includes all humanity, as Thomas Merton among others discovered: "Finding God in his solitude, he found God's people, who are inseparable from God and who . . . are at one with one another in God the Hidden Ground of Love of all that is."[18]

One of the most poetic expression of human solidarity is found in Isaiah 25:6–8:

> On this mountain the Lord of hosts will make for all peoples a feast of rich food, a feast of well-aged wines. . . . And he will destroy on this mountain the shroud that is cast over all peoples, the sheet that is spread over all nations; he will swallow up death forever. Then the Lord God will wipe away the tears from all faces, and the disgrace of his people he will take away from all the earth, for the Lord has spoken.

The unity and solidarity of all God's people will be achieved "on God's holy mountain" at the end time, but this vision compels us to make it as real as possible, here and now. War and violence clearly erode the unity and solidarity of the human family and of creation itself. War sets one part of humanity against another. The violence of war, and the violence of abortion, capital punishment, poverty, racism, and "mercy killing" are all contrary to the gospel of life. In the context of the virtue solidarity we turn to the complex question of the Catholic tradition on war and peace. We connect with the lives of two Catholics who wrestled with the meaning of their Catholic faith in the midst of warfare. One was a German priest, the second was an American laywoman.

Father Max Josef Metzger

When Hitler plunged the Western world into war by attacking Poland in 1939, German Catholics felt it was their duty to support their government; they followed Hitler into battle without complaint. As Thomas Merton explains, "The

Catholic who might perhaps have suffered from some pangs of conscience was officially reassured that this was a perfectly 'just war.'"[19] That is why the witness of Father Max Josef Metzger and others, like the Austrian peasant Franz Jägerstätter, is so remarkable.[20]

Max Josef had been a chaplain in World War I. His experience at the front lines filled him with a deep revulsion for war. He believed that war achieved nothing, that it only brought about moral and physical destruction and prepared the way for a still greater cataclysm. Because of his firsthand experience of war, he devoted his life to the cause of peace and reconciliation.

He worked with the International Fellowship of Reconciliation, attending many peace conferences and congresses. He worked with the poor through a group called the White Cross. He also founded the World Peace League and the World Congress of Christ the King, devoted to the lay apostolate and works of mercy, particularly to work in the cause of international peace. In a speech in France he expressed his belief that "Only the realization of what is the dream of us all can bring peace: a true league of nations, a coalition of all nations in a genuine Christian family of nations worthy of man."[21] He was also ardently devoted to the cause of Christian unity. He was, with Abbe Couturier in France, one of the most original and farsighted precursors of the Catholic ecumenical movement. His best-known work is the Una Sancta movement, which began in 1939 with the retreat of a group of Catholic and Protestant clergy. This movement promoted dialogue and cooperation between Catholics and Protestants.

From the beginning of the Nazi regime, Father Metzger had conflicts with the state. He was arrested and jailed by the Gestapo in 1934, 1938, 1939, and finally in 1943. In the first three prison terms the Gestapo tried to implicate him in a conspiracy against the Führer. What finally emerged as "treason" sufficient to warrant a death sentence was his sincere, almost naive effort to start a plan for peace that he thought would end the war. Through the intermediary of a Swedish woman, who was interested in Una Sancta, Father Metzger wanted to get letters out of Germany to bishops in various warring and neutral countries. He thought that the bishops would be able to influence their governments to seek a negotiated peace instead of the "unconditional surrender" that was to cost Germany so many burned and gutted cities and the lives of thousands of civilians. The Swedish lady turned out to be a Gestapo agent. The Metzger letters which argued for a negotiated peace to spare the destruction of German cities was regarded as treason by Hitler.

His final arrest came in June 1943. He spent almost a year incarcerated in various jails in Berlin. Much of the time he was kept in irons, yet he managed to send hopeful messages to friends on the outside and he encouraged his fellow prisoners with his courage and solid faith. Finally, on April 17, 1944, he was beheaded.

Thomas Merton reflected on the example of Father Max Josef Metzger, suggesting that it "should make us realize that not everyone needs to be a passive utensil of the militarist. Father Metzger was a true patriot. He never failed his country, even though in Hitler's eyes he was a 'traitor to Reich and Fuehrer.' He died for Germany just as heroically and just as wholeheartedly as any soldier who fell on the battlefield. And he died for peace."[22]

Merton continues with a message that is for all ages:

> Let us remember this formula: in the madness of modern war, when every crime is justified, the nation is always right, power is always right, the military is always right. To question those who wield power, to differ from them in any way, is to confess oneself subversive, rebellious, traitorous. Father Metzger did not believe in power, in bombs. He believed in Christ, in unity, in peace. He died as a martyr for his belief.[23]

While Father Metzger was working for peace in Germany, a young woman, born of Scot-Irish Calvinist parents, was working with the poor and calling for pacifism in the United States.

Dorothy Day

Dorothy was born in Brooklyn in 1897; her family subsequently relocated to Chicago. At age sixteen, she headed to the University of Illinois at Urbana where she joined the Socialist Party. After two years she left college and moved to New York City, where she found a job with the Socialist daily, *The Call*. She wrote about poverty from a radical perspective, covering speeches by people like Leon Trotsky, and writing about poverty, labor strikes, and the women's suffrage movement. In 1917, at the age of twenty, Dorothy was arrested in Washington, D.C., while protesting with the suffragettes. Several of the women including Dorothy were given thirty-day jail sentences, which they protested with a hunger strike. After ten days of fasting, they were released on the eighteenth day by order of President Woodrow Wilson.

In 1925 she moved into a beach house on Staten Island with her common-law husband Forster Batterham, an anarchist and biologist. Dorothy admitted that Forster's "ardent love of creation brought me to the Creator of all things." Her appreciation of creation led her to prayer, not as the "opiate of the people," but as a way of thanking God for creation. At this point in her life, she started to attend Mass, to the consternation of Forster. Dorothy and Forster had a child in March 1927, even though Forster did not think it was right to bring a child into a world that he perceived was evil. The birth of their daughter, Tamar Theresa, was a turning point for Dorothy. Dorothy did not want her daughter to flounder through many years as Dorothy had done—doubting, undisciplined, and amoral. She wanted more structure for her daughter, so she had Tamar baptized. Later that same year Dorothy was baptized. The immediate impact of this decision was the painful end of her common-law marriage.

Between 1927 and 1933 Day traveled and worked at a variety of jobs, including as a nurse, and writing for the Catholic periodicals *Commonweal* and *America*. She met and was captivated by the vision of Peter Maurin. Maurin was a French peasant and wanderer. He was a student of the Christian Brothers and former member of the liberal Catholic Sillon Movement. Maurin espoused a "gentle personalism," which was a Catholic radicalism based on a literal interpretation of the Beatitudes. He rejected the liberal institutions of capitalism and the modern state and their faith in material progress and technology. He replaced all that with a personal commitment to love and a vision of the Christian mission. He proposed a radical imitation of the gospel by living in voluntary poverty in solidarity with the weak, the poor, the sick, and the alienated.

Peace historian Ronald Musto noted how Day and Maurin complemented each other perfectly: "To the pacifism and abstract social concerns of the intellectual and bohemian Day, Maurin added the fundamental realities of human community and commitment, the radical social gospel, and the French peasant's disdain for institutions." From these roots they shaped a new movement: "Both drew strength and inspiration from the Sermon on the Mount; they combined the commitment to nonviolence with the struggle for social justice that has always characterized true Catholic peacemaking. The result of this combination of talents and spirits was the Catholic Worker movement."[24]

Together, they founded *The Catholic Worker*, a monthly newspaper that was launched on Workers' Day, May 1, 1933. Maurin and Day did not want to simply denounce injustice, but they wanted to announce a new social order based on the recognition of Christ in one's neighbor. Maurin's plan of action included houses of hospitality, roundtable discussions, and rural communes. They turned the *Catholic Worker* office into a "house of hospitality" to offer food for the hungry and shelter for those uprooted by the Depression. By 1941, thirty-two Worker houses had sprung up around the country. While allowing the supervision of the hierarchy through a chaplain, this movement came from the people and was not controlled by the hierarchy.

Pacifism was not of immediate concern to the Catholic Worker movement, but the events of the 1930s soon made war a central issue. In 1935 the *Catholic Worker* came out against Mussolini's invasion of Ethiopia, alienating many of its Italian readers. Day was also outspoken in her opposition to the Spanish Civil War. This commitment to pacifism was not accepted by all in the Catholic Worker movement, and certainly it was divisive in the Catholic community.

In August 1940 Dorothy Day published an open letter to all Catholic Workers insisting on the pacifist position of the movement. "The result was disastrous."

Those who believed in the primacy of the social mission of the Worker or who supported the church's just war tradition abandoned the movement. By 1945, twenty of the thirty-two Catholic Worker Houses had closed, and the *Catholic Worker* newspaper lost more than one hundred thousand subscribers.[25]

Because of Day's insistence on pacifism, the peace issue became the predominant characteristic of the Catholic Worker movement after 1940. The Catholic Worker Movement helped to establish the groundwork for Catholic resistance during the war and became the seed for Catholic peacemaking after World War II. By her unrelenting stand against war, Dorothy Day "assured a tradition of conscientious objection within the American Catholic Church that would survive the barren winter of World War II and blossom into a new spring of protest in the 1960s."[26]

In 1955, Dorothy joined Ammon Hennacy and others who refused to participate in the mandatory civil defense drills. She argued that these drills fanned the fear of the Soviet Union, led to an attitude of the inevitability of nuclear war, and gave a false sense of security from the devastation of war. The group was jailed, but they repeated the protest the next year. By 1961, several thousand people refused to take shelter during the drills. Eventually, the drills were discontinued.

During the Second Vatican Council, Dorothy lobbied the bishops to include nonviolence as an essential element of living the gospel. The *Catholic Worker*, under her guidance, prepared a special edition on peace and the moral problem of modern warfare. In that issue she wrote:

> One of our Catholic pacifists asked me to write a clear, theoretical, logical pacifist manifesto, and he added so far in these thirty-two years of the Catholic Worker, none had appeared from my pen.
>
> I can write no other than this: unless we use the weapons of the spirit, denying ourselves and taking up our cross and following Jesus, dying with Him and rising with Him, men will go on fighting, and often from the highest motives, believing that they are fighting defensive wars for justice and in self-defense against present or future aggression.[27]

She airmailed the *Catholic Worker* to the bishops gathered in Rome. Then she went to Rome and brought copies of this special edition entitled "The Council and the Bomb." She joined a group of women on a ten-day fast in the hope that the council would speak out clearly against war. Their efforts were not in vain as the *Pastoral Constitution on the Church in the Modern World* (*Gaudium et Spes*) condemned total war and destruction of civilians as a "crime against God" (par. 80).

Dorothy Day left a legacy that the bishops of the United States have acknowledged by naming her in their 1983 pastoral letter on peace. They noted that "the nonviolent witness of such figures as Dorothy Day and Martin Luther King has had a profound impact upon the life of the Church in the United States."[28] Her witness continues to ripple through the church through the Catholic Worker Movement and its commitment to pacifism and nonviolence.

WAR AND PEACE IN THE BIBLICAL TRADITION

The Catholic tradition, with its return to the Bible as a central resource for shaping its social ethic, is becoming more critical of war as an appropriate response to international threats. In the Christian Scriptures we discover that Jesus "renounces violence as a strategy for promoting God's kingdom." Scripture scholar Richard Hays concludes: "The evangelists are unanimous in portraying Jesus as a Messiah who subverts all prior expectations by assuming the vocation of suffering rather than conquering Israel's enemies. Despite his stinging criticism of those in positions of authority, he never attempts to exert force as a way of gaining social or political power. . . ."[29] We may recall that St. Paul talked about using the sword. Hays argues that "there is not a syllable in the Pauline letters that can be cited in support of Christians employing violence." In other words, "from Matthew to Revelation *we find a consistent witness against violence* and a calling to the community to follow the example of Jesus in accepting suffering rather than inflicting it."[30] Roman Catholic moralist Lisa Cahill of Boston College concurs that "nothing is more clear in the moral message of Jesus than his exhortation to and example of forgiveness, mercy, and meekness in the face of abuse or assault."[31]

As we try to draw on the insights of the New Testament to shape our attitude toward war, it is fair to ask if it is possible to follow the teachings of first-century Christianity in the twenty-first century. Weren't conditions drastically different during the time of Jesus and the early church in comparison with today? Those are important questions to reflect on as we try to use the Bible as a guide of our present concerns.

Victor Paul Furnish, a noted Scripture scholar, has pointed out three factors that influenced the way the early church approached the question of war. First, the early Christians saw themselves as inhabiting a new way of life that was "in" but not "of" the surrounding culture. They saw themselves apart from the secular culture. Second, prior to the time of Emperor Constantine in the early fourth century, Christianity itself had never been the religion of a nation-state, and thus had no interest in the problem of religion and political power. Finally, the historical and political setting of the early Christian movement was a Roman Empire relatively secure from international aggression. More than one early theologian praised the *Pax Romana* as a blessing for allowing travel and communication that made spreading the gospel an easier task.[32] The early evangelizers took advantage of the efficient roads and means of transportation afforded by the Roman system.

Jesus and the early leaders of the church articulated their attitude toward war and peace in that political and cultural setting.

After the reign of Emperor Constantine in the mid-fourth century and after the Roman Empire fell apart, the political, religious, and cultural landscape changed dramatically. Christianity became the official religion of the decaying empire, and the church became more responsible for public order and security. These changes meant that the church's attitude toward war also changed.

THE EARLY CHURCH AND ITS LEGACY

The Christian leaders of the first three centuries were generally adamant that discipleship requires close adherence to the nonviolent and countercultural example of Jesus' own life. This was not true after the reign of Constantine (305–327). Early Christians set about to convert individuals and the entire Roman Empire. Their efforts at conversion worked on two levels: theory and practice. They attempted to persuade their Greek and Roman counterparts by explaining Christian doctrine and morality. Second, the Christian tradition of pacifism was made concrete and visible in the lives of the early confessors and martyrs. So a look at the theology and the actions of the early church is important.

Those who explained Christian teaching were known as apologists, that is, one who speaks or writes in defense of Jesus and the Christian way of life. Clement of Alexandria (c. 150–210) was typical of the apologists who tried to win over the Hellenic world through a synthesis of philosophy and Scripture. He pointed out that Christians are educated not for war, but for peace. Christians are soldiers of peace and handle the arms of peace, justice, faith, and salvation. Justice and peace need no arms except the word of God, and "nowhere will they inflict wounds."[33] Tertullian, around 210, is remembered for saying that "Christ in disarming Peter ungirt every soldier." This became the motto for nonviolence. The document known as the "Apostolic Tradition" offered guidance for the early church, maintaining that "a soldier of the civil authority must be taught not to kill men and to refuse to do so if he is commanded."[34]

While the apologists defended the Christian ethic of pacifism, the martyrs put that vision into action by their living and their dying. The martyrdom of Peter and Paul gave Rome a special recognition among the early churches. The total number of martyrs is uncertain—perhaps a few thousand. The message in their suffering and dying is that so many Christians were willing to suffer death rather than inflict it. Their witness was not lost on those observing it. Their witness became the catalyst for the conversion of many fellow citizens. We know the power of martyrdom today as we recall the death of Father Jerzy Popieluszko in Poland or the legacy of Oscar Romero, the martyred archbishop of El Salvador.

Based on the New Testament and the witness of the pre-Constantinian Christians, justifying the use of force by Christians is difficult, if not impossible. Some would argue that we must recover the vision of the early church. Others argue that, as the world has changed drastically from that of first-century Christianity, so its ethic must change. Those stressing nonviolence reply that discipleship permits no compromise with the violence that a sinful world employs to achieve historical ends. What is called for is fidelity to our call, not effectiveness in the world.[35] These are the voices of the early church, Reformation thinkers like Menno Simons, the historic peace churches, Dorothy Day, and others.

Other theologians such as Augustine, Aquinas, Luther, and Calvin, and twentieth-century American theologians Reinhold Niebuhr and John Courtney Murray, see the kingdom as more distant and the obligation to intervene in present injustice as more pressing. These Christians, who are sometimes called "realists," do not abandon attempts to live the radical message of love in the real world, but they do see the demands of love as entailing measures that seem to contradict the requirements of love. These measures can include political coercion, violence, even killing. The example of Lutheran pastor Dietrich Bonhoeffer, who felt he had to resist the evil of Hitler by participating in an attempt to assassinate him, typifies this line of reasoning. "Realists" would state that sometimes Christians must confront evil and injustice, even to the extent of taking life. In this line of thinking, love is limited by the injustice and sin in the world. Christians may have to act with coercion to bring about justice, which is a primitive form of love.

The debate focuses on how faithful our discipleship can be in these sinful times. If true peace is possible only in the kingdom, and if the kingdom is to be fulfilled eschatologically—that is, at the end of time—by God's action, then we may not always be able to live the Christian ideal of nonviolence. On the other hand, we know that Jesus calls his disciples to a converted life, transformed by the Spirit. As such, how can Christians justify any use of violence, even against enemies in self-defense? The Christian just war theory often goes hand-in-hand with an insistence that because the kingdom is not yet fully present, Christian behavior cannot be expected to conform fully to its demands in the present age.

Those who are most insistent on the presence of the kingdom breaking into the present reality tend to be pacifists. By contrast, those who support the just war ethic do not deny the New Testament mandate to live a transformed life, but they give that mandate less practical force. Just war proponents give more weight to the social context and more freedom to interpret the New Testament message.[36] Another way of phrasing this ongoing debate is to ask: Is the teaching of Jesus an *absolute principle* for every situation where we may face violence, or is the teaching of Jesus *an ideal* that encourages us onward, but which we will never completely achieve in this life?[37]

JUST WAR ARGUMENTS

St. Augustine was the first Christian theologian to articulate a framework for a just war—that is, a war in which Christians could participate. He argued on the basis of biblical love, just as pacifists use love as the argument for not going to war. Augustine used the example of a group of people walking through a dangerous area. If attacked by thieves and murderers, Augustine argued that a Christian could repel the attackers, especially to defend the women and children. Christian love could justify one in taking up arms and doing violence to the attackers. Augustine also argued that, in imitation of Jesus, he would not use violence to defend his own life, but only to defend the lives of others.

Those who follow Augustine's line of thinking argue that following the biblical love command is possible even when killing another person. This tradition tends to see the relationship between love and killing, or love and justice, as a paradox. They would argue that "killing someone in the name of love" is a paradox, but may be necessary. The example of Dietrich Bonhoeffer is illustrative of this position. Bonhoeffer and his fellow conspirators were willing to kill Hitler in the name of love.

Reinhold Niebuhr, a famous American Protestant ethicist, believed that Christians are sometimes forced by the ambiguities of human historical experience to employ violence to secure the contingent peace of the temporal order. He would argue that inaction could be an abdication of moral responsibility for the world in which God has placed us.

Niebuhr and Augustine would contend that historical realities have changed drastically from New Testament times. The social and political context for Christian moral decision-making is radically different from the time of Jesus. This approach would argue that the Sermon on the Mount was addressed to a marginal community outside the circle of power. Therefore, the pacifist teaching of the New Testament cannot be directly applied in a context where Christians hold positions of power and influence, or where Christians constitute the majority in a democratic political order.[38]

Another strand of the just war ethic is connected with the thinking of Thomas Aquinas. This version removes killing from the framework of Christian love and thereby does not see killing as a paradox. Rather, war and killing are evaluated in terms of the natural order, natural justice, and the common good. This approach would argue that it may be necessary to use violence to protect the common good from internal or external threats. In other words, for the sake of the good of the many, it may be necessary to take the life of a marauding killer, or another nation that attacks its enemy. In the natural law approach, criteria for discriminating among types of killing and their moral evaluations can be more carefully elaborated. But again, the ideal of kingdom discipleship becomes more distant.[39]

Just War Criteria

The just war tradition consists of a body of ethical reflection on the justifiable use of force. As we saw above, it is a combination of theological and ethical traditions. The Catholic bishops note in their 1993 document, *The Harvest of Justice Is Sown in Peace*, that the goals of the just war ethic are to overcome injustice, reduce violence, and prevent the spread of violence. To achieve these goals the just war tradition aims at

- Clarifying when force can be used
- Limiting the resort to force
- Restraining damage done by military forces during war

The just war tradition begins with a strong presumption against the use of force, and then it establishes the conditions when this presumption may be overridden for the sake of preserving the kind of peace that protects human dignity and human rights.

In a disordered world, where peaceful resolution of conflict sometimes fails, the just war tradition provides an important moral framework for restraining and regulating the limited use of force by governments and international organizations. Since the just war tradition is often misunderstood or selectively applied, we summarize its major components, which are drawn from traditional Catholic teaching.

First, whether lethal force may be used is governed by the following criteria:

- *Just cause*: Force may be used only to correct a grave, public evil, that is, aggression or massive violation of the basic rights of whole populations.
- *Comparative justice*: While there may be rights and wrongs on all sides of a conflict, to override the presumption against the use of force the injustice suffered by one party must significantly outweigh that suffered by the other.
- *Legitimate authority*: Only duly constituted public authorities may use deadly force or wage war.
- *Right intention*: Force may be used only in a truly just cause and solely for that purpose.
- *Probability of success*: Arms may not be used in a futile cause or in a case where disproportionate measures are required to achieve success.
- *Proportionality*: The overall destruction expected from the use of force must be outweighed by the good to be achieved.
- *Last resort*: Force may be used only after all peaceful alternatives have been seriously tried and exhausted.

These criteria, taken as a whole, must be satisfied in order to override the strong presumption against the use of force. These criteria must be satisfied before going to war (*jus ad bellum*). Once a war has started, a second set of principles come into play (*jus in bello*):

- *Noncombatant immunity*: Civilians may not be the object of direct attack, and military personnel must take due care to avoid and minimize indirect harm to civilians.
- *Proportionality*: In the conduct of hostilities, efforts must be made to attain military objectives with no more force than is militarily necessary and to avoid disproportionate collateral damage to civilian life and property.
- *Right intention*: Even in the midst of conflict, the aim of political and military leaders must be peace with justice, so that acts of vengeance and indiscriminate violence, whether by individuals, military units, or governments, are forbidden.[40]

As is clear from this discussion, Catholics do not have a finished product on the morality of war. It is an evolving tradition. One theologian, Michael Schuck, has made suggestions about how it may continue to evolve. He believes that we need not only principles for *going to* war (*jus ad bellum*) and moral guidelines *during* war (*jus in bello*), but also ethical guidelines for conduct *after* war (*jus post bellum*).

Such rules of conduct after war ends would include: 1) the principle of repentance to express remorse for the death and suffering inflicted by war, 2) a principle of honorable surrender to ensure that the peace does not turn into retribution or revenge, and 3) the principle of restoration to ensure that the damage done by the war be repaired.

I believe the sense of repentance and remorse is especially important. While we may be relieved that the fighting is over, a Christian should find it hard to celebrate such a terrible loss of life and suffering. Moral theologian Thomas Shannon notes that "Such principles should not only make us hesitant to enter a war but also encourage our government to plan carefully for the aftermath of the war so that the last state is not worse than the first."[41]

The just war tradition is clearly not a fast track to endorsing the use of violence and war. Rather, it is a rigorous layering of principles that make it very difficult to declare a specific war "just." It shares with pacifism the same underlying assumption against the use of force. In simplified terms, the only difference is that pacifism does not allow any exceptions to the assumption against the use of force, whereas the just war ethic allows exceptions to the rule. But, of course, the pacifist argument is more complex than that.

PACIFISM

Pacifists believe that Christians who accept the use of force are betraying the Christian message and have been co-opted by an ethic that thinks war is the way to peace. John Howard Yoder, a Mennonite ethicist, points out that the "irony of history" ought to lead us to recognize the inadequacy of our reason to shape a world that tends toward justice through violence. How can violence lead to justice and peace? The pacifist approach means that, practically speaking, Christians would have to relinquish positions of power and influence insofar as the exercise of such positions becomes incompatible with the teaching and example of Jesus. This might well mean that the church would assume a peripheral status in our culture, because our culture seems deeply committed to the necessity and glory of violence. The task of the church, then, would be to tell an alternative story, to train disciples in the disciplines necessary to resist the seduction of violence, to offer an alternative home for those who will not worship the Beast.

Richard Hays concludes that

> it is increasingly the case in Western culture that Christians can partici-
> pate in public governance only insofar as they suppress their explicitly
> Christian motivations. Paradoxically, the Christian community might
> have more impact upon the world if it were less concerned about appear-
> ing reasonable in the eyes of the world and more concerned about faith-
> fully embodying the New Testament's teaching against violence.[42]

The Christian Church has not resolved this historic debate about the morality of war. It centers on how much responsibility the church should have for protecting the common good and the social order. Those who maintain that Christians have a responsibility in this area argue that, because of our sinful world, we may have to take up arms. The pacifist tradition argues that we serve the common good more effectively if we witness to the truth of Jesus' pacifism and not compromise the gospel ideals. This tension between these two approaches, I believe, is healthy for both. The Catholic tradition is becoming less convinced about its long commitment to the just war ethic and paying more attention to the pacifism of the early church.

NONVIOLENCE

It is important to distinguish between pacifism and nonviolence. While today we may use the terms interchangeably, the notion of nonviolence is a twentieth-century term. The concept of nonviolence has come into modern moral reflection through the life and witness of Mahatma Gandhi. Gandhi was a pacifist in that he rejected war and violence as a way to address social injustice. But he developed active non-violence, which was different than the pacifist not going to war. Instead, he taught a nonviolence that was more active than violence, because it presupposes the courage both to die and to absorb the violence of the other. Gandhi's nonviolence was not passive; rather it struggled to be victorious. Gandhi called this new form of nonviolence *satyagraha*, the nonviolent struggle. "The victory to be won is not against the enemy but against the enemy's evil. The struggle seeks not to humiliate the aggressors but to elevate and free them."[43]

Gandhian nonviolence was picked up by various Catholic activists in Europe and the United States. In the United States Robert Ludlow, a member of the Catholic Worker movement, was among the first Catholic intellectuals to absorb and interpret Gandhi's theory of nonviolence. Through the 1940s and the 1950s he developed a Catholic theology of nonviolence. He believed that Gandhi's notion of nonviolence could be "a new *Christian* way of social change."[44] This thinking transformed pacifism from an individual opposition to violence to a social effort, a social movement. Ludlow urged Catholic pacifists to move the Catholic Church toward a commitment to peace and then to transform American society.

Martin Luther King Jr. also absorbed and utilized the power of Gandhian nonviolence as a means of social change in the civil rights struggle. The tradition of nonviolent struggle against injustice as a means of social change is a recent development in the history of pacifism. While this tradition may have theological and religious underpinnings it has become a means of social change that is no longer necessarily linked to religion. Nonviolence is seen as a creative force of social change. It focuses on social justice in the secular society. People with diverse religious backgrounds or no religious background are able to work together in the common cause of social justice.

With the development of nonviolent resistance as a social movement it is more accurate to identify three attitudes toward violence:

1. Pacifism, in the classic sense of individual imitation of the pacifism of Jesus
2. Nonviolent resistance, as a social movement and a means of strategic change
3. The just war tradition

Most recently, a fourth category of "preventive war" must be added to the list.

"PREVENTIVE WAR" AFTER SEPTEMBER 11, 2001

A new school of thought regarding the justification for war has emerged in the United States after the terrorist attacks on the World Trade Center, the

Pentagon, and the failed attack that ended in Pennsylvania on September 11, 2001, known as 9/11. This new doctrine asserts that it is justifiable to launch a "preventive war" to confront the new threats of terrorism, weapons of mass destruction, and rogue states. The case has been made not only by George W. Bush's administration but also by political philosopher Jean Bethke Elshtain, a professor of social and political ethics at the University of Chicago, and Michael Novak, contributing editor of the *National Review Online.*

Michael Novak created a controversy when he was invited by the U.S. Ambassador to the Holy See Jim Nicholson to deliver remarks in support of preventive war at a public audience in the Vatican City on February 10, 2003, three weeks before the second war with Iraq was started. Even though Novak is a Catholic, he was not considered an official representative of the U.S. government nor of American Catholics. Novak argued that war against Iraq was justified even though Iraq had not first attacked the United States. He argued that war had been "preemptively declared upon the United States on 09/11/01" and "No major moral authority had any difficulty in recognizing that a war to prevent this new type of terrorism is not only just but morally obligatory."[45] His reasoning is based on the argument that preemptive or anticipatory use of force is sometimes morally permissible, but only in the exceptional case where there is a clear and present danger, or a grave and imminent threat. Elshtain and Novak argued that Iraq posed such a threat.

Just war scholar Michael Walzer points out that "No one expects an Iraqi attack tomorrow or next Tuesday, so there is nothing to preempt. The war that is being discussed is preventive, not preemptive—it is designed to respond to a more distant threat." Such an approach is not consistent with Catholic social teaching. Cardinal Joseph Ratzinger (now Pope Benedict XVI), when he was head of the Vatican Congregation for the Doctrine of the Faith, bluntly noted that such a concept "does not appear in the Catechism of the Catholic Church."[46]

In their November 2002 statement the U.S. bishops expressed grave concerns over the expansion of just cause to include preventive wars. Three months later in February 2003 the bishops, with the strong support of Pope John Paul II, were again highly critical of "preemptive, unilateral use of military ... [because this] would create deeply troubling moral and legal precedents." The bishops conclude that: "Based on the facts that are known, it is difficult to justify resort to war against Iraq, lacking clear and adequate evidence of an imminent attack of a grave nature or Iraq's involvement in the terrorist attacks of September 11."[47]

Bishop Wilton Gregory, president of the U.S. Conference of Catholic Bishops, reiterated the U.S. bishops' rejection of preventive war on the anniversary of the atomic bombings of Hiroshima and Nagasaki: "The United States Conference of Catholic Bishops will continue ... and intensify our work on other pressing issues of war and peace, including opposing notions of preventive war, supporting the long-term task of building a just peace in Afghanistan and Iraq. . . ."[48]

Finally, Pope John Paul II sent his delegate Cardinal Pio Laghi, who had previously served as papal nuncio in the United States, to visit President Bush in March 2003 to ask the president not to engage in a preventive war. A year later on June 4, 2004, the pope met personally with President Bush to argue—as he had in his message for the 2004 World Day of Peace—that "the struggle against terrorism cannot only be 'repressive,' but must start with the 'elimination of the causes' of injustice."[49] Clearly, the Catholic Church has not accepted the arguments of the morality of "preventive war."

PEACEMAKING CHURCH

Since the time of St. Augustine in the fifth century the Catholic Church has been identified with the just war ethic. While many peace movements began within the church, as have declarations to limit warfare and violence, the Roman Catholic Church is not a historic peace church.[50] According to Father Drew Christiansen, a counselor for international affairs at the U.S. Conference of Catholic Bishops, the identification of the Catholic Church as primarily a defender of the just war ethic is no longer true. He believes it is better to describe the Catholic Church as a "peace-making church."[51]

This shift from just war to peacemaking happened gradually since the Second World War. The experience of the Holocaust and two very bloody wars in Europe in less than thirty years led German and French theologians to question the ethics of war. The threat of nuclear weapons challenged the applicability of the just war ethic. The leadership of Pope John XXIII signaled a new direction. As Father Ken Himes notes, "John never explicitly denied the just-war theory in *Pacem in Terris*, but his silence about the right of national self-defense coupled with his opposition to nuclear war created a mood of questioning on the topic of warfare."[52] In 1965 the Second Vatican Council gave expression to those concerns by calling, in paragraph 80 of *Gaudium et Spes*, for "an evaluation of war with an entirely new attitude." In that same paragraph the bishops uttered the only condemnation of all the Vatican II documents: "Any act of war aimed indiscriminately at the destruction of entire cities or of extensive areas along with their population is a crime against God and man himself. It merits unequivocal and unhesitating condemnation."

The U.S. bishops also helped to create a new ethic and attitude toward war. In their 1983 pastoral letter *The Challenge of Peace*, the bishops lifted up nonviolence and peacemaking as a parallel tradition to the just war ethic. This shift resulted in part from the renewed focus on the Bible, especially the New Testament, as the source of the church's moral theology and social ethic.

Previously, the church's teaching was rooted in the Hebrew Scriptures and the writing of St. Augustine. On the tenth anniversary of *The Challenge of Peace* the U.S. bishops issued a statement, *The Harvest of Justice Is Sown in Peace*, which continued to promote the peacemaking tradition. This document quoted Pope John Paul II's perspective on war as found in his 1991 encyclical, *Centesimus Annus*. As mentioned above, in this encyclical we find the strongest statement by the pope on the futility of war:

> No, never again war, which destroys the lives of innocent people, teaches how to kill, throws into upheaval even the lives of those who do the killing and leaves behind a trail of resentment and hatred, thus making it all the more difficult to find a just solution of the very problems which provoked the war. (no. 52)

Catholic social teaching has been become more critical of the just war ethic. While still utilizing it, the tradition has tried to emphasize the framework for building a lasting peace based on justice and human rights. To be effective in peacemaking the Catholic tradition is based on four structures, four foundational elements:

1. Economic and social development; as Pope Paul VI taught, "development is the new name for peace."
2. Human rights that recognize the dignity of every person and the right to have their civil, social, and economic rights respected.
3. The virtue of solidarity.
4. An international world order such as the United Nations.[53]

This is a positive and constructive agenda for the nations of the world—a daunting challenge, but the alternative is to continue the cycle of violence and fear.

The Catholic tradition is moving toward being a "peace-making church," no longer confident that the just war ethic is an effective, long-term response to the question of war. This trajectory of moral reflection suggests that peacemaking strategies, pacifism, and effective nonviolence are the better roads for Catholics to pursue. There may be times when war is regrettably necessary, but all of our human creativity and energy should be used to make sure that option is never forced upon us.

ONGOING CONVERSION

I would like to end this chapter on solidarity and peace by turning to the words of Thomas Merton. He reminds us that "Christ our Lord did not come to bring peace as a kind of spiritual tranquilizer. He brought to his disciples a vocation and task: to struggle in the world of violence to establish His peace not only in their own hearts but in society itself."[54] William Shannon, an expert on the Merton tradition, directs us to the core of Merton's nonviolent vision:

> We shall only learn to deal effectively with violence when we discover (or recover, for it is really always there) in ourselves that contemplative awareness that enables us—as it had enabled Merton—to see the oneness we share with all God's people—indeed with the whole of God's creation.

As we conclude this book on Catholic social teachings, we come around to where we began: our connectedness and solidarity with all of creation. Our wars destroy not only human lives, but also vegetation, trees, rivers and fields, animals, and insects. All of creation pays a price when humans turn to war to solve complex problems.

Shannon continues:

> Once a person has achieved this contemplative insight, nonviolence ceases to be a mere option and becomes a choice that brooks no rejection. But let no one think that becoming nonviolent is an easy task. It calls for painful, ongoing conversion, as slowly and almost imperceptibly we begin to realize what it asks of us and to experience the wisdom it imparts to us.[55]

May that ongoing conversion continue in our lives and in our faith communities.

∞

A Muslim, Jewish, Christian Prayer for Peace

O God, you are the source of life and peace.

Praised be your name forever.

We know it is you who turn

our minds to thoughts of peace.

Hear our prayer in this time of war.

Your power changes hearts.

Muslims, Christians, and Jews remember,

and profoundly affirm,

That they are followers of the one God,

Children of Abraham, brothers and sisters;

Enemies begin to speak to one another;

Those who were estranged

Join hands in friendship;

Nations seek the way of peace together.
Strengthen our resolve to give witness
   to these truths by the way we live.
Give to us: Understanding that puts an end to strife;
Mercy that quenches hatred, and
Forgiveness that overcomes vengeance.
Empower all people to live in your law of love. Amen.[56]

NOTES

Introduction / A New Breed of Men and Women

1. David O'Brien and Thomas Shannon, eds., *Catholic Social Thought* (Maryknoll, NY: Orbis Books, 1992), 5.
2. Synod of Bishops 1971, *Justice in the World*, in O'Brien and Shannon, *Catholic Social Thought*, 295.
3. Francis Schussler Fiorenza, "Church, Social Mission of," in Judith Dwyer, ed., *The New Dictionary of Catholic Social Teaching* (Collegeville, MN: Liturgical Press, 1994), 152.
4. Ibid.
5. *Justice in the World*, in O'Brien and Shannon, *Catholic Social Thought*, 289.
6. Fiorenza, "Church, Social Mission of," 153.
7. Ibid.
8. Joe Holland and Peter Henriot, *Social Analysis: Linking Faith and Social Justice,* rev. ed. (Maryknoll, NY: Orbis Books, 1983).
9. Gustavo Gutiérrez, *A Theology of Liberation* (Maryknoll, NY: Orbis Books, 1973).
10. For a concise overview of the content of official teachings of Catholic social teaching, consult Peter Henriot, Edward DeBerri, and Michael Schulteis, *Catholic Social Teaching: Our Best Kept Secret* (Maryknoll, NY: Orbis Books, 1992). For a helpful analysis of the methodology and content of Catholic social teaching, see Charles Curran, *Catholic Social Teaching, 1891–Present: A Historical, Theological, and Ethical Analysis* (Washington, DC: Georgetown University Press, 2002).
11. O'Brien and Shannon, *Catholic Social Thought*, 1.
12. National Conference of Catholic Bishops, *Sharing Catholic Social Teaching: Challenges and Directions* (Washington, DC: United States Catholic Conference, 1998). The three committees that worked on this project were the Committee of Education, the Committee on Domestic Policy, and the Committee on International Policy. The statement was approved by the bishops on June 19, 1998.
13. Ibid., 3. The thirteen principles identified by the "Content Subgroup" (pp. 23–26) are: (1) the life and dignity of the human person, (2) human equality, (3) the rights and responsibilities of the human person, (4) the call to family, (5) the call to community and participation, (6) the dignity of work and the right of workers, (7) the option for the poor and vulnerable, (8) solidarity, (10) the common good, (11) the

universal destination of goods, the right to private property, and the integrity of creation, (12) economic initiative, and (13) charity and justice.

14. Ibid., 6.
15. *Gaudium et Spes,* no. 43.
16. Richard Sklba, "Theological Diversity and Dissent within the Church," in *Shepherd Speak: American Bishops Confront the Social and Moral Issues That Challenge Christians Today,* ed. Dennis Corrado and James Hinchey (New York: Crossroad, 1986), 26.
17. In this text I quote official church documents by noting the paragraph number when that is available. This is the standard method of noting social documents. It allows the reader to find the quoted text in any of the variety of anthologies of Catholic social teaching as well as the online versions of the texts. This method of notation is preferable to quoting the page number of a specific edition.
18. *Octogesima Adveniens,* no. 4.
19. Task Force on Catholic Social Teaching and Catholic Education, "Report of the Content Subgroup," *Sharing Catholic Social Teaching* (Washington, DC: United States Catholic Conference, 1998), 23.
20. John Coleman, "Development of Church Social Teaching," *Origins* 11 (June 4, 1981): 41.

Chapter 1 / The Challenge of Being Prophetic: Gospel and Culture

1. Richard Rohr and Joseph Martos, *Why Be Catholic? Understanding Our Experience and Tradition* (Cincinnati, OH: St. Anthony Messenger Press, 1989), 11.
2. John Kavanaugh, *Following Christ in a Consumer Society,* rev. ed. (Maryknoll, NY: Orbis Books, 1991), xxviii.
3. Juliet Schor, *The Overworked American: The Unexpected Decline in Leisure* (New York: Basic Books, 1992), as quoted by Charles Murphy, "The Good Life from a Catholic Perspective: The Problem of Consumption," Environmental Justice Program, National Conference of Catholic Bishops Web site www.nccbuscc.org.sdwp/ejp/articles/goodlife.htm.
4. Robert Ellsberg, *All Saints: Daily Reflections on Saints, Prophets, and Witnesses for Our Time* (New York: Crossroad, 1997), 388.
5. Ibid., 389.
6. Murphy, "The Good Life," 2.
7. *Centesimus Annus,* no. 37.
8. Ibid., 3.
9. United States Conference of Catholic Bishops, "Global Climate Change: A Plea for Dialogue, Prudence, and the Common Good," www.nccbuscc.org/sdwp/international/globalclimate.htm.
10. "And God Saw That It Was Good: A Pastoral Letter of the Bishops of the Boston Province," www.environment.harvard.edu/religion/publications/ statements/boston_bishops.html, 2.
11. Luke T. Johnson, *Sharing Possessions: Mandate and Symbol of Faith* (Philadelphia: Fortress Press, 1981), 79.
12. Ibid.
13. Ibid., 49.
14. Ibid., 62–63.
15. Ibid., 108.
16. Ibid., 108–10.
17. Ibid., 128–29.

18. Ibid., 102.
19. William Walsh and John Langan, "Patristic Social Consciousness—The Church and the Poor," in *The Faith That Does Justice,* ed. John Haughey (New York: Paulist Press, 1977), 114.
20. Ibid., 115.
21. Martin Hengel, *Property and Riches in the Early Church,* trans. John Bowden (London: SCM Press, 1974), 58.
22. Walsh and Langan, "Patristic Social Consciousness," 117.
23. Ibid., 126, 118, 129.
24. Ibid., 127, 128.
25. Michael Blastic, "Francis of Assisi, St.," in *The Modern Catholic Encyclopedia,* ed. Michael Glazier and Monika Hellwig (Collegeville, MN: Liturgical Press, 1994), 326.
26. Ellsberg, *All Saints,* 432.
27. Leonardo Boff, *St. Francis: A Model for Human Liberation* (New York: Crossroad, 1982), 39.
28. Ibid., 35.
29. Ellsberg, *All Saints,* 433.
30. Rohr and Martos, *Why Be Catholic?* 66.
31. Kavanaugh, *Following Christ,* 170–71.
32. Walsh and Langan, "Patristic Social Consciousness," 116–17.
33. Ibid., 1156, 117.
34. Campaign for Human Development, *A Justice Prayer Book* (Washington, DC: United States Catholic Conference, 1982), 20.

Chapter 2 / God's Gift of Creation

1. Maureen Abood, "Chef's Special," *U.S. Catholic* 68 (September 2003): 17.
2. Paul Jeffery, Catholic News Service, "Honduras 'March for Life,'" *Catholic Courier* (Diocese of Rochester), July 3, 2003, 3.
3. Barbara Fraser and Paul Jeffery, "Lasting Change: Helping the Poor, without Paternalism," *National Catholic Reporter,* July 16, 2004, 12–13.
4. *National Catholic Reporter,* July 30, 2004, 4.
5. Lynn White Jr., "The Historical Roots of Our Ecological Crisis," *Science* 155 (March 1967): 1207.
6. Dianne Bergant, "The Earth Is the Lord's," in *Renewing the Face of the Earth: A Resource for Parishes* (Washington, DC: United States Catholic Conference, 1994), 11.
7. "The Religious Community Looks Toward the 1992 Earth Summit," *Woodstock Report* (Woodstock Theological Center, Georgetown University) (December 1991): 7–8.
8. Michael Himes and Kenneth Himes, "The Sacrament of Creation: Toward an Environmental Theology," *Commonweal* 117 (January 26, 1990): 44.
9. Ibid., 46.
10. Ibid., 43.
11. National Conference of Catholic Bishops, *Renewing the Earth: An Invitation to Reflection and Action on Environment in Light of Catholic Social Teaching,* November 14, 1991 (Washington, DC: United States Catholic Conference), 5.
12. Luke T. Johnson, *Sharing Possessions: Mandate and Symbol of Faith* (Philadelphia: Fortress Press, 1981), 97.
13. Robert Ellsberg, *All Saints: Daily Reflections on Saints, Prophets, and Witnesses for Our Time* (New York: Crossroad, 1997), 247.
14. Leonardo Boff, *St. Francis: A Model for Human Liberation* (New York: Crossroad, 1982), 39.

15. Ibid., 35.
16. Ellsberg, *All Saints*, 433.
17. Ibid., 558–59.
18. Pope John Paul II, *The Social Concern of the Church*, #34, 1987.
19. Roland Lesseps and Peter Henriot, "Genetically Modified Organisms and Catholic Social Thought," *Blueprint for Social Justice* 57 (January 2004): 2.
20. Bishop Anthony Pilla, "Christian Faith and the Environment," *Origins* 20 (November 1, 1990): 338.
21. Himes and Himes, "The Sacrament of Creation," 45 (emphasis added).
22. Thomas Merton, *New Seeds of Contemplation* (New York: New Directions Books, 1961), 30–31.
23. National Conference of Catholic Bishops, *Renewing the Earth*, 5–6.
24. United States Conference of Catholic Bishops, *Global Climate Change: a Plea for Dialogue, Prudence, and the Common Good*, www.nccbuscc.org/sdwp/international/globalclimate.htm.
25. *The Columbia River Watershed: Caring for Creation and the Common Good, An International Pastoral Letter by the Bishops of the Region*, January 8, 2001 (Seattle: Columbia River Project), 13–14. The text is also available online at www.columbiariver.org. (The bishops have picked up a theocentric vision as suggested by Sister Bergant, who was one of the consultants during the drafting process.)
26. John Paul II, "Peace with All Creation," *Origins* 19 (December 14, 1989): 465.
27. Ibid., 467.
28. Elizabeth Johnson, "The Cosmos: Astonishing Image of God," *Catholic International* 12 (February 2001): 43.
29. Aaron Gallegos, "A Partnership for the Earth: Churches and the Environmental Movement," *Sojourners* 26 (March–April 1997): 14.
30. John Paul II, "Peace with All Creation," 468.
31. Drew Christiansen and Walter Grazier noted that by 1996 there were forty-eight known statements on ecology issued by bishops' conferences or individual dioceses. See Christiansen and Grazier, *"And God Saw That It Was Good": Catholic Theology and the Environment* (Washington, DC: United States Catholic Conference, 1996), 16 n. 4.
32. *Columbia River Watershed*, 5–6, 14.
33. Ibid., 18.
34. Rembert Weakland, "The Economic Pastoral: Draft Two," *America* 153 (1985): 132.
35. The National Religious Partnership for the Environment, established in 1993, brought together the U.S. Catholic Conference, the National Council of Churches of Christ, the Coalition on the Environment and Jewish Life, and the Evangelical Environmental Network. In its first three years the Partnership distributed educational and action kits to nearly ten thousand congregations and held leadership training for two thousand clergy and laypeople. Much of the funding for the Partnership came from secular foundations, such as the Nathan Cummings, Pew, and Rockefeller foundations.
36. *Columbia River Watershed*, 20.
37. Frank Fromherz, "Coming to Know the Common Good," *America* 181 (September 25, 1999): 17–18.
38. Johnson, "The Cosmos," 43.
39. Ibid.
40. Charles Murphy, "The Good Life from a Catholic Perspective: The Problem of Consumption," Environmental Justice Program, National Conference of Catholic Bishops Web site, www.nccbuscc.org/sdwp/ejp/articles/good life.htm.

41. All of these resources may be found at the National Catholic Rural Life Conference Web site, www.ncrlc.com.

42. Indiana Catholic Conference, *Care for the Earth,* May 2000, www.ncrlc.com/indiana. htm.

43. *Basic Call to Consciousness,* rev. ed. (Rooseveltttown, NY: Akwesasne Notes, Mohawk Nation, 1986), 49.

44. Lesseps and Henriot, "Genetically Modified Organisms and Catholic Social Thought," 2.

Chapter 3 / Human Dignity: Respect for Every Life

1. Dorothy Day, in *Peace and Nonviolence,* ed. Edward Guinan (New York: Paulist Press, 1993), 50.

2. Tom Roberts, "Project H.O.M.E.," *National Catholic Reporter* 35 (December 10, 1999): 3–4 (emphasis added).

3. National Conference of Catholic Bishops, *Economic Justice for All* (Washington, DC: United States Catholic Conference, 1986), no. 32 (emphasis added).

4. Ibid., no. 28.

5. Joseph Cardinal Bernardin, *Consistent Ethic of Life* (Kansas City: Sheed and Ward, 1988), 2.

6. Ibid., 5.

7. Ibid., 14.

8. At least three people articulated the connection between war and abortion in 1971, twelve years before Bernardin's first speech on the topic: Archbishop Humberto Medeiros of Boston, Catholic journalist Margaret O'Brien Steinfels, and Eileen Egan of the Catholic Worker movement. See my discussion of this in *Catholic Social Teaching and Movements* (Mystic, CT: Twenty-Third Publications, 1998), 210–14.

9. Bernardin, *Consistent Ethic of Life,* 17.

10. Robert Ellsberg, *All Saints: Daily Reflections on Saints, Prophets, and Witnesses for Our Time* (New York: Crossroad, 1997), 495.

11. Ibid., 495.

12. Ibid., 494–96.

13. Congregation for the Doctrine of the Faith, *Declaration on Euthanasia,* 1980, www.usccb.org/prolife/docs/euthanasia.htm.

14. United States Conference of Catholic Bishops, *Pastoral Plan for Pro-Life Activities: A Campaign in Support of Life* (Washington, DC: United States Catholic Conference, 2001), www.usccb.org/prollife/pastoralplan.htm.

15. Ibid., Web site edition, 3–4.

16. Pope John Paul II, "The International Situation Today," *Origins* 32 (January 30, 2003): 544.

17. We have seen evidence of this at Catholic Family Center in Rochester, New York. Our staff reports a lack of respect toward our clients from some county officials and social workers. These incidences are not just isolated, but seem an expression of a cultural attitude. Monroe County embarked on revision of county services to save $31 million. Many in the religious community and human service sector were alarmed that "efficiency" seemed to be the highest value in this restructuring. The county used consultants from the business community who tried to apply their productivity models to complex human problems. At this writing the process is still under way, and the religious community is trying to monitor any abuses or efforts to maximize "efficiency" at the expense of human lives.

18. Ellsberg, *All Saints*, 306.

19. Quoted by Ronald Musto, in *The Catholic Peace Tradition* (Maryknoll, NY: Orbis Books, 1986), 143.

20. Ellsberg, *All Saints*, 307.

21. John Kavanaugh, *Following Christ in a Consumer Society*, rev. ed. (Maryknoll, NY: Orbis Books, 1991), 32.

22. United States Conference of Catholic Bishops, *Living the Gospel of Life: A Challenge to American Catholics* (Washington, DC: United States Conference of Catholic Bishops, 1998), no. 25.

23. New York State Catholic Conference, *Pursuing Justice: Catholic Social Teaching and Issues in Contemporary Society* (Albany: New York State Catholic Conference, 2002), 2–3.

24. Bernardin, *Consistent Ethic of Life*, 92–93.

25. United States Conference of Catholic Bishops, *Living the Gospel of Life*, no. 24.

26. United States Conference of Catholic Bishops, *A Matter of the Heart: A Statement of the United States Conference of Catholic Bishops on the Thirtieth Anniversary of Roe v. Wade*, November 12, 2002 (Washington, DC: United States Conference of Catholic Bishops, 2002), 2.

27. Rob Cullivan, "A Birthday for Abortion," *Catholic Courier* (Diocese of Rochester) January 30, 2003: 6.

28. Rob Cullivan, "Teens Speak for Those Never Born," *Catholic Courier* (Diocese of Rochester), January 30, 2003, 8.

29. Bernardin, *Consistent Ethic of Life*, 8–9, 83.

30. James Megivern, *The Death Penalty: An Historical and Theological Survey* (New York: Paulist Press, 1997), 444.

31. "Statements by the Holy Father on the Death Penalty," found on the Web site of the United States Conference of Catholic Bishops, www.usccb.org/sdwp/national/criminal/stlouissmt.htm.

32. "Statement by Catholic Bishops of Texas on Capital Punishment," October 20, 1997, at www.usccb.org/sdwp/national/criminal/death/txecu98.htm.

33. Bill Appleby Purcell, *Being Neighbor: The Catechism and Social Justice* (Washington, DC: United States Conference of Catholic Bishops, 1998), 4.

Chapter 4 / Community, Family, Participation

1. Thomas Merton, *Dialogues with Silence: Prayers and Drawings*, ed. Jonathan Montaldo (New York: Harper Collins, 2001), ix–x.

2. William H. Shannon, ed., *Thomas Merton: Passion for Peace: The Social Essays* (New York: Crossroad, 1995), 2–3.

3. Thomas Merton, *Conjectures of a Guilty Bystander* (Garden City, NY: Doubleday, 1965), 140–42.

4. Shannon, *Thomas Merton*, 4.

5. United States Catholic Conference, *Sharing Catholic Social Teaching* (Washington, DC: United States Catholic Conference, 1998), 22.

6. John Coleman, *An American Strategic Theology* (New York: Paulist Press, 1982), 10.

7. John G. Gager, *Kingdom and Community: The Social World of Early Christianity* (Englewood Cliffs, NJ: Prentice Hall, 1976), 96; quoted in William Walsh and John Langan, "Patristic Social Consciousness—The Church and the Poor," in *The Faith That Does Justice*, ed. John Haughey (New York: Paulist Press, 1977), 113.

8. Walter Brueggemann, *Prophetic Imagination*, 2nd ed. (Philadelphia: Fortress Press, 2001), 6, 7, 5.

9. Ibid., 8.

10. Ibid., 21, 24.

11. Ibid., 31–32.

12. Ibid., 33.

13. Ibid., 40.

14. D. N. Premnath, *Eighth-Century Prophets: A Social Analysis* (St. Louis: Chalice Press, 2003), 188.

15. Brueggemann, *Prophetic Imagination,* 66.

16. Ibid., 68.

17. Ibid., 82.

18. Ibid., 84.

19. Ibid., 88.

20. Ibid., 91.

21. Robert Ellsberg, *All Saints: Daily Reflections on Saints, Prophets, and Witnesses for Our Time* (New York: Crossroad, 1997), 259.

22. Ibid., 260.

23. Ibid., 258.

24. Martin Hengel, *Property and Riches in the Early Church,* trans. John Bowden (London: SCM Press Ltd., 1974), 2–3.

25. This is the Jerusalem Bible translation. The New Revised Standard Version (1989) reads: "Then he [Jesus] went home; and the crowd came together again, so that they could not even eat. When his family heard it, they went out to restrain him, for people were saying, 'He has gone out of his mind'" (3:19–21).

26. Margaret Farley, "Family," in *The New Dictionary of Catholic Social Thought,* ed. Judith Dwyer (Collegeville, MN: Michael Glazier/Liturgical Press, 1994), 372.

27. Ibid.

28. Ibid.

29. William Lazareth, *Luther on the Christian Home* (Philadelphia: Muhlenberg, 1960), 133, quoted by Farley, in "Family," 373.

30. Farley, "Family," 374.

31. *The Catechism of the Catholic Church* (Liguori, MO: Liguori Publications, 1994), no. 2204ff.

32. Farley, "Family," 374.

33. Ibid., 379.

34. Lisa Sowle Cahill, *Family: A Christian Social Perspective* (Minneapolis: Augsburg Fortress, 2000), 27–82. I am following the parameters of Cahill's discussion of domestic church as found in the draft of her paper, "Familiaris Consortio," in the commentary on Catholic social thought edited by Kenneth Himes to be published in 2005 by Georgetown University.

35. Michael Fahey, "The Christian Family as Domestic Church at Vatican II," in Lisa Sowle Cahill and Dietmar Mieth, *The Family* (London and Maryknoll, NY: Orbis Books and SCM Press, 1995), 91.

36. Pope John Paul II, *Familiaris Consortio,* no. 42.

37. Ibid., no. 43.

38. Ibid., nos. 64, 41, 47, and 48.

39. National Conference of Catholic Bishops, *Communities of Salt and Light: Reflections on the Social Mission of the Parish* (Washington, DC: United States Catholic Conference, 1993), 7.

40. Ibid., 6.

41. At the supper table we had an hourlong conversation about the event and the meaning

of stealing. My daughter stood her ground and felt it was not necessary to return to the store because it had been in our favor. She might have been standing firm for the sake of the argument. Either way, it showed us as parents how our children's morality is shaped by the cultural norms of "looking out for number one" and "it's not wrong unless you get caught." If she gets married and has children, I would like to hear what she tells her children.

42. National Conference of Catholic Bishops, *Communities of Salt and Light*, 6–7.
43. Ibid., 7.
44. Barbara Fraser and Paul Jeffery, "Lasting Change: Helping the Poor, without Paternalism," *National Catholic Reporter*, July 16, 2004, 11.
45. Ibid., 12.
46. *Octogesima Adveniens*, nos. 22, 47.
47. Robert Sirico and Maciej Zieba, *The Social Agenda: A Collection of Magisterial Texts* (Vatican City State: Libreria Editrice Vaticana, 2000), 72.
48. United States Conference of Catholic Bishops, *Faithful Citizenship: A Catholic Call to Political Responsibility* (Washington, DC: United States Conference of Catholic Bishops, 2003), 7. Web site edition: www.usccb.org/faithfulcitizenship.
49. Ibid., 3, 5.
50. Ibid., 7.
51. Ibid.
52. Ibid., 16 (emphasis in the original).
53. Bill Appleby Purcell, *Being Neighbor: The Catechism and Social Justice* (Washington, DC: United States Catholic Conference, 1998), 5; rewritten by author.

Chapter 5 / Option for the Poor

1. Rob Cullivan, "Woman Lives Life to Help Homeless," *Catholic Courier* (Rochester, NY), January 9, 2003, 12.
2. Jorge Pixley, *Biblical Israel: A People's History* (Minneapolis: Fortress Press, 1992), 12.
3. Ibid.
4. David Blanchard, "Session One: Background Piece," in *Journey to Justice Retreat* (Washington, DC: Catholic Campaign for Human Development, n.d.), 1.
5. Jim Dinn, *Catholic Wisdom on Welfare Reform* (Chicago: Claretian Publications, n.d.), 8.
6. "Session Two: Background Piece," *Journey to Justice Retreat*, 4.
7. Robert Ellsberg, *All Saints: Daily Reflections on Saints, Prophets, and Witnesses for Our Time* (New York: Crossroad, 1997), 479.
8. Ibid., 480.
9. Joseph Gremillion, *The Gospel of Peace and Justice: Catholic Social Teaching since Pope John* (Maryknoll, NY: Orbis Books, 1976), "Justice" section of Medellín Documents, par. 20, 453.
10. Alfred Hennelly, ed., *Liberation Theology: A Documentary History* (Maryknoll, NY: Orbis Books, 1990), 89.
11. Curt Cadorette, "Medellín," in *New Dictionary of Catholic Social Teaching*, ed. Judith Dwyer (Collegeville, MN: Michael Glazier/Liturgical Press, 1994), 593.
12. Curt Cadorette, "Puebla," in *New Dictionary of Catholic Social Teaching*, ed. Judith Dwyer (Collegeville, MN: Michael Glazier/Liturgical Press, 1994), 801.
13. Daniel Hartnett, "Remembering the Poor: An Interview with Gustavo Gutiérrez," *America* 188 (February 3, 2003): 14.
14. Ellsberg, *All Saints*, 527.

15. Ibid.
16. Ibid.
17. Ibid., 526.
18. Ibid.
19. "Martyrs of El Salvador," a card from the Religious Task Force on Central America; www.rtfcam.org.
20. National Conference of Catholic Bishops, *Economic Justice for All* (Washington, DC: United States Catholic Conference, 1986), no. 52 (author's formatting).
21. Blanchard, "Session One: Background Piece," *Journey to Justice Retreat.*
22. Ellsberg, *All Saints,* 439.
23. Ibid.
24. Ibid., 439–40.
25. Donal Dorr, "Option for the Poor," in *New Dictionary of Catholic Social Teaching,* ed. Judith Dwyer (Collegeville, MN: Michael Glazier/Liturgical Press, 1994), 755.
26. Ibid., 757.
27. Ibid., 758.
28. Denis Murphy, "Is 'Church of the Poor' Just Rhetoric?" *America* 188 (January 6–13, 2003): 12–14.
29. Ibid., 12–13.
30. Ibid., 13.
31. Ibid., 14.
32. Jack Jezreel, *Catholic Wisdom on Option for the Poor* (Chicago: Claretian Publications, n.d.), 4–7.
33. Department of Social Development and World Peace, *Communities of Salt and Light: Parish Resource Manual* (Washington, DC: United States Catholic Conference, 1994), 21–22.
34. National Conference of Catholic Bishops, *Sharing Catholic Social Teaching* (Washington, DC: United States Catholic Conference, 1998), 5.
35. Bill Appleby Purcell, *Being Neighbor: The Catechism and Social Justice* (Washington, DC: United States Catholic Conference, 1998), 7 (rewritten by author).

Chapter 6 / Rights and Responsibilities

1. Rob Cullivan, "Woman Lives Life to Help Homeless," *Catholic Courier* (Rochester, NY), January 9, 2003, 12.
2. *Sharing Catholic Social Teaching* (Washington, DC: United States Catholic Conference, 1998), 5.
3. John Donahue, "Biblical Perspectives on Justice," in *Faith That Does Justice,* ed. John Haughey (New York: Paulist Press, 1977), 69.
4. H. H. Schrey, *The Biblical Doctrine of Justice and Law* (London: S.C.M. Press, 1955), 50; quoted by Donahue, "Biblical Perspectives on Justice," 68.
5. Gerhard von Rad, *Old Testament Theology,* trans. D. M. G. Stalker (New York: Harper and Bros., 1962), 1:370; quoted by Donahue, "Biblical Perspectives on Justice," 68.
6. Walter Brueggemann, *The Covenanted Self* (Minneapolis: Fortress Press, 1999), 49.
7. Ibid., 50.
8. Ibid.
9. Ibid., 51.
10. D. N. Premnath, *Eighth-Century Prophets: A Social Analysis* (St. Louis: Chalice Press, 2003), 182.
11. Walter Brueggemann, "Voices of the Night—Against Justice," in Walter Brueggemann,

Sharon Parks, and Thomas H. Groome, *To Act Justly, Love Tenderly, Walk Humbly* (New York: Paulist Press, 1986), 16.

12. The parable of the Workers in the Vineyard is discussed in chap. 7.

13. Vincent Taylor, *The Gospel According to St. Mark,* 2nd ed. (New York: Macmillan and Co., 1966), 462.

14. William Herzog II, *Jesus, Justice, and the Reign of God: A Ministry of Liberation* (Louisville, KY: Westminster John Knox Press, 2000), 133–42.

15. Ibid., 142–43.

16. Matthew Lamb, "Solidarity," in *New Dictionary of Catholic Social Teaching,* ed. Judith Dwyer (Collegeville, MN: Michael Glazier/Liturgical Press, 1994), 911.

17. Thomas Hoppe, "Human Rights," in *New Dictionary of Catholic Social Teaching,* ed. Judith Dwyer (Collegeville, MN: Michael Glazier/Liturgical Press, 1994), 460.

18. R. Scott Appleby, " 'In Truth, Justice, Charity, and Liberty': Contesting *Pacem in Terris* in Our Time," *Journal of Catholic Social Thought* 1 (Winter 2004): 37. The entire first issue of this new journal focused on the meaning of *Pacem in Terris* on its fortieth anniversary.

19. Pope John Paul II, "Address at the United Nations" (Washington, DC: United States Catholic Conference, 1979), no. 13.

20. *Mater et Magistra,* no. 109.

21. *Populorum Progressio,* no. 23.

22. *Gaudium et Spes,* no. 69.

23. National Conference of Catholic Bishops, *Pastoral Letter on Marxist Communism* (Washington, DC: United States Catholic Conference, 1980), no. 44.

24. Robert Ellsberg, *All Saints: Daily Reflections on Saints, Prophets, and Witnesses for Our Time* (New York: Crossroad, 1997), 352.

25. Jon Nilson, "Confessions of a White Catholic Racist Theologian," *Origins* 33 (July 17, 2003): 131.

26. Cyprian Davis, "Two Sides of a Coin: The Black Presence in the History of the Catholic Church in America," in *Many Rains Ago: A Historical and Theological Reflection on the Role of the Episcopate in the Evangelization of African American Catholics,* Secretariat for Black Catholics (Washington, DC: United States Catholic Conference, 1990), 50.

27. Ibid., 59.

28. National Conference of Catholic Bishops, *Brothers and Sisters to Us: U.S. Bishops Pastoral Letter on Racism in Our Day* (Washington, DC: United States Catholic Conference, 1979), 1.

29. Ibid.

30. Archbishop Sean O'Malley, "Solidarity: The Antidote to Resurgent Racism," *Origins* 29 (February 3, 2000): 531–32.

31. Bishop Dale Melczek, "Created in God's Image: The Sin of Racism and a Call to Conversion," *Origins* 33 (September 25, 2003): 271.

32. In *Peace and Nonviolence: Basic Writings,* Edward Guinan, comp. (New York: Paulist Press, 1973), 86.

33. United States Conference of Catholic Bishops, *A Place at the Table: A Catholic Recommitment to Overcome Poverty and to Respect the Dignity of All God's Children, A Pastoral Reflection of the U.S. Catholic Bishops* (Washington, DC: United States Conference of Catholic Bishops, 2002), 4, Web site edition, www.usccb.org/bishops/table.htm.

34. Ibid., 1.

35. Ibid., 8.

36. Ibid., 8–9.
37. Monika Hellwig, "Principle of Subsidiarity," in *The Modern Catholic Encyclopedia,* ed. Michael Glazier and Monika Hellwig (Collegeville, MN: Liturgical Press, 1994), 836.
38. *Sharing Catholic Social Teaching,* 25.
39. United States Conference of Catholic Bishops, *A Place at the Table,* 10–12.

Chapter 7 / Dignity of Work and Workers' Rights

1. Smriti Jacob, "The Power of Disclosure," *Rochester Business Journal,* December 5, 2003, 33.
2. Email correspondence to the author from Bob Fien, December 23, 2003. Two associations that promote employee stock ownership are: National Center for Employee Ownership (NCEO), 1736 Franklin Street, 8th floor, Oakland, CA 94614, (510) 208-1300, and Employee Stock Ownership Plan (ESOP) Association, 1726 M Street, Suite 501, Washington, D.C. 20036, (202) 293-2971.
3. *Voices and Choices,* A Pastoral Letter from the Catholic Bishops of the South (November 2000), Web site version, www.americancatholic.org/News/PoultryPastoral/english.asp.
4. John Rausch, "Cheap Chicken Actually Costs a Lot," National Catholic Rural Life Conference Web site: www.ncrlc.com/poultrypastoral.html. For a view of the working conditions in a poultry processing plant, read Steve Striffler, "Undercover in a Chicken Factory," *Utne* (January–February 2004): 68–74.
5. *Voices and Choices,* 12.
6. Ibid.
7. Ibid., 4.
8. John Paul II, "Address on Christian Unity in a Technological Age," in Gerald Darring, *A Catechism of Catholic Social Teaching* (Kansas City, MO: Sheed and Ward, 1987), 29.
9. William R. Herzog II, *Parables as Subversive Speech* (Louisville, KY: Westminster John Knox Press, 1994), 79–97.
10. Scriptural texts that address workers' rights include: Exod. 23:9; Lev. 25:23–38; Deut. 27:19; Ps. 72; 103:6; Jer. 7:1–11; Isa. 3:11–15; 58; 61; Amos 2:6–7; 6:4–8; 8:4–7; Mic. 6:8; Luke 4:18; Matt. 25:31–46.
11. "Bishops Issue Call to Justice," *Catholic Courier* (Rochester, NY) (November 21, 1996), 1. Also found in *A Decade after Economic Justice for All: Continuing Principles, Changing Context, New Challenges* (Washington, DC: United States Catholic Conference, 1996).
12. Salvador Solis, "Free Migrant Workers from Shadows of Outlaw Status," *Democrat and Chronicle* (Rochester, NY), September 28, 2003.
13. Tom Schindler, "Work," in *The Modern Catholic Encyclopedia,* ed. Michael Glazier and Monika Hellwig (Collegeville, MN: Michael Glazier/Liturgical Press, 1994), 917.
14. Christine Firer Hinze, "Dirt and Economic Inequality: A Christian-Ethical Peek under the Rug," *Annual of the Society of Christian Ethics* 21 (2001): 59.
15. Michael Pennock, *Catholic Social Teaching: Learning and Living Justice* (Notre Dame, IN: Ave Maria Press, 2000), 228.
16. National Conference of Catholic Bishops, *Economic Justice for All* (Washington, DC: United States Catholic Conference, 1986), par. 104.
17. Tom Schindler, "Unions," in *The Modern Catholic Encyclopedia,* ed. Michael Glazier and Monika Hellwig (Collegeville, MN: Michael Glazier/Liturgical Press, 1994), 881–82.

18. Maryanne Stevens, "Strike, Right to," in *The New Dictionary of Catholic Social Thought*, ed. Judith Dwyer (Collegeville, MN: Michael Glazier/Liturgical Press, 1994), 926.

19. Mary (Harris) Jones, *Autobiography of Mother Jones* (Chicago: Charles H. Kerr and Co., 1925; reprint ed., New York: Arno Press, 1969), 12.

20. Dumas Malone, ed., *Dictionary of American Biography*, vol. 10 (New York: Charles Scribner's Sons, 1933), 195.

21. Dale Fetherling, *Mother Jones, the Miners' Angel: A Portrait* (Carbondale: Southern Illinois University Press, 1074), 8.

22. Ibid., 41–42.

23. Ibid., 48–57.

24. Ibid., 121; 107–8.

25. Frank Almade, "Just Wage," in *The New Dictionary of Catholic Social Thought*, ed. Judith Dwyer (Collegeville, MN: Michael Glazier/Liturgical Press, 1994), 493.

26. Ibid., 493–94. "Indirect employers" is found in *Laborem Exercens*, no. 17.

27. Michael J. Naughton, "Distributors of Justice: A Case for a Just Wage," *America* 182 (May 27, 2000): 14.

28. Ibid.

29. National Conference of Catholic Bishops, *A Fair and Just Workplace: Principles and Practices for Catholic Health Care* (Washington, DC: United States Catholic Conference, 1999), Web site edition, www.nccbuscc.org/sdwp/national/workplace.htm.

30. Ronald Taylor, *Chavez and the Farm Workers* (Boston: Beacon Press, 1975), 81.

31. Jean Maddern Pitrone, *Chavez: Man of the Migrants, A Plea for Social Justice* (New York: Alba House, 1971), 53.

32. Robert Ellsberg, *All Saints: Daily Reflections on Saints, Prophets, and Witnesses for Our Time* (New York: Crossroad, 1977), 180–81.

33. http://www.nfwm.org/nfwmresources/farmworkerprayers.shtml.

Chapter 8 / Solidarity: War and Peace

1. "India Mourns Loss of Native-born Hero on 2nd Spaceflight," *Democrat and Chronicle* (Rochester, NY), February 2, 2003, A13.

2. The *Langenscheidt's New College Merriam-Webster English Dictionary* (Maspeth, NY: Langenscheidt Pub., 1998), cites 1841 as the first time "solidarity" was used in English.

3. Matthew Lamb, "Solidarity," *The New Dictionary of Catholic Social Thought*, ed. Judith Dwyer (Collegeville, MN: Michael Glazier/Liturgical Press, 1994), 909.

4. Robert Ellsberg, *All Saints: Daily Reflections on Saints, Prophets, and Witnesses for Our Time* (New York: Crossroad, 1997), 457.

5. Ibid., 457–58.

6. Lamb, "Solidarity," 912.

7. Ibid.

8. Patrick McCormick, "Centesimus Annus," *The New Dictionary of Catholic Social Thought*, ed. Judith Dwyer (Collegeville, MN: Michael Glazier/ Liturgical Press, 1994), 141.

9. Ibid.

10. Ibid., 142.

11. Ibid.

12. *Centesimus Annus*, no. 52

13. Paul Tillich, *Love, Power and Justice* (London: Oxford University Press, 1954), 63ff.

14. Donald Shriver Jr., *An Ethic for Enemies* (London: Oxford University Press, 1995), as quoted by William Bole, "Forgiveness: A Radical New Factor," *America* 189 (April 21, 2003): 18.

15. Bole, "Forgiveness," 18.

16. Pope John Paul II, "The International Situation Today," *Origins* 32 (January 30, 2003): 544.

17. Ibid.

18. William H. Shannon, ed., *Thomas Merton: Passion for Peace: The Social Essays* (New York: Crossroad, 1995), 2–3.

19. Ibid., 54.

20. Ellsberg, *All Saints*, 341–43.

21. Ibid., 172.

22. Shannon, *Thomas Merton*, 54.

23. Ibid., 55.

24. Ronald Musto, *The Catholic Peace Tradition* (Maryknoll, NY: Orbis Books, 1986), 242.

25. Ibid., 243.

26. Ibid.

27. *The Catholic Worker* (July–August 1965), 7.

28. *The Challenge of Peace: God's Promise and Our Response*, no. 117.

29. Richard Hays, *The Moral Vision of the New Testament* (New York: Harper Collins, 1996), 329–30.

30. Ibid., 331, 332 (emphasis added).

31. Lisa Cahill, *Love Your Enemies: Discipleship, Pacifism, and Just War Theory* (Minneapolis: Fortress Press, 1944), 3.

32. Ibid., 39.

33. Musto, *The Catholic Peace Tradition*, 35.

34. Ibid., 36.

35. Cahill, *Love Your Enemies*, 7.

36. Ibid., 12.

37. Ibid., 13.

38. Hays, *The Moral Vision of the New Testament*, 342.

39. Cahill, *Love Your Enemies*, 14.

40. Excerpts from *The Harvest of Justice Is Sown in Peace: A Reflection of the National Conference of Catholic Bishops on the Tenth Anniversary of "The Challenge of Peace"* (Washington, DC: United States Catholic Conference, 1993), Web site edition, www.usccb.org/sdwp/harvest.htm.

41. Thomas Shannon, "What is 'Just War' Today?" *Catholic Update* (May 2004): 4.

42. Hays, *The Moral Vision of the New Testament*, 342–43. The official Catholic position would argue that pacifism and nonviolence can be seen as "reasonable," and participating in public governance can actually be a Christian vocation.

43. Musto, *The Catholic Peace Tradition*, 200.

44. Ibid., 247.

45. Michael Novak, "'Asymmetrical Warfare' and Just War: A Moral Obligation," *National Review Online*, www.nationalreview.com (February 10, 2003).

46. Gerard Powers, "An Ethical Analysis of War against Iraq," *Blueprint for Social Justice* 56 (March 2003): 3.

47. Quoted by Shannon, "What is 'Just War' Today?" 4.

48. Wilton Gregory, "Blessed Are the Peacemakers: Reflections on Two Anniversaries," www.uscsb.org/sdwp, August 4, 2003.

49. Zenit News Agency, "Pope to Ask Bush for Radical Shift in Policy, Says Cardinal Laghi, Changes Sought in Approach to Iraq and Holy Land," www.Zenit.org/English, May 13, 2004.

50. For a treatment of peace history within Catholicism, see Musto, *The Catholic Peace Tradition*.

51. Drew Christiansen, "Catholic Theology of Peace—and War," Lecture delivered at Nazareth College, Rochester, NY, October 30, 2003.

52. Kenneth Himes, "War," *The New Dictionary of Catholic Social Thought*, ed. Judith Dwyer (Collegeville, MN: Michael Glazier/Liturgical Press, 1994), 979.

53. Christiansen, "Catholic Theology of Peace—and War."

54. Shannon, *Thomas Merton*, 3–4.

55. Ibid., 4.

56. Distributed by Pax Christi USA and the Fellowship of Reconciliation, www.paxchristi usa.org.

INDEX

Notes

Notes

Notes

Notes

Notes

Notes